The Market as God

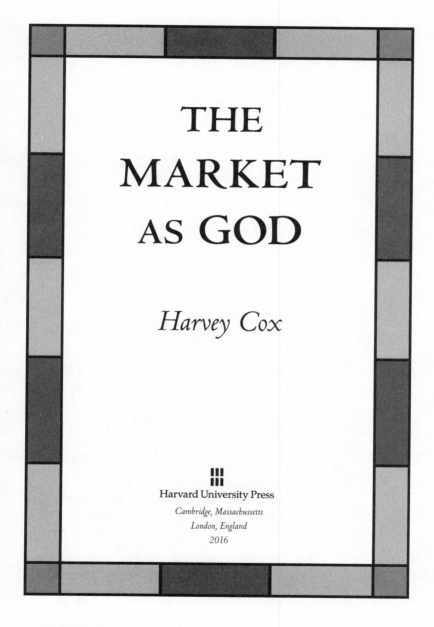

THE
MARKET
AS GOD

Harvey Cox

Harvard University Press

Cambridge, Massachussetts
London, England
2016

First printing

Library of Congress Cataloging-in-Publication Data
Names: Cox, Harvey, author.
Title: The market as god / Harvey Cox.
Description: Cambridge, Massachusetts : Harvard University
Press, 2016. | Includes bibliographical references and index.
Identifiers: LCCN 2016014998 | ISBN 9780674659681 (alk. paper)
Subjects: LCSH: Money market—Moral and ethical aspects. | Financial
institutions—Moral and ethical aspects—United States. | Economics—
Moral and ethical aspects. | Economics—Religious aspects.
Classification: LCC HG226 .C69 2016 | DDC
174/.4—dc23 LC record available at
https://lccn.loc.gov/2016014998

This book is dedicated to
Pope Francis
with gratitude and hope

Contents

Contents

The Market as God

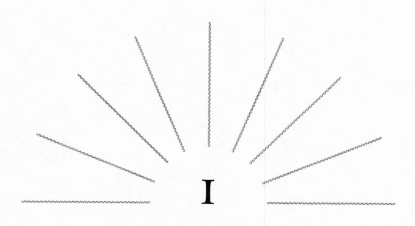

I

Overview

I

The Market as God

> We have created new idols. The worship of the ancient
> golden calf (cf. *Ex* 32:1–35) has returned in ... the idolatry
> of money.... In this system ... whatever is fragile, like the
> environment, is defenseless before the interests of a deified
> market.
>
> —Pope Francis

I n November 2013, the recently elected Pope Francis issued a document entitled "Evangelii Gaudium" (The Joy of the Gospel).
Neither in Latin nor in English was the title designed to attract a
huge readership. But as the news began to spread of what it said, the
fifty-thousand-word "apostolic exhortation" became one of the most
controversial and widely discussed writings in recent memory. Undoubtedly the reason for its instant notoriety was that the pope
includes a stinging critique of today's unbridled consumerism and
"economy of exclusion and inequality." He notes that "some people
continue to defend trickle-down theories which assume that economic growth, encouraged by a free market, will inevitably succeed
in bringing about greater justice and inclusiveness in the world." His
Holiness begs to differ. "This opinion," he says, "expresses a crude
and naïve trust in the goodness of those wielding economic power
and in the sacralized workings of the prevailing economic system."
Meanwhile, "the excluded are still waiting ... [and] a globalization

of indifference has developed." Later he speaks about a "deified market" and "ideologies which defend the absolute autonomy of the marketplace"—a system, he says, "which tends to devour everything which stands in the way of increased profits."[1]

These are bold and controversial claims, of a kind one does not normally expect from papal statements. But Francis is speaking as someone who, unlike most previous prelates, knows poverty firsthand. He has spent many days visiting his people in the crowded tarpaper slums of Argentina. His first trip as pope was to the Mediterranean island of Lampedusa, where the bodies of desperate refugees who tried to flee hunger wash up on the shore. More recently he visited with the excluded and exploited indigenous people of Chiapas, Mexico.

The importance of this document, however, is that Francis goes beyond the moral outrage many feel about these injustices. What caught my eye in particular was the pope's use of explicit religious language like "the sacralized workings of the prevailing economic system" and "a deified market." What was Francis intending with these phrases? Was he just waxing metaphorical, or was he lifting the ordinary critique of the suffering caused by economic inequality out of the strictly moral idiom in which it is usually phrased, and raising it to a theological level? Did he really believe that what he called "unrestricted consumer capitalism" had become a quasi-religion, maybe even a heresy?

These questions piqued my interest because I had personally spent some time considering the nature of our society's faith in markets.[2] Some years ago, a friend advised me that if I wanted to know what was going on in the real world, I should skip the front page of the *New York Times* and turn immediately to the business section. Although my lifelong interest has been in the study of religion, I am always willing to expand my horizons, so I took the advice, vaguely fearful that I would have to cope with a new and baffling vocabulary.

I did not. Instead I was surprised to discover that most of the concepts I ran across were strangely familiar. Expecting a terra incognita, I found myself instead in the land of déjà vu. The lexicon of the *Wall Street Journal, Financial Times,* and *Economist* turned out to bear a striking resemblance to Genesis, the Epistle to the Romans, and Saint Augustine's *City of God.* Behind descriptions of acquisitions and mergers, monetary policy, and the convolutions of the Dow and the NASDAQ, I gradually made out the pieces of a grand narrative about the inner meaning of human history, why things go wrong, and how to put them right. Theologians call these myths of origin, legends of the fall, and doctrines of sin and redemption. Here they were again, and in only thin disguise: chronicles about the creation of wealth, the seductive temptations of over-regulation, captivity to faceless business cycles, and, ultimately, salvation through the advent of free markets, with a small dose of ascetic belt-tightening along the way for those economies that fall into the sin of arrears. I realized then that my many years of studying religion and theology had prepared me to approach this mysterious thing called the economy more knowingly than I could have guessed.

On June 18, 2015, Pope Francis released a longer teaching he entitled "Laudato Si" which addresses the growing planetary crisis brought on by climate change. In this encyclical the pope continued to decry those who put profits above the health of the earth, and questioned the idea that "current economics" or "market growth" could head off the climate catastrophe toward which we are hurtling, or the starvation and poverty it will bring. I have never believed the old Vatican adage *Roma locuta, causa finita* ("Rome has spoken, the matter is closed") but I was gratified to see that, at least in this matter, the bishop of Rome and I were on the same page. The crisis that our current economic practices have created for what he calls "our common home" is not just an economic one, and even more than a moral one. It is a spiritual, even theological, crisis and must be understood at that level.

I do not believe Pope Francis is speaking just metaphorically any more than I believe he is indulging in hyperbole when he equates the early death caused by economic inequality with the murder forbidden by "thou shall not kill." He is drawing our collective attention to what has become a powerful and all-encompassing worldview, a vision of reality that pulls everything into its orbit and that should therefore be recognized as a kind of religion. The phrase "religion of the market" is not just a figure of speech. Faith in the workings of markets actually takes the form of a functioning religion, complete with its own priests and rituals, its own doctrines and theologies, its own saints and prophets, and its own zeal to bring its gospel to the whole world and win converts everywhere. The fact that acolytes of the market faith do not formally acknowledge it as a religion does not change this reality. Only when we have seen it for what it is can we appreciate the profound challenge the market faith poses and the depth and scope of our global crisis.

Encouraged by the example of Pope Francis, I took up again my excursions into what had been for me the unexplored continent of business and finance. I soon found that a theological lens provides an illuminating way to understand economic debates. The troubles with countries from Japan to Greece, I recognized the Market's votaries to be arguing, derive from their heretical straying from free-market orthodoxy—they are practitioners of "crony capitalism," or "ethno-capitalism," or "statist capitalism." Like those of ancient Arians or medieval Albigensians, their theories are all deviations from the one true faith—in other words, heresies. In the Great Recession of 2007–2009, I saw the kind of crisis that shakes the foundations of belief. But faith is strengthened by adversity, and the market religion emerged buttressed and renewed from its trial by financial heterodoxies. The banks that were "too big to fail" are bigger than ever. In a modern age when arguments from design no longer suffice to prove any god's existence, the god of the market is like Pascal's deity—believed in despite the evidence. A decade ago Alan Greenspan evinced this tempered but stalwart faith as he testified before Congress. A leading hedge fund had just lost billions of dollars, shaking market confidence and precipitating calls for new federal regulation. Greenspan, usually Delphic in his comments, was decisive. He believed, he said, that regulation would only impede these markets, and that they should continue to be self-regulated. True faith, Saint Paul tells us, is "the evidence of things unseen."

To begin exploring the market theology is quickly to marvel at just how comprehensive it is. There are sacraments to convey salvific power to the lost, a liturgical year, a calendar of entrepreneurial saints, and even what theologians call "eschatology"—a teaching about the "end of history." My curiosity was piqued. I began cataloguing these strangely familiar doctrines, and gradually concluded that there lies embedded in the rhetoric of business journalism and the curricula of business schools an entire theology, which is comparable in scope if not in profundity to that of Thomas Aquinas or Karl Barth. It needed only to be systematized for a whole new *Summa* to take shape. The purpose of this book is to bring that theology out of the shadows. I want to demonstrate that the way the world economy operates today is not simply "natural" or "just the way things work," but is shaped by a powerful and global system of values and symbols that can best be understood as an *ersatz religion*. Both words are important. It is a religion because, as we will see in the chapters that follow, it exhibits all the characteristics of a classical faith. But it is ersatz because the market, like the graven idols of old, was constructed by human hands.

Let us begin, as many theologians do, with the pinnacle. At the apex of any theological system, of course, is its doctrine of God. In the new theology this celestial peak is occupied by The Market, which I will henceforth capitalize to signify both the mystery that enshrouds it and the reverence it inspires in its adepts. "The Market" in this book will serve as synecdoche, a figure of speech in which a part is made to signify the whole. Thus "The Market" stands for the entire economic and cultural system which it pervades and in which it is the supremely powerful part.

Different faiths have, of course, different conceptions of divine attributes. In Christianity, God has sometimes been defined as omnipotent (possessing all power), omniscient (having all knowledge), and omnipresent (existing everywhere). Most Christian theologies, it is true, hedge a bit. They teach that these qualities of the divinity are indeed there, but are hidden from mortal eyes both by human sin and by the transcendence of the divine itself. In "light inaccessible" they are, as the old hymn puts it, "hid from our eyes."

Likewise, although The Market, we are assured, possesses these divine attributes, they are not always completely evident to earthlings but must be trusted and affirmed by faith. "Farther along," as another old gospel song says, "we'll understand why."

In the arguments and explanations of the economist-theologians who justify The Market's ways to men, I spotted the same dialectics I have grown fond of across many years of pondering the Thomists, the Calvinists, and the various schools of modern religious thought. In particular, the business theologians' rhetoric resembles what is sometimes called "process theology," a relatively contemporary trend influenced by the philosophy of William James, who advocated a "finite deity"—that is, a divinity that was only moving toward these ultimate attributes, maybe for an infinite amount of time. This conjecture is of immense help to theologians for obvious reasons. It answers the bothersome puzzle of theodicy: why a lot of bad things happen that an omnipotent, omnipresent, and omniscient God—especially a benevolent one—would presumably not countenance. Likewise for the theologians of The Market, still-imperfect capacities might help to explain the boom-and-bust cycles of dislocation, pain, and disorientation that people who live within its ever-expanding sphere undergo. Their suffering is tragic, but should not cause doubt as to the ultimate benevolence of the Market God.

For quite a long time in human history, of course, there have been bazaars, rialtos, and trading posts—all markets. But they arose only when certain conditions permitted, and for centuries people got along without them. Eventually, when the market did appear it was not God, because there were other centers of value and meaning, other "gods." The Market operated within a plethora of assorted institutions that restrained it. As Karl Polanyi demonstrates in his classic work *The Great Transformation,* only in the past three centuries has The Market risen above these demigods and chthonic spirits to become today's unrivaled First Cause.[3] Initially The Market's rise to Olympic supremacy replicated the gradual ascent of Zeus above all the other divinities of the ancient Greek pantheon, a climb that necessitated the defeat of a previous generation of deities, the Titans, and was never quite secure. Zeus, it will be recalled, had to keep storming down from Olympus to quell this or that threat to his sovereignty. Recently, however, The Market is becoming more like the Yahweh of the Old Testament—not just one superior deity contending with others but the Supreme Deity, the only true God, whose reign must be universally accepted and who allows for no pretenders.

Divine omnipotence means the capacity to define what is real. It is the power to make something out of nothing and nothing out of something. The willed-but-not-yet-achieved omnipotence of The Market means that there is no conceivable limit to its inexorable ability to convert creation into commodities. But again, this is hardly a new idea, though it has a new twist. In Catholic theology, through what is called "transubstantiation," ordinary bread and wine become vehicles of the Holy Presence. In the mass of The Market's religion, a reverse process occurs. Things that have been held sacred are transmuted into interchangeable items for sale. Land is a good example. For millennia it has held various meanings, many of them numinous. It has been Mother Earth, ancestral resting place, holy mountain, enchanted forest, tribal homeland, aesthetic inspiration, sacred turf, and much more. But when The Market's Sanctus bell rings, and the elements are elevated, all these complex meanings of land melt into one: real estate. At the right price no land is not for sale, and this includes everything from the forefathers' burial grounds to the cove of the local fertility sprite. This radical desacralization dramatically alters the human relationship to land; the same happens with trees, water, air, space, and soon (it is predicted) the heavenly bodies.

At the high moment of the mass the priest says, "This is my body," meaning the body of Christ and, by extension, the bodies of all the faithful people. Christianity and Judaism both teach that the human body is made "in the image of God." Now, however, in a dazzling display of reverse transubstantiation, the human body has become the latest sacred vessel to be converted into a commodity. The process began, fittingly enough, with blood. But now, all bodily organs— kidneys, skin, bone marrow, sperm, the heart itself—can miraculously be changed into purchasable items, and those that are not already soon will be.

Still, the liturgy of The Market is not proceeding without some opposition from the pews. A few years ago a considerable battle broke out in the United States over the attempt to merchandise human genes. Banding together for the first time in memory, virtually all the religious institutions in the country, from the liberal National Council of Churches to the Catholic bishops to the conservative National Association of Evangelicals, opposed the gene mart, at that time the newest theophany of The Market. But these critics are followers of what some now call the "old religions," which, like the goddess cults that were thriving when the worship of the vigorous young Apollo began sweeping ancient Greece, might not have the muscle to slow the spread of the new devotion. Also, the ingenuous opponents of gene vending did not recognize the full scope of what they were up against, a total world-shaping ethos in which there is nothing that is not for sale.

Occasionally backsliders try to bite the Invisible Hand that feeds them. On October 26, 1996, the German government ran an ad offering the entire village of Liebenberg, in what used to be East Germany, for sale—with no previous notice to its some 350 residents. Liebenberg's citizens, many of them elderly or unemployed, stared at the notice in disbelief. They had certainly loathed communism, but when reunification brought with it a market economy they hardly expected this. Liebenberg includes residences, a thirteenth-century church, a Baroque castle, a lake, a hunting lodge, two restaurants, and three thousand acres of meadow and forest. Once a favorite site for boar hunting by the old German nobility, it was entirely too valuable a parcel to overlook. Besides, having been expropriated by the East German Communist government, it was now legally eligible for sale under the terms of German reunification. Overnight Liebenberg became a living parable, providing an invaluable glimpse of the kingdom in which The Market's will is indeed done. But the outraged burghers of the town did not feel particularly blessed. They complained loudly, and the sale was postponed.[4] Everyone in town realized, however, that it was not really a victory. The Market, like the Lord God of Hosts, may lose a skirmish, but in a war of attrition like the one Joshua waged against the luckless Canaanites, The Market will win in the end.

Of course, religion in the past has not been reluctant to charge for its services either. Prayers, masses, blessings, healings, baptisms, funerals, and amulets have been hawked, and still are. Nor has religion always been sensitive to what the traffic would bear. When, in the early sixteenth century, Johann Tetzel jacked up the price of indulgences and even used one of the first singing commercials composed to push sales ("When the coin into the platter pings, the soul out of purgatory springs"), he failed to realize that he was overreaching. The customers balked, and a young Augustinian monk brought the traffic to a standstill with a placard tacked to a church door.

It would be a lot harder for a Luther to interrupt sales of The Market's amulets today. As the people of Liebenberg discovered, everything can now be bought. Lakes, meadows, church buildings—everything carries a sticker price. But this practice itself exacts a cost. As everything in what used to be called creation becomes merchandise, human beings begin to look at one another, and at themselves, in a funny way, and they see colored price tags. There was a time when people spoke of the "inherent worth"—if not of things, then at least of persons. The Liebenberg principle changes all that. One wonders what would become of a modern Luther who tried to post his theses on the church door, only to find that the whole edifice had been bought, crated, and reassembled by an American billionaire who thought it would give his estate just the old-world touch it needed. It is comforting to note that the citizens of Liebenberg, at least, were not put on the block.

But that raises a good question. What is the value of a human life in the theology of The Market? Here the new deity barely pauses. The relevant numbers could be expressed in monetary terms, although the computation might be complex. We should not presume, for example, that if a child is born severely handicapped, unable to be "productive," The Market will decree its death. One must remember that the profits derived from medications, leg braces, and CAT-scan equipment should also be figured into the equation. Such a cost-benefit analysis might result in a close call—but the inherent worth of the child's life, since it cannot be quantified, would be hard to include in the calculation.

Calculating the worth of a human life may sound degraded, but in the age of The Market it goes on all the time. A few years back, during the presidency of George H. W. Bush, the Environmental Protection Agency decided that the value of a life for people under seventy was $3.7 million, and for people over seventy it was $2.3 million. After the uproar that followed, Obama's EPA decided all American lives should be equally valued, at $9.1 million a person.

That the value of some things is incalculable does not mean a price will fail to be named. How much, for example, is a tradition worth? On September 10, 2014, the *Harvard Crimson* reported that a wealthy Hong Kong real-estate magnate, Gerald L. Chan, had phoned his old friend William F. Lee, a member of "the Corporation" (or more formally, the President and Fellows of Harvard College), the small group that governs the university. After some pleasant chatter, Mr. Chan got to the point. How much would it cost to rename the Harvard School of Public Health for his late father? Lee quickly brought the matter to the attention of the Harvard Corporation, which fixed the amount at $350 million, which would be the largest single gift ever received by the university. Chan quickly accepted. The school is now officially the Harvard T. H. Chan School of Public Health.[5]

To be sure, this was not the first example of renaming things at Harvard. In the early seventeenth century, when it was only a small college in the wilds of New England with no particular name, it was christened to honor its first benefactor, John Harvard, whose private collection of books became its library. Three centuries later, in 1966, its School of Government was renamed "the John F. Kennedy School of Government," after the Harvard graduate who had become president of the United States and recently been assassinated.

But somehow this seemed a little different. The open asking of how much such a naming would cost, and the rapid response, sounded to some people too much like a cash-on-the-barrelhead transaction, and perhaps just a bit unseemly. At a minimum, it signaled a change in the way Harvard thinks about tradition and money. Fred Hess, director of education-policy studies at the market-friendly American Enterprise Institute, told the *Crimson*, "I think this makes it clear that Harvard weighed the value of tradition against an enormous contribution and decided the contribution was worth it." He also thought the transaction would set a precedent for other Harvard graduate schools as they met with potential donors, all of them now "aware that Harvard is open to selling naming rights." University administrators did not blink at the significance of the precedent. Treasurer Paul J. Finnegan said the university should be ready to enter into similar negotiations. "If anyone is considering a gift at this level or higher, and is proposing naming rights, the Corporation should give it full consideration."

Whatever else the renaming of the School of Public Health means, it suggests that The Market's reach is becoming more and more extensive, indeed "omnipresent"—a divine attribute we will return to in a moment. Further, its reach moves in all directions. Like the biblical God, whether one climbs to the highest heaven or descends into the lowest depths, The Market is impossible to escape. As Stacy Palmer, editor of the *Chronicle of Philanthropy,* informed the Harvard reporters, one now sees names of donors on seats in classroom theaters, "and some schools have gone to the extreme of putting names on bathrooms and bathroom fixtures."

It is sometimes said that since everything is for sale under the rule of The Market, nothing is sacred. But this is not quite true. Some years ago a nasty controversy erupted in Great Britain when a railway pension fund that owned the small jeweled casket in which the remains of Saint Thomas à Becket are said to have rested decided to auction it off through Sotheby's. The casket dates from the twelfth century and is revered as both a sacred relic and a national treasure. The British Museum made an effort to buy it but lacked the funds, so the casket was sold to a private Canadian citizen. Only last-minute measures by the British government prevented removal of the casket from the United Kingdom. In principle, however, in the theology of The Market, there is no reason why any relic, coffin, body, or national monument—say, the Statue of Liberty or Westminster Abbey—should not be listed. Does anyone doubt that if the True Cross were ever really discovered, it would eventually find its way to Sotheby's? The Market is neither omnipotent nor omnipresent—yet. But the process is under way and it is gaining momentum.

Omniscience is a little harder to gauge. Maybe The Market has already achieved it but is unable—temporarily—to apply its gnosis until its kingdom and power come in their fullness. Nonetheless, current thinking already assigns to The Market a comprehensive wisdom that in the past only the gods have known. The Market, we are taught, is able to determine what human needs are, what copper and capital should cost, how much barbers and CEOs should be paid, and how much jet planes, running shoes, and hysterectomies should sell for. But how do we know The Market's will?

I was happy to discover one day that, at least according to one prominent economist, votaries of the Market God run into exactly this problem. As the Nobel-winning economist Paul Krugman writes:

> In the Middle Ages, the call for a crusade to conquer the Holy Land was met with cries of "Deus vult!"—God wills it. But did the crusaders really know what God wanted? Given how the venture turned out, apparently not.
>
> Now, that was a long time ago, and, in the areas I write about, invocations of God's presumed will are rare. You do, however, see a lot of policy crusades, and these are often justified with implicit cries of "Mercatus vult!"—the market wills it. But do those invoking the will of the market really know what the markets want?[6]

In days of old, seers entered a trance state and then informed anxious seekers what kind of mood the gods were in, and whether this was an auspicious time to begin a journey, get married, or start a war. The prophets of Israel repaired to the desert and then returned to announce whether Yahweh was feeling benevolent or wrathful. Today, The Market's fickle will is clarified by daily reports from Wall Street and other sensory organs of finance. Thus we can learn on a day-to-day basis that The Market is "apprehensive," "relieved," "nervous," or even at times "jubilant." On the basis of this revelation, awed devotees make critical decisions about whether to buy or sell. Like one of the devouring gods of old, The Market—aptly embodied in a bull or a bear—must be fed and kept happy under all circumstances. True, at times its appetite may seem excessive—the mammoth banks that constitute its store often seem to need votive offerings of, say, a $350 billion bailout now, another $500 billion later—but the alternative to assuaging its hunger is too terrible to contemplate.

The diviners and seers of The Market's moods are the financial consultants and CEOs of major investment houses. They are the high priests of its mysteries. To act against their admonitions is to risk excommunication and possibly damnation. If, for example, any government's policy vexes The Market, those responsible for the irreverence will be made to suffer. That the Market is not at all displeased by downsizing or by a growing income gap, but can be gleeful about the expansion of cigarette sales to Asian young people, should not cause anyone to question its ultimate omniscience. Like Calvin's inscrutable deity, The Market may work in mysterious ways, "hid from our eyes," but ultimately it knows best.

Omniscience can sometimes seem intrusive. The traditional God of the Episcopal Book of Common Prayer is invoked as one "unto whom all hearts are open, all desires known, and from whom no secrets are hid." Like Him, The Market already knows the deepest secrets and darkest desires of our hearts—or at least would like to know them. But one suspects that divine motivation differs in these two cases. Clearly The Market wants this kind of x-ray wisdom because by probing our inmost fears and desires and then dispensing across-the-counter solutions, it can further extend its reach. Like the gods of the past, whose priests offered up the fervent prayers and petitions of the people, The Market relies on its own intermediaries: motivational researchers. Trained in the advanced art of psychology, which has long since replaced theology as the true "science of the soul," the modern heirs of the medieval confessors delve into the hidden fantasies, insecurities, and hopes of the populace. The "secrets of the heart" they uncover provide the raw material for sales campaigns, the evangelistic missions of the Market faith—which despite its rhetoric really does not want people to make rational decisions. Like all successful evangelists, its appeal is to the heart, and to the unconscious.

One sometimes wonders, in this era of Market religion, where the skeptics and freethinkers have gone. What has happened to the Voltaires who once exposed bogus miracles, and the H. L. Menckens who blew shrill whistles on pious humbuggery? Such is the grip of current orthodoxy that to question the omniscience of The Market is to question the inscrutable wisdom of Providence. The metaphysical principle is obvious: If you say it's the real thing (think Coca-Cola), then it must be the real thing. As the early Christian theologian Tertullian once remarked, "Credo quia absurdum est" ("I believe because it is absurd").

In recent years we have witnessed a series of books by alleged atheists like Sam Harris and Richard Dawkins skewering religions and exposing the damage they are said to cause. But one wonders why these self-styled dogma slayers are so cautious, and some even reverential, when it comes to the most powerful religion of our era, the one with its curia in the basilicas of Wall Street.

Finally, as mentioned above, there is the divinity's will to be omnipresent. Virtually every religion teaches this idea in one way or another and the religion of The Market is no exception. The latest trend in economic theory is the attempt to apply market calculations to areas that once appeared to be exempt, such as dating, family life, marital relations, and child-rearing. Saint Paul reminded the Athenians that their own poets sang of a God "in whom we live and move and have our being." The Market likewise is not only around us but inside us, informing our senses and our feelings. There seems to be nowhere left to flee from its untiring quest. Like the Hound of Heaven, it pursues us home from the mall and into the nursery and the bedroom.

It used to be thought—mistakenly, as it turns out—that at least the innermost, or "spiritual," dimension of life was resistant to The Market. It seemed unlikely that Saint Teresa's interior castle would ever be listed by Century 21. But as the markets for material goods become increasingly glutted, such previously unmarketable states of grace as serenity and tranquility are now appearing in the catalogs. Your personal vision quest can take place in unspoiled wildernesses that are pictured as virtually unreachable—except, presumably, by the other people who consult the same catalog. Furthermore, ecstasy and spirituality, often accompanied by massages, crystals, and psychic readings, are now offered in convenient generic forms. Thus The Market makes available the religious benefits that once required prayer and fasting, without the awkwardness of extended commitment or the tedious ascetic discipline that once limited their accessibility. All can now handily be bought without an unrealistic demand on one's time, in a weekend workshop at a Caribbean resort with a sensitive psychological consultant replacing the crotchety retreat master.

Discovering the theology of The Market made me begin to think in a different way about the conflict among religions. Not long ago violence flared between Catholics and Protestants in Ulster, and between Hindus and Muslims in India. Now the strife seems most heated within Islam, with radical jihadists harassing and murdering each other and the unfortunate religious minorities that fall within their power. But I have come to wonder whether the real clash of religions (or even of civilizations) may be going unnoticed. I am beginning to think that for all the religions of the world, however they may differ from one another, the religion of The Market has become the most formidable rival. The traditional religions and the religion of The Market, for example, hold radically different views of nature. In

Christianity and Judaism, "the earth is the Lord's and the fullness thereof, the world and all that dwell therein." The Creator appoints human beings as stewards and gardeners but, as it were, retains title to the earth. Other faiths have similar ideas.

In the religion of The Market, however, human beings, more particularly those with the wherewithal, own anything they buy and— within certain limits—can dispose of whatever they own in any way they choose. Other contradictions can be seen in ideas about the human body, the nature of human community, and the purpose of life. The older religions encourage archaic attachments to particular places. But in The Market's eyes all places are interchangeable. The Market prefers a homogenized world culture with as few inconvenient particularities as possible. It longs to "make the rough places smooth."

Disagreements among the traditional religions sometimes seem picayune in comparison to the fundamental differences they all have with the religion of The Market. Will this lead to a new jihad or crusade? Before Pope Francis began to speak out, it seemed highly unlikely that traditional religions would rise to the occasion and challenge the doctrines of the new dispensation. Most of them seemed content to become its acolytes or to be absorbed into its pantheon, much as the old Nordic deities, after putting up a game fight, eventually settled for a diminished but secure status as Christian saints.

But is that now changing? Again, I believe that Pope Francis is serious, and not merely engaging in a flight of rhetorical fancy. The market economy, with its consumer culture, does in fact bear all the marks of a religion. No religion, new or old, is subject to empirical proof, so what we see is a contest between faiths. Much is at stake and The Market, once aroused, is like the Yahweh of the Old Testament conquest narratives, willing to go to war if necessary. During the recent row over the emission standards, for example, the *New York*

Times editorialized that a "war on coal" was being waged, but not by government regulators. Rather, "the real war has been waged by the market and technology."[7] The Market God has understandable reasons to go to war. It has its own causa belli. It strongly prefers radical individualism and instant mobility. Since it needs to shift people to wherever production requires them, it becomes wrathful when they cluster or cling to local traditions and locations. Will these vestiges of older dispensations—like the "high places" of the Baalim—simply be plowed under? Maybe not. Like previous religions, the new one has ingenious ways of incorporating preexisting ones. Hindu temples, Buddhist festivals, and Catholic saints' shrines can look forward to new incarnations. Along with native costumes and spicy food, they will be allowed to provide local color and authenticity in what could otherwise turn out to be an extremely bland Beulah Land.

There is, however, one contradiction between the religion of The Market and the traditional religions that seems to be insurmountable. All of the traditional religions teach that human beings are finite creatures and that there are limits to any earthly enterprise. A Japanese Zen master once said to his disciples as he was dying, "I have learned only one thing in life: how much is enough." He would find no niche in the chapel of The Market, for whom the First Commandment is "There is never enough." Like the proverbial shark that stops moving, The Market that stops expanding dies. At the moment this seems most unlikely, but it could happen. Faced with intractable natural limits, the endless growth of the economy might end. And if it does, then Nietzsche's announcement about the death of God will have been right after all. He will just have had the wrong God in mind.

Pope Francis has launched a crucial conversation, one that is bound to continue for some time to come. The question is whether our civilization can draw on the obvious strengths of the market but avoid its self-divinizing excesses. It is important to note that nowhere in his "Joy of the Gospel" or his subsequent speeches and writings does the pope call for the abolition of The Market. He wants it to recover its appropriate role as the servant of society rather than its master. To invent a word derived from the religious realm, he wants to "de-deify" The Market, so it can once again become the market. But is this reverse apotheosis possible?

I believe it just may be. Indeed, there are indications that the process might already be under way. But it can proceed only if we understand the extent to which The Market has really become a functioning, if usually unrecognized, pseudo religion. That understanding is what—with some help from both religious and business history—I hope to provide in the pages that follow.

2

Sciences, Regal and Divine

Much of the debate [about market efficiency] involves theological tenets that are empirically undecidable.

—John Campbell, Andrew Lo, and Craig MacKinlay

During its heyday, theology was once called "The Queen of the Sciences." Economics is still sometimes tagged with the label "the dismal science." Neither appellation is entirely fair. Once closer to the intellectual throne, theologians now prefer to think of their work as more that of a partner in conversation rather than a suzerain. As for economics, it is hard to dismiss a discipline that has produced Thorsten Veblen, R. H. Tawney, and John Kenneth Galbraith as drab or dull. It is even a question whether the term "science" as currently understood is appropriate to either of these fields. Our question in this book is how these two intellectual pursuits relate to each other. The answer, as we will see in the following chapters, is that the relationship has been sporadic, convoluted, and a sometimes troubled one. But where does this relationship stand now? And what might it become in the future?

As I picked my way with increasing fascination through the debates of economists and economic theorists, one can imagine how pleased I was to stumble on the sentence quoted above from a book entitled *The Econometrics of Financial Markets* by a group of prestigious practitioners of the trade.[1] So, there is indeed a "theological" dimension to the "dismal" science! I felt vindicated.

My vindication waxed and my curiosity was further piqued when I ran across a book entitled *The Economist as Preacher and Other Essays* by George J. Stigler, himself an economist.[2] I also thought it telling (and picturesque) that the author had chosen to pose in the pulpit of the University of Chicago's famous Rockefeller Memorial Chapel for the photo that appears on the cover of his book. Indeed, the juxtaposition of the words "Rockefeller" and "chapel" spoke volumes. I was feeling less and less like an interloper in what for me had at first seemed a strange new world.

As I read further, however, there was something that continued to bother me. There was a time in the history of the West when people killed each other by sword and fire over what now seem like theological fine points. Theologians developed polemics into an art form. Opponents and spokesmen of divergent interpretations of the great mysteries often went after one another with unseemly ferociousness. Accusations of stupidity, lack of adequate preparation, obtuseness, and other ad hominem pejoratives were not unusual. Luther called the pope a "vulgar boor," a "crude ass," and "the devil's mouthpiece." And these were among his less scurrilous appellations for the Holy Father.

Some of that *odium theologicum* has lasted into our century in the Middle East. But by and large theologians now use much more nuanced language, and there is more ecumenical and interfaith mutuality. Even in the papacy, or maybe I should say especially in the papacy, nowadays the tone of infallibility is fading.

Today the polemics are not as barbed or the invective as biting as they once were. Disputes among theologians tend to be considerably more nuanced and no one has the authority to burn those guilty of lacking theological correctness at an auto–da–fé. True, when he was prefect of the Congregation for the Doctrine of the Faith, Pope Benedict XVI (then Monsignor Joseph Ratzinger) condemned and even excommunicated some liberation theologians. But the pope no longer sends people to the stake. The faggots no longer crackle. On the whole, the language employed by theologians is noticeably more modulated. But is the same trend noticeable among economists?

Well, not always. Just as in the theology of a previous era, economists today still seem to delight in splitting into parties and schools that further fragment into sub-schools, and then defaming each other. Thus we have what is usually called "classical economic theory" represented by the Thomas Aquinas of the field, Adam Smith, whose foundational text *An Inquiry into the Wealth of Nations* is cited just as often as theologians refer to Aquinas's *Summa Theologica*. But after "classical theory" came neoclassical and, more recently, something called "new classical" economics. Somewhere in the sequence came Keynesian economics, after John Maynard Keynes (who, according to some historians I consulted, might not himself have been very "Keynesian"). Then there were neo-Keynesians and, inevitably, those who tried to combine and synthesize these warring sects.

Again, in reading these sages I found myself in strangely familiar terrain. In theology we are also accustomed to rival schools of thought, some bearing the names of their founders. During my training in the field I had learned about Thomism (from Thomas Aquinas), for example, and a twentieth-century neo-Thomism movement that attracted impressive thinkers like Jacques Maritain and Etienne Gilson. On the Protestant side there were Lutheran Orthodoxy and Calvinist Orthodoxy (neither to be confused with Eastern Orthodoxy), and then twentieth-century neo-Orthodoxy, which was said to include Karl Barth and Reinhold Niebuhr (neither of whom relished the label). We later saw Barthians and Niebuhrians and, some years ago at Yale, a theological current of neo-Barthians. As far as I know, although Rein-hold Niebuhr received a new lease on recognition when Barack Obama named him as his favorite philosopher, there are no neo-Niebuhrians.

When I dipped into the language that representatives of the hostile camps of economic theory deploy in their debates, I was carried back to the nasty skirmishes I know about between John Calvin and the Anabaptists, and to Pascal's barbs against the Jesuits found in his Provincial Letters. Keynesians accuse neoclassicists of being "products of the Dark Ages." The neo-Classicists reciprocate with accusations that the Keynesians (and I suspect the neo-Keynesians as well) base their thought on discredited "fairy tales." Theology has its schismatics and heretics, but economics seems to have their functional equivalents, often lacking tenure at prestigious universities and rarely publishing articles in the established journals of the field.

Maybe the intensity of the rhetoric is understandable when one considers what is at stake in the argument, and not only for those doing the arguing. What theologians decide about the exact relationship among the persons of the Trinity is unlikely to cause death or even very much interest for most people. But what economists decide can be literally life-and-death matters. When Pope Francis writes that those who advocate certain current fiscal and trade policies which turn out to cause deaths by starvation are guilty of violating the "thou shalt not kill" commandment, he is being quite serious.

Many economists are painfully aware that their voices do shape actual policy choices of great consequence. This was once true for theology as well. There was a time when bishops and popes and preachers counseled princes, who often heeded their advice. The clergy ruled on matters of marital status, just war, and—very relevant to our present discussion—labor practices and what constituted a "just price." This is no longer the case, which may explain why so many Catholic bishops and many conservative Protestants, understandably nettled because policy-makers no longer pay them much heed on the larger issues, have often seized on more domestic ones such as gay marriage and contraception. Today it is the economists, not the confessors, who have the ears of princes and presidents. This may be one reason that Pope Francis is trying to shift the focus of ecclesial attention away from the bedroom and back to the boardroom, from contraception to deprivation.

In an age when The Market rules and nervous national statesmen get up each morning to ask what the Dow is doing, the admonitions of economists are harkened to. The president of the United States has a council of economic advisors, but not a conclave of divines. There is no Nobel Memorial Prize in theology. This is comprehensible because economic doctrines make a real difference in the real world. Take, for example, the ongoing argument between the classical economists and the Keynesians. When the former hold sway, there tends to be less government intrusion in the private economy, but when the latter get a turn, state participation (and spending) usually increases. Theory, even economic theory, makes a difference, even down to what is eaten or not eaten across the globe. The election-year mantra "It's the economy, stupid" makes sense.

For theologians of the past, the issues were more than even life-and-death ones. They had to do with *everlasting* life and *eternal* death. Now, the questions for theology have less to do with delivering people from the flames of Hades. They have more to do with helping them to escape the peonage of poverty, or—if they are not trapped in that captivity—to rise above the emptiness and triviality of the age and to recognize the interests we share in common. Salvation remains of overriding concern, but now finds expression in a concern for how to save humankind from self-destruction, and the planet from destruction by humans.

For the economists, the issues are equally urgent. In today's capitalist systems, economists are the ones who tell us how to stabilize currencies, reduce unemployment, and stave off depressions. But there is one serious problem. What happens, as Saint Paul asks, "if the trumpet gives an uncertain sound?"[3] What if the experts differ in identifying the right road to salvation or the proper path to prosperity? In truth, the "what if" could be deleted from that sentence: differences of opinion among economics experts have been going on for centuries, and were only exacerbated by the recent global financial crisis and recession. Not since Adam and Eve blamed the serpent for their misadventure with the apple has such a wave of finger-pointing and impugning swept through the land.

These debates are about specific policy questions. But in the background lurk what sometimes sound like highly esoteric theoretical disputes that eventually influence the practical realm. And here, too, the parallel with theology is evident. It is useful to look at two burning issues, one in theology and the other in economics, which turn out to be strikingly similar.

One of the most divisive theological disputes of the past two hundred years was the torrid battle over "papal infallibility." The disagreement had arisen many years before it was allegedly resolved in Rome at the First Vatican Council in 1870. One group within the Roman Catholic Church, the ultramontanists (called that because their allegiance was to the man "beyond the mountains" from northern Europe, which is to say in Rome), was trying to center more authority in the papacy and to counter the anticlericalism and nationalistic divisiveness that began to spread after the French Revolution. Its members believed that designating the pope as the final arbiter in matters of faith and morals would quell some of the threats.

Other equally committed churchmen, including the esteemed John Henry Cardinal Newman (after whom hundreds of Catholic student groups are named today), opposed the idea of infallibility as both an innovation and a novelty that would unduly centralize spiritual power, which had been highly decentralized for centuries. They also feared it might lead to a kind of religious authoritarianism. In the preliminary vote at the Vatican Council, 457 bishops voted in favor (*placet*), 88 against (*non placet*), and 62 in favor if the measure were amended (*placet iuxta modum*). Then, however, sixty-eight of the opposing bishops left Rome, undoubtedly to avoid having to go on record. The final vote was 433 to 2 in favor, and the pope was declared infallible.

The decision evoked indignant criticisms from Protestants and Eastern Orthodox Christians and it remains one of the major obstacles to the hope of their ever reuniting with Catholics. It also caused a split in the Catholic Church itself. The question has continued to roil a hundred and fifty years later, even though only one pope has ever actually invoked this infallible power. That was Pius XII as, in 1950, he proclaimed the Doctrine of the Assumption of the Virgin Mary.

The disagreement over infallibility may be hard to grasp today. But I was intrigued to find that a similar dispute over a strangely comparable question still rages among economists. It concerns what is called the "efficient market hypothesis." The originator of this controversial item of economic dogma is the University of Chicago's Eugene Fama, who in a series of books and articles developed the assertion that, since The Market operates on the basis of all existing and available information, it is never wrong. However, just as the doctrine of papal infallibility hedges a bit by stating that the pope is infallible only under certain conditions (namely, when he is peaking ex cathedra to the whole church on matters of faith and morals) so what might be dubbed the infallible market hypothesis claims infallibility only for The Market that is "efficient." Fama writes, "market efficiency means that the market is aware of all available information and uses it correctly."[4]

Comparing these two doctrines is a beguiling exercise. Since the enactment of papal infallibility by Vatican One, shelves of articles and books have been written about what it "really" means. One of the best is Catholic theologian Hans Küng's *Infallible? An Inquiry*, but the shelves of learned treatises continue to fill with nearly every papal statement.[5] To what extent, if any, is this latest one authoritative, if not infallible? Are there degrees of infallibility? Who is to decide? Who is to decide who is to decide? What if it happens someday that a pope suffers a nervous breakdown, becomes schizophrenic, or simply gets carried away by an idea that seems to everyone else far outside the limits of Catholic teaching? What if a pope becomes heretical? There have been, after all, popes in the past who wound up as "antipopes"— which is to say they were deemed to be heretics and had their names retroactively stricken from the list of Peter's successors. Is it ever safe to say that even the pope does not really know all that needs to be known about the mind of God? Likewise, debates about the "actual" meaning of market efficiency continue to seethe. The finance textbook that gave this chapter its epigraph is only one of many acknowledging the controversies over when, how, and if the market is "correct."

Sometimes as I perused these two parallel discussions I came close to a startling conclusion, and one that no theologian or economist I know of has drawn: in these two instances, "infallible" and "correct" are being redefined in a manner not in keeping with the way we usually use these words. In the meaning these doctrines attach to them, a statement is not just true but infallibly true not just because the pope enunciates it, but because he has listened, as the popes actually do, to the prevailing sentiment of the people (what theologians call the *sensus fidelium*). Even though there may be many who disagree, when the pope proclaims something as official dogma it becomes "true" in a new sense. All Catholics, whatever their views were on the day before the doctrinal proclamation, are now obligated to believe it is true.

Similarly, The Market (when it is efficient) is always correct because that is what The Market is: an accurate reflection and distillation of the countless millions of decisions made by buyers and sellers and investors. The true worth of a stock, for example, is what The Market says it is. There is no other way of judging its worth. There is no higher court of appeal. One cannot help, however, musing over a scenario comparable to that of a mad pope. The Market, after all, even its most zealous defenders concede, is a human artifice, if a hugely complex one. Only a few thinkers, like Adam Smith with his "invisible hand," imply that it was divinely instituted, although those who find it a "natural" phenomenon like seasonal change come close. Could the market go crazy? There are some observers who suggest that it already has on occasion.

I think there is a way out of this double dilemma, but it requires something neither theologians nor economists are particularly well known for: humility. One of the seven classical Christian virtues, *humilitas* is not terribly popular nowadays. But even in an age of self-assertiveness training and the super-rich aggregating an increasingly large piece of the pastry every year, humility is not dead—at least not quite. We still claim to admire it when we see it in some rare individual like Mother Teresa, and often such people are inspired by their faith. It seems to have largely vanished, however, among economists; they advance answers to our economic woes with an assurance once found only among medieval prelates. Hence it was with considerable relief that one day I discovered an exception. When David Colander,

31

a card-carrying member of the guild, published an article promisingly entitled "How the Economists Got it Wrong," I saw that humility, while perhaps on life support, was at least still breathing in the profession. It is at least acknowledged if not often practiced by economists. Just after the 2008 economic disaster, the British newspaper *The Telegraph* reported that Queen Elizabeth had visited the London School of Economics and, while there, asked a professor why nobody had noticed the brewing crisis. The answer she got was vague and unrepentant. But in Colander's article we find the *mea culpa* the royal query deserved: "we pretend we understand more than we do." He writes that the "main body of academic economists pretended, and some of them actually believed, that they understood a complex system that they did not (and still do not) understand. Therefore they failed to express their ideas and arguments with the appropriate humility."[6]

It is comforting to discover that economists, or at least some of them, may be traveling the same road theologians once traversed. They may be discovering how to acknowledge their mistakes and learn from them. They may be learning to listen to their fellow practitioners, even those who have previously been dismissed as heretical or outside the mainstream, and to apply their collective wisdom to the most urgent issues of our era. We might even see the return of an era when philosophers, theologians, and moralists worked with the new kid on the block, economics, to tackle these concerns together. But to move in that direction we need to look into how the market became The Market—how it arose from its position as one institution among many to reach the overwhelmingly powerful, quasi-deified place it now holds. That ascent is the subject of the next chapter.

3

How The Market Became Divine

Apotheosis: n. I. The elevation or exaltation of a person to
the rank of a god.

—Random House Dictionary of the English Language

I said, "You are 'gods'; you are all sons of the Most High."
But you will die like mere mortals; you will fall like every
other ruler.

—Psalm 82:6–7

The relationship between religion and The Market is a long and
convoluted saga. When did it start? One day a Cro-Magnon man
traded a chiseled-stone spearhead with a hunter for a slice of newly
slain saber-toothed tiger. He was so pleased with the exchange that
the next morning he laid out some other tools he had made on a large
rock and watched for passersby to stop and deal. The first market was
born, and that was about forty-three thousand years ago.

This, of course, is a myth, and like any other myth it takes place
on some other plane of time and space. It has no basis in fact; its purpose is to explain or justify some feature of our own times. But there
are good myths and bad ones: some deepen our tenuous understanding
of human life, and some obscure or distort it. In my view, the myth
of the Fall of Adam and Eve still tells us something significant about
who we are today. The Nazi myth of a superior Aryan race was a vicious

and destructive one. What about the Cro-Magnon man and his spearhead? It is a myth that may seem harmless enough in some respects, but the way it is often used today places it in the bad-myth category. It is deployed misleadingly to construct an impressive but spurious lineage, and even to assert a virtually timeless and therefore "natural" quality of the market.

Its lack of any basis in real history is not what makes it a bad myth. Many good myths share that quality. Still, since those who use it often assert it is historical, it is important to remember that anthropological and historical research has shown that the earliest people did not have markets. Rather, theirs were "gift cultures," at least within social groups. One was expected, of course, eventually to reciprocate for gifts accepted. But the reciprocation was not expected to happen right away; otherwise it would amount to tit-for-tat bargaining. What little barter did happen took place only with outsiders. Thus trust, reciprocity, and the importance of community are more primal and more "natural," if that word is relevant in this case. They were present before markets or even bartering appeared.

Also, when two people met each other in even the most primitive of exchanges, they were already embedded in social and symbolic worlds which overlapped in both conflict and mutuality. There had probably been previous encounters and there would be more to come. As intertribal connections increased, the role of traders, once peripheral, grew as well. But even when simple forms of currency appeared (in the form of shells or beads, for example) both the buyer and seller knew they were part of larger interlaced worlds that relied on some common assumptions. The spearhead-for-a-slice or any of its variants is ahistorical. It may be a useful fiction, for some people, because it serves as what theologians call a "myth of origin" for the religion of the Market God. It suggests that market values are primal, even ingrained in the human psyche. We are, as the T-shirt has it, "Born to Shop." But the truth is that market economies are not timeless. They appeared in human history under certain ascertainable conditions. The fact that they have existed for a long time does not make them eternal and it does not guarantee they will always be with us.[1]

So much for our Cro-Magnon spearhead marketer and his stone-top display. It is also important to recall that, even before gifting gave way to marketing, some form of religion was also on the scene. Markets may eventually have performed an important human service. But they did so surrounded and constrained by a host of other institutions—families, tribes, religion, customs, rituals, and governing institutions.

Markets contributed one voice to the choir, but have never sung an unaccompanied a cappella solo or drowned out all the altos and tenors. The Market never reveled before in the celestial centrality it has enjoyed in recent western history and especially in the past two centuries. How did the change come about?

It took a while. Ages in human history have always been defined by key metaphors or webs of metaphors, often unnoticed grids through which people see themselves, others, and the world. An age's metaphor is not just invented. It grows out of the conflicts and convergences of ordinary human efforts and the perception of the wider horizon of life within which daily life unfolds. Philosopher Charles Taylor and other scholars have recently begun to call this metaphor the "social imaginary." Lewis Mumford once pointed out that historians might have placed undue emphasis on man as toolmaker because tools, being crafted out of stone, flint, or iron, were the surviving artifacts of otherwise lost civilizations. But, Mumford reminds us, in addition to making axes and hammers, our earliest ancestors also spun out stories to try to make sense of their often threatening world.[2]

Man the toolmaker was also man the tale-teller. Archeologists can recover the tools, but the stories woven from sounds and gestures—the elements from which religion is made—have been lost. Hardly an echo survives, although sometimes we can catch a glimpse of what they might have been about in the carefully executed paintings that scroll across the walls of the cave dwellers. Enticing and elusive, these sketches tell us little but hint at much. They suggest that the imaginative worlds, and perhaps the dream worlds, of our forebears were rich and complex.

One such cave was discovered as recently as 1994 by speleologist Jean-Marie Chauvet in France. Its vivid drawings are dated to a time thirty thousand years ago, making them ten thousand years older than the most ancient cave art found elsewhere. When the German director Werner Herzog made his superb film about the Chauvet Cave, he significantly titled it *Cave of Forgotten Dreams*. But his film raises a profound question: Why did people who clung to life so close to the edge of hunger and cold devote precious hours to portraying animal and human forms by the light of flickering torches? They lived in an environment that was unpredictable and threatening. They had to stave off wild animals, insects, and storms. They hunted and gathered, then later planted and picked, but their lives were always precarious.

Imagine how a sudden flash of lightning or ear-splitting peal of thunder, both totally inexplicable, pierced their quotidian routines. What did the Chauvet Cave mean to those people? No one knows the entirety. But surely it performed at least two closely related functions. First, it provided a safe place where they could gather and be reminded of the irreducibly corporate and communal character of their lives. No sane person would venture out alone to hunt or gather. They knew they needed each other. And second, it offered a location where they could placate the terrifying forces that constantly threatened them.

In a deep recess of one of the branches of the Chauvet Cave stands a large, flat boulder with what appear to be stone containers on each side. What is this? Again, no one can be sure. But the consensus among scholars is that it is a primitive altar. Looking upon it amidst the vivid colors of the wild bison and human torsos makes the mind race. What lost rituals and incantations might have been intoned here? What plants or animals would have been offered to keep the menacing powers at bay? Could this have been the location of the earliest fore-runner of the Eucharist and Passover Seder?

The cave is reluctant to reveal its secrets. But clearly, our ancestors were not just crafting handaxes and hide-scrapers; they were also imag-ining, dreaming, drawing, and perhaps praying. As *Los Angeles Times* film critic Kenneth Turan writes, the Chauvet Cave is "a sacred space where the human and the mystical effortlessly intertwine."[3] Perhaps the people who created the paintings and altar needed periodic rit-uals to remind themselves that the welfare of the group—the family, the tribe—was vital to the survival of the individual. And in the face of a frightening world they were doing everything in their limited powers to project some meaning onto it, to prevent it from doing its worst, to stake out a space in which to survive. They had to cope with both the selfish passions of human beings and the capricious moods of the gods. The world-metaphor informing their lives was a dark forest where danger lurked both within and without. Whatever exchanges took place did so surrounded by the symbolic and ritual parameters of a larger human enterprise that placed the value of collective survival far above that of personal gain. The market and the altar both have long histories. But the altar, and some form of spirituality, seems to predate the advent of markets. Still, the epic of their interaction, sometimes friendly, sometimes adversarial, is the stuff of an ongoing drama.

From Tribe to Empire

Step by step, tribal groups clustered into villages and villages became cities. Strong cities conquered weaker ones and empires arose. As we know from the epochal research of archaeologists like Henri Frankfort, it is nearly impossible to find distinct market spaces in ancient imperial cities. Whatever markets existed were located within the temple areas in the cities' physical centers.[4]

Recall the famous account of Jesus knotting a whip of cords and chasing the money changers from one ancient temple, the one in Jerusalem. The story of his overturning their tables and calling them thieves has been subject to a long history of gross misinterpretation. Countless sermons have piously asserted that he was decrying such commercial activity within the walls of a holy place. But this is a patently mistaken reading. Like temples before and after it, the Jewish temple had a place within its walls, in the outer court, for people selling various items, including most importantly the animals and birds to be used as sacrifices. Having come from distant parts of Palestine and the empire, these pilgrims would have carried widely differing coinages. Because they needed to pay for the animals in the local currency, the "money changers" provided an essential service. So why did Jesus, at least temporarily, close them down?

It was not because he objected to ritual sacrifices. Indeed, in another passage he tells his followers that if, while they are on the way to the temple to make a sacrifice, they remember that they bear some grudge against a neighbor, they should first make peace with that neighbor, and then proceed to the temple and make the sacrifice. Jesus lashed out at the money changers not because he objected to the business they were doing or to the practice of ritual sacrifice, but because the prices they were exacting were too high. They had become a "den of thieves." They were cheating poor, defenseless pilgrims, and he probably knew that the temple priesthood was getting a nice cut of their takings. Jesus, in other words, was enforcing a venerable but often violated religious practice: protecting the weak and vulnerable against the predations of calculating profit seekers. He was enacting one episode in the long struggle we will follow in this book between the God of the Bible who has a bias for the poor, and the God of The Market.

As the ancient world gradually becomes what we call the Medieval period, the religions of Chauvet's cave and of the classical empires were absorbed, at least in the West, by Christendom. By this point, wild animals were less of a worry. Hunger still threatened, but food could be smoked and stored. Most people lived in villages within sprawling systems of manors and fiefs in which each owed fealty to the next level up on the social hierarchy.

At the top stood the "head," the lord of the estate, the king, the bishop, or the pope. Below him were nobles and clergy. They were the hands and hearts doing the fighting and the knees doing the praying. Scattered throughout were merchants, tinkers, and peddlers distributing the goods and services the people could not produce on their own. At the bottom were the feet, the peasants who trudged out to their daily toil from sunrise to sunset. In theory all segments fit together into one organic whole.

In Medieval society, shaped by a near universal faith, the controlling metaphor, drawn from the Bible, was that of the human body. But it was not just a physical body. The parts all fit together because they shared a common spiritual purpose. Saint Paul was the main authority for this idea:

> God arranged the organs in the body, each one of them, as he chose . . . the parts of the body which seem to be weaker are indispensable, and

those parts of the body which we think less honorable we invest with the greater honor, and our unpresentable parts are treated with greater modesty, which our more presentable parts do not require. But God has so composed the body, giving the greater honor to the inferior part, that there may be no discord in the body, but that the members may have the same care for one another. (I Corinthians 12:18, 22–25)

As powerful as the image of the body was for medieval people, it was still precarious. Just as among the Cro-Magnons, menace still loomed. The threat became not the thunder clap or the lightning flash. It was human passions that could boil up and corrode the fragile fabric that bound the parts of the body together. Anger, lust, avarice, or gluttony could poison the body and rot the ligaments that keep head and heart and feet laced to each other in a single purpose. In place of the caves, churches and cathedrals reached toward the sky, replete with images of exemplary figures embodying virtues like courage, compassion, and generosity. The walls were also decked with gargoyles and monsters, symbols of such vices as greed, gluttony, and envy that threatened the health of the community. Saints and gargoyles, images of heaven and of hell, all found their niches both inside and outside. The road from the Chauvet Cave to Chartres was a long one, but it can be traced.

As today's tourist can observe, the cathedral at Chartres, like most cathedrals, faces an open square. Markets thrived literally within the shadow of its facade. But as trade and travel and pilgrimage increased, enterprising merchants moved some market functions further from the cathedral, just as their predecessors had in the ancient world. At first such movement was only temporary. Like today's roving falafel carts, vendors went to where the people were. They set up booths and stalls, especially at popular pilgrimage sites, hawking food and drink and whatever else passersby might be tempted to buy. As a saint's day or festival drew to a close, these emporia were easily taken down and moved again. Some tourists today seem offended when they discover rampant commercial activity at pilgrimage destinations such as Lourdes and Fatima, but the fact is that knickknacks, drinks, and religious kitsch have been sold since opening day.

Gradually, more permanent market encampments appeared at points of convergence of rivers and rutted highways. This was another ancient practice. The Sumerian ideogram for market is a Y, suggesting a junction. But wherever they appeared, markets were still expected to do their business within the traditional moral and spiritual restraints that had obtained when they plied their trade within the walls of the temple. These restrictions were enforced by cities and boroughs, and by guilds and confraternities whose members had internalized the theological concept of the "just price" and the recognition that buyers had to be protected against swindlers with thumbs on their scales and false bottoms in their baskets. The idea of *caveat emptor* ("let the buyer beware") was undoubtedly known, but the buyer was aided in his wariness and by a long tradition of moral precepts that shielded him from the worst predations of the unscrupulous. The idea that the market was automatically self-regulating would have seemed bizarre. Traders, buyers, and sellers all transacted their business within a nexus of assumed mutual trust, manners, and obligation that were plaited into the underpinnings of their world. As anthropologist David Graeber points out, our habit of saying "thank you" or even "I'm much obliged" after a purchase (presumably unnecessary in an economic world where perfect pricing means neither side is doing any favor for the other) is a reminder of this larger context, which is a set of shared "assumptions of what humans are and what they owe one another." He also notes that the simple, common act of asking directions

41

from a stranger, and expecting him to share his knowledge with no expectation of being paid, testifies to a baseline recognition of inter-dependence and commitment to social peace underlying whatever pecuniary bargaining we do.[5]

As cities grew, buying and selling also mushroomed exponentially. Markets raced ahead of the power of traditional restraints or explicit rules designed to prevent them from bilking the weak or the gullible. Kings in their palaces and emperors on their thrones often tried to wield the kind of control over the markets that temples once had. But it was usually too much for them. These crowned heads had to borrow money for their sumptuous palaces and their wars, so they needed the merchants and, when they later appeared on the scene, those who plied the business of finance. The investors and bankers were willing to loan the money, but in exchange, they wanted the kings to clear away the obstacles that hindered them from making that money in the first place. The rudiments of a deal were obvious. If your majesty will get the priests and the guilds and any others who are barriers to profit off our backs, we will be more than happy to make the cash you need available—with a hefty interest charge, of course. Things were changing. The twelfth-century monk Alain de Lille may have been exagger-ating a bit when he wrote, "not Caesar now, but money, is all," but he was undoubtedly prescient. Throne and altar were giving way to bourse and counting house as the reigning establishments.

We are a long way now from the Chauvet Cave, or Chartres, where the market was constrained by the temple, and people were suspicious of greed. As the middle ages began to wane, a whole new ethos ap-peared and spread. As Lewis Mumford puts it:

With the extension of the wholesale market ... by means of both money and credit, seeking large speculative profits, there grew up a new attitude toward life: a combination of ascetic regularity and speculative enterprise, of systematic avarice and presumptuous pride. If the prevailing theme of the Middle Ages was protection and security, the new economy was founded on the principle of calculated risks.[6]

Now, as trade among distant cities and even with other peoples developed, a strange new phenomenon appeared. Secured loans, currency exchanges, shipping insurance, and joint stock endeavors emerged. Paper replaced bags of gold. What historians have called "the abstract market" heaved into view. With the appearance of letters of credit and other forms of "paper," fewer stalls or booths were needed. If money could be made from money and even by buying debt, the possibility of containing this overgrown cash box to protect those drawn to it by ruthlessness and fraud diminished. No longer did buyer and seller, or borrower and lender, meet each other and transact their business within the same implicit or explicit code of moral norms. The foundation was laid for the coming era when billions of dollars would be able to be deposited or withdrawn from anywhere in the world with the click of a finger. Securitized mortgages and leveraged buyouts had their seeds sown. The "new attitude" Mumford describes combined with dazzling technology to defeat the best intentions of moralists and regulators. Let the buyer indeed beware.

Today it is no longer helpful to think of markets as just particular zones or as constituting one societal institution among many. We live in a new Marketist era. The Market now pervades our social imaginary. The change in attitude has affected everything. Physical markets escaped towns with their limiting customs and regulations, then escaped physical space altogether. New habits of calculating invaded the arts and family life. Nor was religion unaffected by the change. Practices involving counting up how many days one must endure purgatory for this or that sin, and how many of those days could be cancelled by dispensations or indulgences of a certain price, were perfectly logical extensions of this fiscal thinking. In Milan, a giant market—the first mall in history—was constructed just across the piazza from the cathedral. It replicated its ecclesial opposite number in every detail: the central nave became a sheltered passageway along which the faithful could stroll; side altars, customarily devoted to different saints, became permanent spaces for certain shops. These two buildings still face each other today on different sides of the stone pavement where tourists photograph both and pigeons flutter. But any sense of equality was not to last long. By the end of the eighteenth century, it appeared that the protracted conflict between the God of the Bible and the deified Market was over, and The Market had won. Today urban architecture tells the tale. In most western cities the steel and glass towers of insurance companies and financial conglomerates soar over the steeples of even the largest churches.

Still, the long contest was not quite over, and now and then hints of efforts to reinject religious and moral values into The Market, or in some cases even to find a different way of distributing the good things of life, have appeared. Movements have arisen intent on dethroning the sovereign Market and restoring it to the honorable but not almighty place it once held. Popes have issued strongly worded encyclicals, such as Pope Leo XIII's "Rerum Novarum" in 1891, which insisted on the right of labor to bargain collectively.[7] In the first decades of the twentieth century, a Baptist minister, Walter Rauschenbusch, who had been shocked by the conditions he discovered in the parish he served in New York's "Hell's Kitchen" neighborhood, advocated what came to be labeled the "social gospel," which called for the application of Christian principles to the economy. Sometimes he

44

used almost apocalyptic language to express his message: "If the twentieth century could do for us in the control of social forces what the nineteenth did for us in the control of natural forces, our grand-children would live in a society that would be justified in regarding our present social life as semi-barbarous." He called for Christians to "snap the bonds of evil and turn the present unparalleled economic and intellectual resources to the harmonious development of a true social life." Rauschenbusch had come to see that the misery he had found in Hell's Kitchen was caused by deep-set structural injustices, and he became sympathetic to democratic socialism.[8]

Influenced in some measure by Rauschenbusch, but taking another step, the distinguished Protestant theologian Reinhold Niebuhr wrote scathing critiques of the excesses of capitalism, even running for a seat in the New York State Senate on the Socialist Party ticket. Niebuhr's colleague Paul Tillich, prior to immigrating to America, helped found a movement in Germany called "religious socialism." After World War II, dozens of Catholic men in France became "worker priests," living and laboring among the factory and dock workers. Most significantly, in the wake of the Second Vatican Council, a movement called "liberation theology" proliferated throughout Latin America and challenged the church's long alliance with the ruling elites. It thrived for a few years and spread to Africa and Korea as successive popes including John Paul II struggled to contain it. Recently, however, liberation theology has staged a remarkable comeback with Pope Francis emphasizing its central themes in his teachings and publicly endorsing some of its key figures. These include Fr. Gustavo Gutierrez of Peru, sometimes thought of as the movement's founding theologian; Bishop Samuel Ruiz of Chiapas, Mexico; and the martyred Óscar Romero, Archbishop of San Salvador. The episodic surfacing of movements like this suggests that the protracted cold war between the contending deities we have charted in this chapter might still be capable of some heat.[9]

Evidently the age-old confrontation between God and The Market is still not finished. But in order to understand it we will need to explore how The Market has appropriated powers traditionally attributed to God, like creating people. We will turn to that in the next chapter.

4

How The Market Creates People

So God created mankind in his own image, in the image of
God he created them; male and female he created them.

—Genesis I:27

When God created Adam (or so the story goes) he scooped up
a handful of dirt, shaped it, and breathed into it, making the
first human (Genesis 2:7). A little later, He fashioned Eve out of
Adam's rib. In one sense this finished the job of creating human beings, but in another sense the primal pair represents only the first
step in a longer process. When they demonstrated that they were not
content with being merely human and wanted to be "like God" (Genesis 3:5), God expelled them from the Garden and they had to live
henceforth east of Eden with the constant realization of their very
ungodlike mortality.

Beneath all the quaint language of this ancient tale, two points
stand out about what it means to be human. The first is that our mortality or, more correctly, our recognition of our mortality, acutely
shapes our consciousness. It is one, and maybe the most important,
of the features that mark our distinctness as human beings. Anthro-
pologists who puzzle over the question of just when a creature that is
recognizably human emerged from the evolutionary process sometimes
peg the arrival of humankind to the earliest appearance of grave

markers. Even the most advanced chimpanzees, though they appear disquieted by the loss of a fellow primate, never place a pile of stones where its corpse lies. There is no evidence to suggest that they are aware that they too will one day cease to exist. Zoologists confirm, too, that the fable about aging elephants slogging through the bush to "the place where elephants die" is just that: a fable. It is not that being aware of one's mortality necessarily gives rise to speculation about an afterlife, although that happens in some cultures. But it does tend to "focus the mind" on the question of the meaning of this life.

The other insight the Genesis story suggests is that people are not fully human until they accept responsibility for their own decisions. Beyond the tasting of the proscribed fruit, it was also the blame game that followed that sent them packing. Adam was quick to incriminate Eve for having plucked the fruit. Eve tried to pass the buck on to the serpent for deceiving her. But the Creator would not permit them to get away with such brazen finger-pointing. They had done what they had done, and they were accountable. From now on Paradise would be barred by an angel with a flaming sword, and they would have to make their way through life as creatures both aware of their mortality and answerable for their actions. Such is the human condition.

Or at least it was, until the rise to power of the Market God and the legal ethos this god has shaped. In our time we are witnessing a new "creation myth," and the invention of a new form of person. The powers of this new person dramatically exceed those of the primal couple and their billions of descendants. Again the process has been a gradual one, albeit sped up in recent years. During this progression the Market God has breathed a kind of life into the new person, endowing it with the very qualities denied to Adam and Eve: immortality and blamelessness. In legal terms the latter is called "limited liability." I refer here, of course, to corporations, and to the convoluted saga of their legal definition, a history that only became possible as the Market God approached the zenith of its sovereignty.

In Greek religion and mythology, the gods—Apollo, Dionysius, Athena, and the rest—exhibit all the foibles of human beings. They can be deceitful and jealous. They fall in love (even with mere human beings) and they nurse murderous grudges. But there is one big difference: they cannot die.[1] They are immortal. But now, *ecce homo novus*. Behold the contemporary corporation-person. As it has emerged from the long legal tangle of laws and court cases in the past century, the modern corporation has now reached the Olympian status that Zeus and Minerva had. It may live on indefinitely. The mere human beings who found, organize, and manage it grow old and die. But the corporation still exists. It needs no magical elixir, no fountain of youth, no voice crying "Lazarus, come forth!" It need fear no Ides of March. It is created from the outset with an unlimited shelf life. As a "person" the corporation seems, at least at first glance, to demonstrate a distinct advance over the imperfect prototype God molded out of a fistful of mud, but there is more.

The other quality of the new corporate persons that marks a significant change from the old-fashioned model is that in many cases the law grants them "limited liability." This is an intriguing concept. It seems that Adam and Eve tried to invoke it in the historic case of *God v. Primal Pair*. ("The serpent told me . . . but the women told me.") But their creator, who was in this case their judge as well, would have none of it. Out they went, destined in Eve's case to bear children in pain; in Adam's to till the soil with the sweat of his brow; and in the serpent's to crawl on his belly in the dust. There was no limited liability for human beings (or serpents) either in the Garden of Eden or in its aftermath.

At the root of this matter lies a tenacious pair of ideas that theology has consistently attached to the human condition. The first is "free will." The second is "sin." Both have been declared obsolete more than once in the past. Theories of psychological determinism have taught that what we think of as our free will is illusory. We are wired for what we do by evolution, early toilet training, or the chemical interactions in our synapses. The idea of sin has also frequently been declared outmoded. Sometimes its banishment was justified, for example when it was reduced in some Victorian exhortations to violations of petty morals. When the word "sin" began to be affixed to perfumes and chocolate ice cream dishes, those of us in the field of theology realized something had gone badly awry with the concept.

But if not the word "sin," then the reality the word points to could not be so easily dismissed. It refers to the paradoxical quandary we find ourselves in as human persons, realizing that we are making free choices but also aware that we are enmeshed in what one theologian calls "existential alienation" and another terms "tragic entanglement." This is why such titans of modern theology as Paul Tillich and Reinhold Niebuhr both denounced the moralistic reduction of "sin" but at the same time asserted its indispensability.[2] If we compare the original model of the human person with the newly minted corporate model, the difference becomes all too clear. Old-style human beings realize that, wiggle as we will, and despite our "tragic entanglement," we are in fact responsible—liable—for our actions. The ideas of free will and sin and responsibility are indissolubly linked to each other.

Since corporation-persons are not vexed by mortality, and since they can, in many cases, claim limited liability for their actions, what Saint Paul called "the law of sin and death" does not apply to them. But in addition to these extraordinary qualities, Market-created "persons" possess another somewhat spectral feature that one writer has called "shape shifting." Those of us who study comparative religion, especially folk religions, are familiar with the concept. For example, the power to change from a human being into a coyote or a deer is integral to the worldview of some Native American peoples. But it appears in many other areas as well. It is also well known to adepts of recent vampire movies in which werewolves, large black bats, and people seem almost interchangeable.

In the world of corporate persons shape shifting works in the following way. Although immortal, a corporation, when necessary, say, to avoid bothersome litigation, can simply disappear into another corporation. The process is in part shape shifting, but also bears an eerie similarity to reincarnation. The result is that the previous corporation-person is not exactly dead, it just no longer "exists" in the form it previously did, and can therefore obviously not be held responsible for its previous actions. John Dillinger and Whitey Bulger would, I am sure, love to have possessed this capability.

A vivid example of how corporate persons can deploy their shape-shifting power can be seen in the case of the notorious disaster at Bhopal, India. On December 3, 1984 the citizens of this small city in Madhya Pradesh were awakened just after midnight by the sound of crowds surging through the streets and the screams of their neighbors. Minutes before, an accident had occurred at the local Union Carbide plant, releasing twenty-seven tons of a gas five hundred times more toxic than cyanide. There was no warning. All the plant's safety precautions had failed. As the gas swept through the streets and into homes it seared people's eyes, noses, and throats. Some died instantly. Many lost control of their bladders and bowels. Others vomited phlegm streaked with blood, choked, or became blind. People panicked. Unable to see and groping in darkness, some trampled on others. Within hours thousands of bodies littered the streets. Estimates put the number of dead at twenty thousand.

Naturally the survivors of the Bhopal catastrophe turned to the courts for redress and compensation. Due to delays and postponements it was not until 1992, eight years later, that their case was finally litigated. Union Carbide was charged with "culpable homicide." But then the shape shifting began. At first the company refused to respond to the charge, claiming the Bhopal plant was technically the responsibility of the Indian state. The case dragged on. Finally, in 2001, the shape shifting, or partial reincarnation, took place. Union Carbide was acquired by Dow Chemical (incidentally, the originator of "agent orange"). Dow then disavowed any responsibility whatever for the Bhopal incident and refused to consider either compensating the survivors or cleaning up the site which was still affected by the gas. Dow's argument was that since Union Carbide no longer existed, how could it be held responsible for anything? Meanwhile some 120,000 people became ill from the gas while the case dragged on. It has never been resolved. The coyote had become a deer.

The creation of the person-corporation with its attributes comparable to those of a superhero has not gone uncontested. There is a full and absorbing literature about the subject, manly in journals of business law. Sometimes the descriptions of the corporate person wax lyrical if not scriptural. One legal scholar soared into a paean, comparing the parts of the corporation to the head, hands, and feet of the human corpus, each with its own responsibility. His description calls to mind the Vedic Hindu hymn, dated at about 1600 BCE, addressed to the Parusha, who is pictured as a cosmic-sized man. He is sacrificed by the other gods and from his parts the various castes, or varnas, are created. The head becomes the Brahmin or priestly caste, and the arms become the Ksatriyas, the warriors. The torso becomes the Vaisyas who are the merchants, while the feet end up as the Sudras, the laborers. The stubbornly persistent Indian caste system is anchored in this ancient myth, which helps explain why neither Gandhi nor other reformers have ever succeeded in abolishing it.

Turning to the human body as a metaphor for a corporation or a society is a widespread conceit. For those familiar with the Christian scriptures it is, again, hard not to be reminded of Saint Paul's words in I Corinthians 12. Here is more from that chapter:

> Now the body is not a single part, but many. If a foot should say, "Because I am not a hand I do not belong to the body," it does not for this reason belong any less to the body. Or if an ear should say, "Because I am not an eye I do not belong to the body," it does not for this reason belong any less to the body. If the whole body were an eye, where would the hearing be? If the whole body were hearing, where would the sense of smell be? . . . God has so constructed the body as to give greater honor to a part that is without it, so that there may be no division in the body, but that the parts may have the same concern for one another. If [one] part suffers, all the parts suffer with it; if one part is honored, all the parts share its joy. (I Corinthians 12:14–17, 24–26)

But contrary to the equalitarian spirit of this epistle, the different organs of the corporation-persons are often assigned quite different values. Corporations sometimes devolve actions that might incur criminal charges to the lowest levels. According to Robert Monks and Nell Minow's *Corporate Governance*, this means that in reality, "successful prosecutions are all but impossible."[3] There are widely differing opinions about the relations of the levels of the corporate personality to each other. Some judges hold that the corporate person is identical with the people who constitute it. Others, however, for example in the United Kingdom, contend that the corporation is a "living thing," with a "personality at law distinct from the personalities of its members and could therefore sue in the English Courts as a British Subject."[4] Not at all, say other judges: a corporation cannot be hanged or incarcerated. It has no intent, no agency, and no consciousness of its own. Therefore courts should not impute liability to the corporation but should direct it toward its individual members.

The idea of shifting the emphasis in legal actions from "the corporation" to the actual individuals who, in fact, made the decisions being investigated got what many considered a real boost in September 2015 when the Justice Department of the United States issued some new policy directives to federal prosecutors. The guidelines direct them to focus more on the actual executives who were involved in, for example, the housing crisis, the financial meltdown, and various corporate scandals. Throughout the corporate investigations that went on after the great financial meltdown, although large fines were exacted from some corporations, not a single executive spent any time in jail. For example, in the criminal case against France's largest bank, BNP Paribas, the company had to pay $8.9 billion in fines—but no BNP employee faced criminal charges.[5]

This is the dilemma the new directive seems intended to address. Sally Yates, the deputy United States attorney general, put it this way: "Corporations can only commit crimes through flesh-and-blood people. It is only fair that the people who are responsible for committing those crimes be held accountable." The new policy also pushes corporations to produce the evidence needed to pursue prosecutions regardless of the "position, status or seniority" of the accused executives. "We mean it when we say 'you have to cough up the individuals,'" Ms. Yates said.[6]

Of course it remains to be seen how effective these new measures will be in reality. The announcements of the Justice Department are in part symbolic. They are intended to send a message. But the hundreds of prosecutors to whom they are addressed have considerable leeway about just how strictly to apply them. And the corporations involved can afford legions of skilled lawyers who can slow or derail prosecutions. Usually what has happened is that, when they are investigated, the legal teams of these companies conduct what they call "internal inquiries," which amount to self-investigations, with all the weaknesses that implies. The lawyers then turn over what they have found to the Justice Department and what ensues is usually some settlement, which can include a fine. But in the past, banks and other companies have withheld information about individual employees until after the settlement is reached, too late to make it possible to punish the employees themselves. Even the Justice Department of the United States faces a steep challenge in any legal confrontation, given the platoons of skilled lawyers using every available device to protect their high-paid clients from passing any time behind bars. Thus the long debate about the mysterious relationship between corporate persons and the people who constitute them drags on, with no end in sight.

At times, when I read these debates about the nature of the corporate personality, they call to mind the often esoteric deliberations about the nature of the Holy Trinity that have persisted throughout Christian history. I will return to this below. Meanwhile it should be noted that the definition of what a corporate person is continues to be anything but fixed. Courts in the United States—responding to the exigencies of The Market, in which the corporation is the top-billed actor—have continuously expanded its "personhood." Corporations have won rights under the first, fourth, fifth, and seventh amendments. They have been granted immunity from double jeopardy, and given the right to trial by jury. (What would the "peers" of a corporate person be?). They have also been accorded the right to avoid unwarranted search and seizure. The idea of corporate personhood has also migrated into the political arena, which in the realm of The Market is less and less separable from the economic arena where it started. The movement culminated in the famous *Citizens United v. Federal Elections Commission* case adjudicated by the United States Supreme Court in 2010, to which we will return below.

As mentioned above, when one peruses this disputatious history it is impossible not to detect echoes of discussions about the Holy Trinity. In Christianity it all started when the early Church fathers, building on both their Jewish legacy and their Graeco-Roman environment, had to piece together just how Jesus, whom they had come to believe was divine, could be reconciled with Jewish monotheism. Their dilemma was further complicated because they also believed that the Holy Spirit, which had descended at Pentecost, was divine. It was not an easy task. How could God be one, and yet three?

The question riled the Western Church for at least four hundred years, and is still far from settled. Many opinions were advanced, but three dominated. The "Adoptionists" taught that Jesus was an ordinary man until his baptism. When the clouds parted, a dove descended and he was adopted by God as his Son. (The dove has remained the principal symbol of the Holy Spirit in Christian art and iconography.) Incidentally, new evidence has come to light in recent years that strengthens the Adoptionist case. Scholars have discovered that the words used in this text—"This is my beloved son in whom I am well pleased" (Mark 1:9–13)—were borrowed from a legal formula in use at that time in cases of legal adoption. But unfortunately for the ancient advocates of this view, since they were arguing their point some fifteen hundred years before the appearance of modern biblical research, they did not know this at the time.

A second school of thought in the Trinitarian dispute, the Sabellians, disagreed. They argued that the Father, Son, and Holy Spirit are three aspects of same God who plays, as it were, different roles in the cosmic drama. Although it was eventually declared heretical, this view still has its advocates. Sometimes they like to use the analogy of the actor in a Greek drama who steps on stage in different masks to depict different characters. Underneath, he is the same thespian.

The third position was held by the followers of Arius, a prominent priest and theologian of third-century Alexandria. Called "Arians," and trying to find a way out of the impasse, they said that the three persons were indeed coequal and co-substantial, and that Christ was of course the Son of God. But, they maintained, "there was a time when Christ was not," even if that time was before the creation of the world. This did not satisfy the strict Trinitarians who were writing the creeds and who insisted that the Trinity in all three coequal persons had existed for all eternity.

Finally the main outline of the doctrine of the Trinity was allegedly settled by a series of Church Councils, and those who disagreed were excommunicated. But that in no way ended the disputes. Now the question became exactly how these three persons relate to each other. Did they have, as it were, specialties—for example, the Father creating, the Son redeeming, the Spirit comforting? No, the strict Trinitarians asserted, because that would verge on a kind of Greek role-playing. Well then, did they all do everything? If so, then why are there three? This is another argument that awaits a resolution, but in the meantime it was Hilary, the Bishop of Poitiers (300–368 CE) who suggested what has become the classic formulation of the relations among the persons of the Trinity. He used the Greek term *perichoresis,* which means "go around." Hilary sated that the three "reciprocally contain one another so that one permanently envelopes and is permanently enveloped by the others whom he yet envelopes." To a contemporary reader this may sound more like a wordy Zen koan than a theological clarification. But it has persisted as the capstone of Trinitarian theology in many textbooks to this day.

This animated argument has never been confined exclusively to Christian circles. Hindu religious thought speaks of Brahma, Vishnu, and Shiva—the creator, protector, and destroyer of the universe—and discussions about how they relate to each other have gone on for millennia. Raymond Panikkar, an Indian Catholic theologian with a profound knowledge of Hindu thought, has written that the reason the Christian doctrine of the Trinity is true is only because reality itself is tripartite, something he implies Hindus realized long before Christians ever appeared on the scene.

Even Jews, who sometimes suspect that Christians are not true monotheists, are not exempt. A few years ago I was studying with a small group of scholars at the Hartman Center in Jerusalem under the tutelage of a prominent Jewish student of mysticism. One day he handed us the English translation of a medieval polemical Muslim text that inveighed against the failure of the Jews to adhere to the strict monotheism Muslims believe the Koran insists on: "There is no God but Allah. . . ." The polemic quoted Jewish religious texts in which the mercy of God argues with God's judgment. This did not sound like pure monotheism. "Well, were the Muslims wrong?" our teacher asked us. We hesitated. "No, they were right," he said. "Look, there is an incipient, even overt, Trinitarianism in Jewish thought, too, and it's always been there. These Muslims were on to something, so don't you Christians get the idea that you have a monopoly on it."

All of this, I realize, could sound hopelessly esoteric to modern ears, but such debates are simplicity itself compared to the convoluted disputes I have just referred to about the internal and external parts ("persons") of the corporation. These discussions carry esoterica to a level hardly matched by the church fathers. But I found one way to think about them that helped me make some sense out of the discussion. It is to view them through the lenses of developmental psychology.

Could corporate personalities be understood to go through different stages of maturation like most human beings do? Might they fall into depression or paranoia? Or suffer from arrested development or identity crises? Looking at the research of scholars and clinicians who work in this field offers some useful insights. Jean Piaget and Erik Erikson are good examples. Both charted the standard trajectories from infancy through adolescence and adulthood to old age, and both suggest that, for some individuals, making the transition from one stage to the next can be difficult. But in my attempt to apply this school of thought to corporations, the pioneering work of Lawrence Kohlberg, who was influenced by Piaget and Erikson, and who focused on the moral development of persons, appears most pertinent. It illuminates much about the rocky history of corporations, especially in America, and where they now find themselves.

Kohlberg discovered seven stages in human moral development. The first he calls the "obedience and punishment" phase. It is the way most young children reason. They think of morality as adhering to rules that adults make; one follows these rules to avoid punishment. The second stage he calls "individualism and exchange." In this stage, the child, usually now an older one, asks in situations calling for a choice: How can I best look out for my own best interests, not just to avoid punishment but possibly to gain favor and maybe even to get something in return from the other person involved?

By the teenage years, the child begins to think more in terms of maintaining good relations with the people who are important to him, especially in his own family, community, or peer group. One acts not just to curry reciprocity but to maintain a fabric of trust that everyone needs. At this stage, the young person is also becoming more aware of motives, and often tries to discern what a moral actor's inner intentions are. This definitely marks a step toward adulthood, but the developing individual's horizon is still somewhat delimited.

As someone enters young adulthood, a fourth stage in moral reasoning appears. Now the person begins to see that not just their immediate circle is influenced by the choices they make but, in important ways, the structure of the whole society is. Without going so far as to refer to Immanuel Kant, they might ask: What would happen if everyone acted this way? The same recognition of consequences beyond oneself that was there in the previous stage is still in play, but the intimate circle has been enlarged. This stage usually blends into the next one, the fifth, in which moral reasoning begins to take into its purview not just the reciprocal ordering of the society, but its overall health and vitality. This is clearly a mode of reasoning that requires some genuine maturity and a capacity for at least some abstract thinking. It is no longer just a question of how the choice I make will maintain the network, but of how it might improve or impair the network.

At one point in his work, Kohlberg sketched a sixth stage, a "universal" one, in which the individual is prepared to sacrifice his or her own rights and privileges, or possibly even life, for the good of the whole. He recognized, however, that only a very few individuals (such as Gandhi or Martin Luther King Jr.) reach this plateau, so he did not include it in his chart of normal stages of moral development.[7]

Viewed from the perspective of Kohlberg's pioneering work on the stages of moral development, corporations exhibit a peculiar pattern. When they were first chartered in America beginning in the 1790s, they were small and they were licensed by states for particular purposes. Shares in these companies were usually bought by local people who could take an active interest in how they were doing. The charter often stipulated the way they were to be governed, and—significantly—they were not created in perpetuity. Most importantly, the governments that chartered corporations asserted that since they were licensed by the public, they obviously bore some responsibility to the public. In other words, there were not just shareholders, there were also stakeholders—people and institutions whose interests the corporation should serve. It seems that these early corporations possessed at birth some of the qualities ordinary humans grow into during their lives.

But babies and infants do not stay in cradle and nursery. And corporations as they grew began to rebel against parental supervision, a stage human beings exhibit at about age two, as any parent will recognize. When they became even bigger, wealthier, and more politically influential, corporations succeeded in rolling back some of the governmental oversight, which they found cutting unduly into their profit-making. Eventually this ushered in the age of the famous "robber barons," the energetic chieftains of the railroad, oil, and other industries whose deep pockets and high testosterone levels could fend off too much government supervision.

Could this be compared to the stage of adolescent development most parents are familiar with, when many teenagers try to throw off the restraints they find stifling their right to stay out late and play loud music?

It was Theodore Roosevelt who took up the role of the parent in this situation. Supported by a growing popular resentment against the antics of the robber barons, he tried to reinstate some of the original restraints that had been in place when the corporations were born. In his first annual message to Congress in 1901, Teddy said, "Great corporations exist only because they are created and safeguarded by our institutions; and it is therefore our right and duty to see that they work in harmony with those institutions."[8] As a result of Roosevelt's efforts, and many other factors, the boisterous adolescent corporations were tamed, at least to some extent and for a time.

The next phase in the uneven maturation process of the American corporate person has been called the "managerial revolution," brought to the public's attention by an influential book by Adolf Berle and Gardiner Means.[9] The writers show how when corporations got larger, some extraordinarily so, those who had bought the stocks and who were therefore technically the owners could no longer exercise any real authority in governing these companies. They became "passive owners," the equivalent of absentee landlords. Consequently, the professional managers they had originally hired to look out for their interests began to look out for their own (the managers') interest as their first priority. They sometimes began to pick their own board members, often including CEOs of other corporations. Some CEOs even became chairmen of their own boards. Not surprisingly, executive salaries soared. Dispersed and at a distance, the stockholders could do little to thwart this managerial palace coup. An internal corporate contest between managers and stockholders might eventually have brought some of these companies to ruin, but for a very savvy move: the decision to pay the managers in part with stock options. This meant that the financial interests of the stockholders and of the managers would now more or less overlap.

But there was one serious flaw in the plan. These two parties were not the only stakeholders. There were also the employees, the suppliers, the customers, the local community, the country, and the whole planet (which in a period of ecological crisis seems to be a stakeholder worth considering). These other interested parties were all more or less ignored in the cozy new arrangement between managers and stockholders. The stage was set for a burst of self-centered and egotistical entitlement. This is also not an unfamiliar syndrome in young people, especially those from privileged families. The psychologist Robert Coles studied many youngsters in this age and class bracket and coined the term "narcissistic entitlement" to describe their outlook. It seems a particularly similar characteristic for the corporation in which the benefits of productivity are carved up by the managers and stockholders with little thought for any of the other shareholders.

At this stage, it is a powerful temptation for either a person or a corporation to identify its own interests and benefits with those of the larger society, if not the world. Charles Wilson, the flamboyant CEO of General Motors, once famously declaimed that "what is good for GM is good for America and what is good for America is good for GM." Still, even as the corporations were becoming more narcissistic, voices of maturity and a broader moral perspective could be heard in the business community. In 1981, the Business Roundtable stated that, in deciding on policies, corporate management should keep in mind "the impacts of all operating and policy decisions on each of the corporation's constituents. Responsibility to all these constituents *in toto* constitutes responsibility to society," and this includes providing jobs and building the economy as a whole.[10]

No doubt this statement constitutes a kind of ideal that not all corporations can fulfill. But among developmental psychologists, it was Erik Erikson who insisted that such ideal goals and images are integral to the maturation process. He invented the term "identity model," which suggests that as people mature they have in their minds a person or persons, often a parent, whom they sometimes unconsciously try to be like. But as a practicing psychotherapist, Erikson also noticed time and again that the model his patients looked to was not just the father but the father's model, and this in turn was drawn from previous models, thus carrying the process of identity formation into history, including religious and cultural heroes and saints. In other words, for Erikson, the daunting task of becoming a full person is not just an internal psychological one. It is imbedded in culture and history.

Erikson also discovered something else about the pathway through the various stages from infancy to old age. He found that, all too easily, people can become stuck or derailed. For a variety of reasons, both personal and societal, they might fail to negotiate the strenuous transition from adolescence to young adulthood or from adulthood to old age. They can become disoriented and begin to exhibit what Erikson called an "identity crisis," a term he also invented. Sometimes this happens because a person finds it difficult to respond to the changing demands and expectations of those with whom he or she lives. When this happens, it is too easy to shut some of these out and to focus on a much reduced set of obligations. The teenager who, like Peter Pan, just does not want to grow up but prefers to remain a *puer aeternus*, an eternal youth, represents a classic expression of this personality type. It is a type which played a prominent role in the psychological research of Carl Gustav Jung.

For Erikson, an identity crisis can consist of getting mired in one stage, unable to summon the resources or the imagination to move on to the next. This can happen when the individual hits some rough waters, changed circumstances, or unprecedented challenges. This is exactly what happened to American corporations as they hit the 1970s and 1980s. Riding high after victory in World War II, with global markets open to them and the dollar as the universally accepted reserve currency, they suddenly had to face revived and robust economies in Japan and Europe. Toyotas and Volkswagens began to crowd Fords and Chevrolets, even on American roads. This was followed by the spectacular ascent of China, which began to whip out consumer goods, clothing, and electronics that undercut the prices of their American counterparts.

Now the management-stockholder collaboration was faced with policy decisions which did not adhere to the high-minded ideals of the Business Roundtable. Maximizing profit shoved itself onto center stage. If management thought that firing a third of the workforce, or dumping refuse into a nearby river, or moving the whole operation to China would make the bottom line look better, it did so, with little regard to such stakeholders as employees, the local community, or the natural environment. And now, the same Business Roundtable that in 1981 had spelled out its ideal for the responsible corporation changed its tune. In 1997, it declared that the "principal objective of a business enterprise is to generate economic returns for its owners. . . . [I]f the CEO and the directors are not focused on shareholder value, it may be less likely the corporation will realize that value."[11] Notice that in this statement the other stakeholders are not even mentioned. It is remarkable how the conscience, both of individual human beings and of the new corporate persons, can adjust to the demands of the times.

Psychologically speaking, one could say that some corporations are mired in a kind of adolescent rut—a classic "identity crisis." Confronted by a barrage of new challenges from across the Pacific and the Atlantic, and now also from south of the Rio Grande, they have dug into a kind of narcissistic entitlement stance. Some have even convinced themselves that Charlie Wilson was right all along. The way for a corporation to serve the community, its employees, and the society as a whole is to "generate economic returns to its owners." In common parlance, it is to enlarge the whole pie—or better, *my* whole pie—and let others worry about how it is to be sliced and divided. The curious feature of this particular identity crisis, however, is that in some ways the typical corporation was healthier and more mature in the earliest years of its history, when corporations were chartered with a range of worthy and interested parties in mind. Now, that is rarely the case. But as with any psychological malady, the longer people remain in its grip, the worse their capacity to cope with reality becomes.

Business economists today sometimes worry about the effect this single-minded focus on maximizing profits will have on business as a whole, on the economy, and on the natural environment. Thoughtful observers worry about what impact the widening gap in wealth and income distribution will have on democratic governance. All things considered, the prognosis for the immobilized corporation is not good. Is there any way for today's corporation to wrench itself loose and begin to move toward a more mature life as what the Business Roundtable called a "responsible corporation"?

When it comes to individuals, sometimes the jolt comes from an intensified set of circumstances that force him or her to look within and make the necessary changes. Veterans of Alcoholics Anonymous report that when an alcoholic "hits the bottom"—wakes up on his lawn or forgets the whole previous evening, for example—the painful realization dawns that he has run out of resources of his own and will need help from elsewhere. Only then can a healing process begin. But often this self-realization does not happen by itself. In this case, various strategies are sometimes brought into play to facilitate it. One of these strategies is called an "intervention." Important people in the person's life, who have his best interest at heart, come together with the individual to help him to see what, given his own denial and defensiveness, he cannot discern himself. These equivalents of stakeholders do their best, but the next move must ultimately be taken by the individual.

This does not imply that even an obsessively profit-focused corporation is like a drunkard. But it does suggest that parties immobilized in an immature stage of development will often have a hard time recognizing their own conditions or seeing a way out. They need other actors who can both affirm their inner strengths and also help them to enlarge the circle of those to whom they need to be both responsive and responsible, in order to step beyond the distorted view of world and self that an inflated sense of entitlement carries with it. In the case of the corporation, it is especially vital to identify the strengths it has, even in what might seem to be a hopeless situation.

One very serious challenge that many executives see as alarming and even potentially catastrophic, and that might motivate them to think more self-critically about their overall business strategy, is the American trade deficit with China. This deficit now stands at somewhere between two and three trillion dollars, and if—despite China's recent economic difficulties—it continues to balloon, it will not be just this or that corporation in trouble but the whole American economy. Still, many US companies find it profitable to locate manufacturing bases in China, and recently even to move their research-and-development operations there. For some time, the Chinese have been using their colossal stash of dollars to buy US treasury bonds, but recently they have begun to buy American companies, or chunks of them, including a whole division of General Electric.

The report in early 2016 that China had bought the Chicago Stock Exchange was particularly disquieting to many business leaders. This turn of events, like waking up on the front lawn, might shake even the most narcissistic corporation into a new wakefulness. It is encouraging to notice that some leading executives know this. Back in 2001 Jeffrey Immelt, the CEO of General Electric, put it this way: "If the US government wants to fix the trade deficit, it's got to be pushed;

GE wants to be an exporter. We want to be a good citizen. Do we want to make a lot of money? Sure we do. But I think at the end of the day we've got to have a tax system or a set of incentives that promote what the government wants to do."[12] This statement, with its mention of citizenship, the role of government, and even tax incentives, is a clear indication that some corporations do have strengths to draw on. Also, without leaving profit-making out, it suggests that the idea of corporate responsibility to a wider horizon of stakeholders has not been totally forgotten. Might the external pressures on corporations—like increasingly effective foreign competition and the threat of climate change—combine with the kind of internal reflection exhibited by Mr. Immelt? If so, then at least some corporations might emerge from their egotistical adolescence and enter young adulthood. Who knows? At some point they might attain full adulthood. Eventually they might even be willing to recognize that, despite the unlimited lease on life some now claim, no corporation, not even Walmart, Apple, or McDonald's, will live forever. They came into being on earth and within human history and as mortal entities, and they bear some responsibility to see to it that both the earth and human history have a future.

5

Biblical Sources of Conflict over Usury and Phishing

No one can serve two masters. Either you will hate the one and love the other, or you will be devoted to the one and despise the other. You cannot serve both God and money.

—Matthew 6:12

In the previous chapter we saw that the Market God's relations with the Biblical God have often been testy. Almost from the first advent of markets, but especially since the Market's series of victories in the eighteenth and nineteenth centuries, the conflict has flickered and flared, with the Market frequently finding itself opposed by both religious leaders and laymen. At the source of this long clash lie two consistent biblical themes concerning the meaning of wealth.

The first is that God is the original creator of all of it. Therefore God is the true owner of the world's wealth and human beings are created to be its caretakers and stewards. As Psalm 24 begins, "The earth is the Lord's, and the fullness thereof; the world, and they that dwell therein. For he hath founded it upon the seas, and established it upon the floods." Whatever wealth we "own" as people is ours in a kind of trust. And that custodianship is not unconditional.

God's purpose in putting people in charge of his wealth—in lands, animals, or money—is to meet the needs of all human beings and all sentient creatures. Except for occasional fasting, there is little in the Bible to support asceticism. God wants people to be well fed and clothed. He wants us all to "prosper." Our prosperity, if we have it, carries with it the obligation of generosity to those who do not have it. On this point the much maligned "prosperity gospel" has it right. It just goes astray, as we will show later, when it suggests that those who enjoy prosperity do so because of their surfeit of piety, and those who do not prosper are being punished for their deficiency of spiritual zeal.

The second biblical theme that creates inevitable tension with The Market is God's unwavering bias in favor of the poor, "widows and orphans," and others who have no one to defend or speak for them. The Bible also warns that wealth can pose a serious spiritual danger. Those who have it are tempted by the comforts and the security it seems to offer to place their trust in the treasures they have "stored up on earth," even though—as Jesus frequently warned—all that can be swept away overnight. Also, the false comfort wealth brings can cause those who hold it to forget their responsibilities for the poor, the orphans, and the widows. As Pope Francis writes, it can lead to a "globalization of indifference."

Wealth can often be the product of injustice perpetrated by the privileged against those who are excluded from the benefits it brings, and the Bible warns that they will not escape retribution. One need only turn to almost any page in the books of prophets Amos or Isaiah to see this theme emphasized. Here is Amos warning the prosperous and powerful of Israel: "Therefore because you trample on the poor, and take from them levies of grain, you have built houses of hewn stone but you shall not live in them; you have planted pleasant vineyards, but you shall not drink their wine" (Amos 5:11). Jesus picks up and continues this theme, especially in his inaugural sermon in the synagogue of his home town, Nazareth. He declares, "The Spirit of the Lord is on me, because he has anointed me to proclaim good news to the poor. He has sent me to proclaim freedom for the prisoners and recovery of sight for the blind, to set the oppressed free, to proclaim the year of the Lord's favor" (Luke 4:18–19).

These basic biblical principles, God's ownership of the world's bounty and God's bias for the poor, are expressed in the Bible in two institutions that date back to the earliest days of the ancient Hebrews but continue, in one way or another, to our time. The first is the repeated prohibition of usury, or charging interest on a loan. The second is the periodic observance of the "Jubilee Year," a mandate for a regular and radical redistribution of land and wealth. Both these biblical institutions might seem picturesque and antiquated today, but on closer examination they turn out to have an urgent relevance in our time. In the next chapter we will examine the annals of the Jubilee Year. This chapter will look at the prohibition of usury which, despite its biblical clarity and consistency, has had a tangled history of interpretation.

In our era of credit cards, thirty-year mortgages, colossal sovereign debt, the World Bank, and the IMF, we rarely think about usurers. It is easy to forget, unless we witness *The Merchant of Venice* or dip into Dante's *Inferno*, the low regard in which they have been held in history. Take Dante for example:

> From art and nature, if you will recall
> The opening of Genesis, man is meant
> To earn his way and further humankind.
>
> But still the usurer takes another way:
> He scorns nature and her follower, art,
> Because he puts his hope in something else.[1]

Why such a dim view of money lenders? The biblical proscription of taking interest, especially from the poor, is not peripheral to the Hebrew faith. It first appears in the book of Exodus and is integral to the covenant God gives the Hebrews at Mount Sinai: "If you lend money to my people, to the poor among you, you shall not deal with them as a creditor. You shall not exact interest from them" (Exodus 22:25).

As it stands, this command seems unambiguous, but countless pages of exegesis have been devoted to discussing exactly what the term "interest" means here. Does it refer to charging anything at all for money lent, or just an unfair rate? And what if one is not lending to "the poor" but to someone who is not ordinarily in need but requires some temporary financial backing? The Hebrew word for "interest" used here is *nesek*, the same word for "bite," which carries connotations of callousness and malice. Some commentators make a distinction between personal loans, for which no interest should be charged, and loans of a more commercial type which can legitimately demand it.[2]

The Hebrew Bible itself includes several examples of the application of the prohibition of usury. Amongst the miscellaneous laws spelled out in Deuteronomy is a ban on charging interest of a fellow Israelite, although it is lawful to take it from a foreigner (Deuteronomy 23:19–20). In Deuteronomy 24, a lender is forbidden to take away such necessities of life as millstones and cloaks even if they have been pledged as collateral. The catalog of discouraged collateral later expands—surprisingly—to children. In 2 Kings 4, a widow cries out to the prophet Elisha that her husband has died and "now his creditor is coming to take my two boys as his slaves." Did such foreclosures really go on? Since admonishments tend to arise only when there are abuses to correct, we can presume that they did. Children, for example, might have been forced to work in the fields, perhaps until their father's debt was paid.

Notice that when the faith of the luckless Job was being tested, one of his inept "comforters," Eliphaz the Temanite, who is trying to uncover some reason why God is punishing Job, accuses him of exacting pledges from his own brothers and leaving people "stripped of their clothes and naked" (Job 22:6). Later on, when Job has tasted what it is like to be destitute, he rages against those who mistreat the impoverished and warns that a day of reckoning is coming for the wicked who "drive off the donkey belonging to the fatherless, and lead away the widow's ox with a rope." This evidently refers to items put up as collateral for a loan. And again we see disgust for lenders who would even "take the poor person's child in pledge" (Job 24: 3,9).

Another text on usury can be found in book of Leviticus (25:35–37), where it is flatly stated that one must not lend the poor money at interest or even sell them food at a profit. In the later books of the Hebrew Scripture the condemnation of usury (whatever it may have meant) continues. When the writer of Psalm 15 asks who is qualified to come into the presence of the Lord, the implied list of those who are *not* welcome puts people who lend money for interest in some rather sordid company:

> Lord, who may lodge in your tent?
> Who may dwell on your holy mountain?
> One of blameless life, who does what is right
> and speaks the truth from his heart;
> who has no malice on his tongue,
> who never wrongs his fellow,
> and tells no tales against his neighbor;
> who shows his scorn for those the Lord rejects,
> but honours those who fear the Lord;
> who holds to his oath even to his own hurt,

who does not put his money out to usury,
and never accepts a bribe against the innocent.
He who behaves in this way will remain unshaken.

(Psalm 15)

The Prophet Ezekiel's inventory of *personae non gratae* is even more colorful. He catalogs people who lend at interest with those who worship idols, defile their neighbors' wives, commit robbery, and join in abominable rites (Ezekiel 18:11–13). Obviously in these passages—and more could be added—usury is not just a minor offense. It is viewed as a major transgression, at least on paper.

The question, however, is how far the proscription goes beyond paper. Rabbinical commentators often stress that the underlying objective of the Bible's monetary rules—the "spirit of the law," so to speak—was to protect the orphan and the widow, and this could mean that in strictly commercial transactions, where the poor were not involved, lending at interest may have been permitted. Also, in apparent disregard to clear regulations, there are passages (such as Psalm 112:5) in which it seems to be assumed that many lenders charge interest, but that good will come to those who lend freely. These seemingly contradictory or at least ambiguous texts have provided ample evidence and counter-evidence for centuries of debates about what the God of the Bible requires of men of commerce.

Still, once a chink in the wall of the law is discovered, the way is opened for more and more expansive and relaxed interpretations. This inviting line of inquiry has led later generations of casuists—Jewish, Catholic, and Protestant—to find ways around clearly stated prohibitions without ever denying the text in question.

It might seem natural to ask: well, faced with these legal strictures and aware of some of the wiggle room, what did people actually do?

74

Unfortunately, it is next to impossible to find out how the ancient peoples who lived more directly under the sway of the Torah, especially the Law Code in the book of Deuteronomy, interpreted these texts or how closely they followed them. It is never possible to ascertain what was actually going on, or not going on, in any past society simply by scanning its law books. The explicit prohibition of crimes and misdeeds, however, suggests that these things were in fact happening and therefore warnings constantly needed to be posted. All things considered, the Hebrew Bible leaves ample room for quibbling about the fine details of charging interest, but is unequivocal in its insistence on generous treatment of the deprived and the needy.

Then what about the New Testament? Actually there is surprisingly little mention of lending, debt, or usury in the Gospels or the Epistles. The Greek word for both lending and borrowing, *daneizo*, appears only three times. Most famously it appears in parable of the unmerciful servant. As Jesus tells the story, a servant who owed ten thousand talents to his king was unable to pay, and therefore was ordered to be sold "with his wife and his children and everything he had" to make up for the debt. But seeing the man fall on his knees and beg for mercy, the king was moved with pity and utterly forgave the financial obligation. The lesson Jesus wants to teach here, however, is not principally concerned with commercial ethics. The parable continues that, having been dealt with so kindly by the king, the servant in turn meted out an opposite treatment to his fellow servant, who owed him a much smaller sum. He demanded full payment, and when the second servant could not pay, had him thrown in prison. The king soon heard about this and his response was to reinstate the original servant's debt, with jail time and torture added for good measure. Rebuking his debtor fiercely, he asked, "Ought you not to have shown mercy to your fellow servant when I showed mercy to you?"

(Matthew 18:23–25). For Jesus, the point of the parable is to show by analogy how God expects his mercy to be emulated. Indeed the story calls to mind the line in the Lord's Prayer, "Forgive us our debts as we forgive our debtors." It hardly seems that Jesus is intending here to clarify the rules of lending.

The record is not entirely clear. Jesus advises his disciples to lend money to those in need (implying, incidentally, that not all his followers were poor) but then he makes life difficult for those who would act on this instruction by adding that they should "expect nothing in return" (Luke 6:34–35)—which is hardly a policy JP Morgan Chase could adopt. In another of his stories (related somewhat differently by Matthew and Luke), Jesus tells of a man who entrusted servants with the caretaking of portions of his wealth while he spent a long time away. The servant who ended up angering him was the one who chose to bury the money rather than put it to work producing more wealth. The master reproached him for not at least giving it to the bankers and earning interest. This is the only clear reference to lending with interest in Jesus's teachings. As can be imagined it has become a favorite proof text for those latter-day followers who want to reconcile doing good with doing well. But the parable of the talents provides only a slender reed for such purposes. While the servants who increased the assets they managed were handsomely rewarded (and Jesus seems to commend their investment risk-taking) the master who allotted the cash is not depicted as an admirable man. Most commentators stress that Jesus is illustrating how those who take the portion of grace they have already received and put it to work on Earth will see outsized rewards in the Kingdom of God.

All in all, the biblical view of charging interest, although complex, is unequivocal when it comes to the poor. Charging them more than the capital for the money lent to them is not allowable. It is robbery. First, it deprives the disadvantaged of resources they need to live, which is an offence against God. Second, as an expression of avarice, it presents all the serious spiritual pitfalls that wealth and acquisitiveness bear with them. Usury's damage cuts both ways. On this point at least, Shakespeare's garrulous old Polonius ("neither a borrower nor a lender be") was on to something.

After the New Testament, in the early centuries of Christianity, bishops and preachers continued to take a very dim view of lending at interest. Saint Basil, the bishop of Caesarea in Cappadocia and a famously silver-tongued preacher (329–379 CE), warned his people against borrowing and thundered against anyone who would take advantage of the destitute by charging interest for a loan. Instead, he insisted, they should help the poor with outright gifts. Such gifts, he said, were the equivalent of investing in God. His claim had a basis in scripture: "He who is generous to the poor lends to the Lord, who will recompense him for his deed" (Proverbs 19:17).

But just as the Supreme Court is said to keep an eye on the newspapers, bishops and theologians also stayed alert to what was happening in the world outside the parish house, perhaps especially in the marketplace. As the second millennium of Christianity began to unfold, so did the realm of commerce and with it the loaning of money. In the Medieval period, both the Church and the culture at large viewed usury as an abominable immorality. When Dante outlined the nine progressively deep circles of hell, he placed usurers in the innermost ring of the seventh, alongside blasphemers and sodomites deemed to be equally "violent against nature." Worse even than the sinners who commit physical violence against acquaintances and strangers, usurers are described as sitting in agony while they futilely try to swat away the stings they feel from a hot, biting wind (an apt punishment given that, as noted earlier, the Hebrew word used for "interest" is the same as for "bite.") Usury was seen both as a trespass against nature and a crime against the poor, an expression of the deadly sin of avarice. The penalties for practicing it were often harsh. Usurers were not permitted to receive communion and were banned from confession, absolution, and Christian burial. In the thirteenth century, an ecclesial court in Florence collected fines of 7,000 florins from "usurers and blasphemers." The Council of Vienne in 1312 declared that rulers and magistrates who allowed usury were subject to excommunication; and that anyone who preached that usury was not a grievous sin was a heretic and should be dealt with by the Inquisition. On both these fronts, confessors were to make inquiries into possible cupidity or covetousness.

Other inventories of transgressions put moneylenders in very bad company. One such guide for the priest behind the screen instructs him to ask about "rapine, usury . . . barratry, false and lying sales, unjust weights and measures, lying, perjury and craft."[3] Of course, as commerce grew, transactions became more complicated and, as volumes of correspondence between Rome and the bishops testify, the difficulty of enforcing the strictures became trickier. What about selling wares at a price higher than that originally quoted if their value has gone up? When a usurer is compelled to make restitution but the borrower has died, must the restitution be made to the heirs? Sometimes, in response to these queries, the higher clergy resorted to a kind of spirit-of-the-law answer, saying that what really mattered was the intent. One response, for example, states that in general, faithful Christians should "have wide regard for their salvation . . . since the thought of men cannot be concealed from Almighty God."[4] This advice implies a kind of "self-regulation" which, as we have noticed in later centuries, cannot always be relied on.

It is sometimes argued that the Reformation sounded the death knell for religious objections to usury, but this claim oversimplifies a complicated situation. The Catholic Church was itself the biggest landowner in Europe and not always exemplary in the way it treated its tenants and serfs. Nor did it always deal gently with its own children, like the spiritual Franciscans, who warned that ecclesial riches were handicapping its stated mission to preach and exemplify the teachings of the poor carpenter of Galilee. Many of these troublesome monks ended their days on flaming pyres along with other heretics. It is true that John Calvin allowed for moderate interest to be charged in the ultra-reformed (and commercial) city-state of Geneva. The "allowed" part of his doctrine was quickly accepted, but the "moderate" part was soon ignored. In England, the Puritans, direct descendants of Calvin, seized on the "moderate interest" idea and ran with it. Moderation, it seems, could mean almost anything and the Puritans took to interest, as one writer says, "like Turks took to polygamy." One wonders, five centuries later, how today's Swiss bankers interpret Calvin's doctrine, or if they even know about it. But the truth is that neither Protestants nor Catholics could hold out for long against the flood of credit instruments of many kinds that arrived along with the rise of capitalism.

They often tried. In 1552, in Scotland, which came to be renowned not just for its penny-pinching but also for its sharp business practices, the newly Reformed Church nonetheless issued a catechism that condemned usurers, along with covetous merchants, masters who withhold wages, and landlords who grind their tenants. But as the bustle of business grew louder, all but drowned out were the exhortations of preachers and moralists. In a widely read 1572 treatise by Thomas Wilson entitled "Discourse upon Usury," the argument is framed that lending with interest is essential to building new industries, and that merchants and other businessmen "must not be overthwarted by preachers and others that cannot skill their doings." In twenty-first-century English this simply means: don't pay any attention to these religious busybodies and their harping; they don't know what they're talking about.[5]

A careful reading of the history of this critical period in the struggle of the Market to assume its place in the sun suggests that it was not in fact the Reformation that cleared the way for the kinds of financial practices that would have invited excommunication not many decades earlier. Catholics and Protestants who tried to defend traditional restraints both knew they were fighting a losing battle. The theologians tried various tactics. One strategy, as we have seen, was to try to rein in runaway avarice instead of trying to abolish it—a policy that proved largely ineffective.

Another and more creative maneuver by some guilds, parishes, and monasteries was to create alternative institutions from which the poor could secure loans at far lower rates. In 1462 the Franciscans, traditionally concerned about the poor, created the model for a mont-de-piété (or bank of pity) which they spread throughout Italy, and later to France and Germany. It was subsequently picked up by Protestant groups, and its descendants can still be seen in church-sponsored credit unions.

But these noble attempts were dwarfed by the larger currents of economic change. All the ecclesial forces in the world could not turn back the tide of contracts, colonies, trading companies, partnerships, and credit mechanisms. In the seventeenth century, a symbolic climax occurred in the millennia-long dispute when a certain Rev. David Jones decided to preach a sermon against usury in St Mary Woolnoth, a London Anglican church. His text: "The Pharisees who were covetous heard all these things and they derided Christ." For his efforts the preacher was summarily dismissed from his post.[6]

Today the centuries-old prohibitions against usury can seem as archaic as laws against witchcraft or seething a young goat in its mother's milk. But when we look below the surface for the spiritual and moral values that animate them, the injunctions become painfully relevant. This is exactly the approach Jesus took to interpreting the precepts of the Jewish Law in his day. He plainly said that he had "not come to abolish the law, but to fulfill it." And while he warned that "not one jot or tittle of the Law" should be tampered with, his strategy was to dig into the fundamental intention of a law and to base his actions on that. He obeyed the animating "spirit" more than the "letter" of it. Thus, when he appeared to violate the rule forbidding work on the Sabbath by performing acts of healing on that seventh day, he was out to make a larger point—just as he was when he flouted laws specifying with whom Jews should dine. He even sometimes contrasted fellow Jews unfavorably with certain Gentiles he met. If the same approach to upholding the spirit of old laws were taken today regarding usury, what surprising practices might we see?

The original inspiration for the prohibition was simply moral insight into what today we would call "predatory lending." And it would be hard to claim that we no longer have any of that going on. In fact we seem to be surrounded and besieged by it. In their recent book *Phishing for Phools: The Economics of Manipulation and Deceit*, George Akerlof and Robert Shiller make a convincing case that in recent years, predatory lending, enhanced by the newest techniques in communication and marketing, is enjoying a heyday. The thesis of these highly respected economists (both winners of the Sveriges Riksbank Prize in Economic Sciences, called by many the Nobel Prize in Economics) is that The Market, far from exposing and discouraging deception in marketing—for example, of mortgages, credit cards, and property sales with their steep "closing costs"—actually encourages it, practically to the point of making it necessary.[7]

These writers are not trying to make villains of the companies or the individuals who engage in such devious activities. On the contrary, they demonstrate that, given the pressures of The Market, sellers have little choice if they want to stay in business. The logic of The Market does not favor the needy. It favors those who attract the most customers, in whatever way they do it. The word "phishing" in the zany title of their penetrating study is a 1990s coinage referring to the metaphorical fishing an online scam artist does, hoping some unsuspecting Internet users will bite and unwittingly hand over confidential information. (In my own place of work, we are frequently warned to be wary of phishing emails that instruct us to click on seemingly legitimate links and enter private data, lest we become accomplices in delivering our own information to parties only pretending to be who they say they are.) "Phool" is the phishers' term for any individual they manage to dupe.

Akerlof and Shiller broaden the word "phishing" to include a range of corporate practices that involve the use of information gathered from potential customers to push products and services. The deceit involved here is rarely outright lying; rather it is the stretching, shading, and tilting of information to convey impressions that are not in keeping with the facts. Professional magicians and circus barkers are familiar with this level of fabrication and legerdemain. The importance of the insights in *Phishing for Phools* is that they thoroughly undermine one of the most precious doctrines in the creed of The Market: the myth of the rational decision-maker. The fact is that consumers are not fundamentally rational at all. They are easily manipulated creatures of impulse, fantasy, and self-deception. As P. T. Barnum might have said, "There's a phool born every minute." This is a decisive criticism because without a rational decision maker at its base the whole towering campanile of the Market God's basilica totters and crashes into the courtyard. But until that happens, the limitless imagination of the phishermen will continue to transform peoples' idle wishes, uncovered by focus groups, niche research, and surveys, into false perceptions of real needs. The phools who succumb will continue their march on an endless treadmill of consumption, a stairway to a paradise without a top.

How, exactly, do companies hawk their hollow products? For the answer, look to the methods of The Market's equivalent of missionary and evangelistic outreach. The Market's Secretariat for Propagation of the Faith, its division of proselytism, is its advertising department. This wing is not just an adjunct. Without it, the whole juggernaut of modern business would be brought to a standstill. As Akerlof and Shiller move into their chapter in which "Advertisers Discover How to Zoom in on Our Weak Spots" they arrive at the common ground with theology. It is the man-as-tale-teller territory that I touched on in an earlier chapter of this book. They see human beings not as the data-sifting decision makers of classical economic theory, but as creatures who live by narratives, according to the stories they hear and the ones they tell themselves and each other.[8]

The overlap with religion is obvious. The content of traditional religions is made up of narratives: myths, legends, parables, liturgies, and testimonies. These are what enable human beings as habitual storytellers to grasp the precepts of traditional religions and to weave them into their own internal narratives. But Madison Avenue knows this secret, too. Modern advertising is a compendium of graphic stories, endlessly repeated, that lure listeners and watchers into internalizing them or at least into retaining them in their semi-conscious psyches.

No analysis of Market civilization by any other economists so dramatically illuminates the fact that what we are seeing today is a contest between rival faiths (even if, again, the flame keepers of the Market God fail to recognize or refuse to admit it). Phishing is just a modern form of what our ancestors called usury, taking advantage of the weak, uninformed, and vulnerable for purposes of profit taking. And those who practice it deserved to be placed, as those ancestors placed them, in the company of the worst of bottom-feeders.

Luis Borges once remarked that "the future belongs to those who tell the best stories." But what stories are "best" and how do we judge among them? What I have tried to do in this book is to suggest that the rhapsodic chronicle we hear so often about the beauty and benefits of The Market, and how "natural" it is, is just one story among others. Current-world conditions of stubborn joblessness and growing economic inequality are putting that story to a severe test. But the story is not yet over. Current signs indicate that much of the human race has now totally forgotten how unjust and humiliating it is to take from people the resources they need to live, and to exact personal gain from their misery. We will turn to this in the next chapter.

6

Biblical Sources of Conflict over Redistribution

> Set aside and consecrate the fiftieth year to declare liberty throughout the land for all of its inhabitants. It is to be a jubilee for you. Every person is to return to his own land that he has inherited. Likewise, every person is to return to his tribe.
>
> —Leviticus 25:10

In addition to prohibiting usury, the Hebrew Bible also mandates a program for the radical redistribution of wealth. It calls this the "Jubilee Year." Plainly the ancient Hebrews not only were uneasy with economic inequality and the dangers it posed to their nation, they also took extraordinary measures to counter it. Maybe the origin of their disquietude and action is that they believed they were living as members of a covenant community (the Hebrew term is *berith*), which involved a permanent contractual agreement between the people and God, and among the people themselves.[1] Like so many recent observers, they recognized that no society afflicted by excessive inequality could survive for long, because it would erode all sense of common belonging—still a dangerous development, especially for a democracy which can function properly only if all citizens feel they have a genuine stake in its future.

This point is made with special forcefulness by Thomas Piketty in his surprise bestseller *Capital in the Twenty-First Century*.[2] Piketty also amply demonstrates that since wealth tends to accumulate and perpetuate itself, political and social countermeasures are needed. The Hebrews recognized this and saw that they needed more than exhortations. They needed institutions to accomplish the regular redistribution of that wealth. The "Jubilee Year" eventually became the principal vehicle for that reallocation.

Like many biblical institutions, the Jubilee Year developed over a period of centuries. It grew out of the more fundamental tradition of observing the Sabbath every seven days. The account of creation in Genesis states that, having created the world in six days, on the seventh day, "God rested." Human beings and animals (and later the land itself) were therefore commanded to rest as well. This rule was sanctified as the Fourth Commandment on the tablets believed to have been given to Moses and the Hebrew people at Mount Sinai:

> Remember the Sabbath day, and keep it holy. Six days you shall labor and do all your work. But the seventh day is a Sabbath to the Lord your God; you shall not do any work—you, your son or your daughter, your male or female slave, your livestock, or the alien resident in your towns. For in six days the Lord made heaven and earth, the sea, and all that is in them, but rested the seventh day; therefore the Lord blessed the Sabbath day and consecrated it. (Exodus 20:8)

Keeping the weekly Sabbath in one way or another has survived among Jews for thousands of years, and is understood by many rabbis to be the most important of all the commandments. There is a tale the activist Rabbi Abraham Joshua Heschel used to tell about a rabbi who was taking a stroll in his garden on the Sabbath when he noticed that one of his apple trees needed pruning. Recognizing that he should not do the trimming on the Sabbath, the rabbi decided he would attend to it the following day. But when he walked into the garden the next day, he saw that the apple tree had shriveled into a dried stump. Annoyed, the rabbi prayed to God, "Why have you withered my tree? Did you not notice that I conscientiously postponed pruning it until after the Sabbath?"

"Not good enough," God replied. "You should not even *think* about work on the Sabbath!"

The Jubilee Year evolved out of this strong habit. First came the "Sabbath Year" (Exodus 23:10 and Leviticus 25). This is an entire twelve months in which fields are to remain fallow, and thus be given a rest, after six years of sowing and harvesting. Food has to be stored from what are presumably bumper crops in year six. Next, in more of the spirit of the Jubilee Year, came the observance of a "year for canceling debts." As specified in Deuteronomy, the rule is that "At the end of every seven years you must cancel debts. This is how it is to be done: Every creditor shall cancel any loan they have made to a fellow Israelite. They shall not require payment from anyone among their own people, because the Lord's time for canceling debts has been proclaimed" (Deuteronomy 15:1–2).

Finally, in the book of religiously based legal provisions called Leviticus, a full-blown year of redistribution is decreed. God himself instructs Moses:

Count off seven sabbath years—seven times seven years—so that the seven sabbath years amount to a period of forty-nine years. Then have the trumpet sounded everywhere on the tenth day of the seventh month; on the Day of Atonement sound the trumpet throughout your land. Consecrate the fiftieth year and proclaim liberty throughout the land to all its inhabitants. It shall be a jubilee for you; each of you is to return to your family property and to your own clan. (Leviticus 25:8–10)[3]

The very term "Jubilee" derived from the *jubel*, the trumpet-like ram's horn that was to be sounded to announce its start. This statute adds that all debts were to be either reduced or canceled (the record is not clear). Mortgages were annulled. All slaves were to be freed. Bonded servants could return to their families.

The Jubilee Year was intended to be an across-the-board wiping of the slate, a "Return to 'Go,'" and the opening of a new game on what is now called a level playing surface. And it is important to recognize that this institution was not instituted by the prophets, whom we are used to seeing as the main advocates for the poor, but is imbedded in the holy law of the people. It is foundational.

But was the Jubilee Year ever really observed? Or was it seen as a kind of ideal worth striving for but never realized in actuality? Scholars have puzzled over this question for hundreds of years. Skeptics ask how any sort of borrowing or loaning could have survived such a sweeping debt-elimination policy. Why would lenders risk making loans, especially in those years when the Jubilee was nearing? But scholars who maintain that the Jubilee Year was observed, at least in some measure, point out the surprising level of detail of the debt forgiveness policy spelled out in subsequent verses. They specify, for example, the different treatment of property inside town walls versus in the open country. (The first was exempted from the redistribution but the second was not. Why? Was it because the farming and grazing areas so clearly belonged to God, while there was some doubt about the city properties? There is no clear answer.)

The Jubilee Year was probably not being practiced in the time of Jesus. The harsh taxation polices of the Roman occupiers and their oppressive land-control situation might have made it impossible. But people obviously still knew about it. In his initial announcement of his mission at the synagogue in Nazareth (Luke 4:16–19) Jesus first reads from portions of the Torah. Just before "closing the scroll" he announces "the year of the Lord's favor," which scholars agree refers to the Jubilee Year. Knowing this clarifies the words Jesus uses in teaching his disciples to pray: "Forgive us our debts as we forgive our debtors." Unfortunately in many denominations, the words "trespass" and "trespass against us" are substituted for the language of debt. But "trespass" in colloquial English has become trivial. It conjures up the idea of walking across a meadow or someone's front yard where a "No Trespassing" sign is posted. The phrase has been emptied of its original economic substance.

And what has happened to the Jubilee Year itself? Its post-biblical history presents a noteworthy example of the complex interaction between the biblical God and the Market Deity. The Jubilee Years proclaimed by popes for the past several centuries began with Boniface VII in his bull "Antiquorum Habet Fida Relatio." The year 1300, he announced, was to be a Holy Year. The big event was to be the opening of all the historic churches of Rome for pilgrims from all over Europe with the papal assurance that such a pilgrimage, preferably on foot, would gain an indulgence for their sins. There were other enticements. Judges sometimes sentenced convicted criminals to go on this pilgrimage rather than to prison. For some young folks it sounded like a lark. There were undoubtedly also people along who were trying to get away from a family or a village they didn't like, or even from the wrath of an angry cuckolded husband. A wide variety of people went on pilgrimages, as we can see in Chaucer's *Canterbury Tales*. But the papal promise of the "plenary indulgence" capped the deal for many. This was too good a chance to miss, and thousands began descending on Rome in the Christmas season of 1299.

The innkeepers and restaurant owners were exultant, and had a very good year, and so did the church. Christ and The Market were co-operating splendidly, to the profit of both. The tradesmen were selling large quantities of pasta and Chianti. The churchmen were filling the treasury by the sale of indulgences since people wanted even more than the arduous slog to Rome merited them, and were willing to pay. Both the businessmen and the ecclesiastics liked the Jubilee so much they immediately pressed for another one as soon as possible. But Pope Clement VI, not wanting to overdo even a very good thing, ruled that there had to be fifty years between Holy Years.

The pressure continued, however, and a few decades later Pope Urban VI decided to reduce the period to thirty-three years—in memory, he said, of the earthly life of Jesus. Customer demand, un-dergirded by the shopkeepers' and the prelates' eagerness to keep up the cash flow, sparked new interest in more Jubilees. And popes began adding features to make the journey to Rome more attractive. Thus when Pope Boniface IX opened a Holy Year in 1390, he set what was to become a landmark precedent: with considerable ceremony he opened the Holy Door of Saint Peter's Basilica on Christmas Eve. Pilgrims arrived in hordes, and he called a second Holy Year of his reign for 1400. All kinds of people, from princes to paupers, made the trek—among them Dante Alighieri, no friend of the papacy, who writes of the event in his *Divine Comedy* in canto XXXI of *Il Paradiso*.

As years went by it became evident that the thirty-three-year rule was not being adhered to, and still more special features were added to the Jubilees. In 1425, Pope Martin V proclaimed a Holy Year, and this time a special Jubilee Medal that the pilgrims could take home with them was struck. Also, another "Holy Door," this one in the Cathedral of Saint John Lateran, was ceremonially opened. Again the Jubilee was highly successful, and Pope Nicholas V, ignoring the thirty-three year policy, called for a Holy Year in 1450. Tens of thousands of people swarmed into Rome, but the year turned out to be anything but a blessing for some of them. Plague tore through their camps. Hundreds were crushed to death or drowned during a stampede on one of the city's bridges—reminding us that the tragedy in 2015, when over two thousand Muslims crowding toward Mecca lost their lives, was the latest but hardly the first such catastrophe at a holy site.

Some people have wondered why the mere opening of a door, even a very large one, should be treated as such a special event. The reason becomes clearer when one remembers the many years of Rome's history filled with factional disputes and bloodletting among rival families, some of whom controlled one church or another. Church buildings also served as fortresses. Opening their doors to virtually anyone signaled both a period of relative civic peace and also that the pope rather than any feuding clan, like the Borgias or the Colonnas, was in charge. Thus, when Pope Alexander VI announced in 1500 that the doors in all four major basilicas would be opened, and that he himself would open the Holy Door of Saint Peter's, he renewed a ritual that every pope since him has continued.

Seeing what was happening with the Jubilees, Pope Paul II had in 1470 issued a Bull to limit them to every twenty-five years. As soon as the twenty-five years passed, Pope Sixtus IV called for one in 1475. This one is important in history because the pope spent vast amounts of money to beautify Rome for the occasion. Artists like Verrocchio, Botticelli, Perugino, and Pinturicchio were commissioned to produce work, and the pope also ordered the construction of the Sistine Chapel (named after himself), which Michelangelo later decorated with the murals that now draw millions of people every year.

Crowd control and public health were not the only troubles rising with Holy Years; discontent was brewing on another level. Even before Luther took up the cause against the sale of indulgences, the practice was coming under severe criticism by Catholic theologians. According to the Church's teaching at the time, every sin must be purified either here on earth or after death in a state called purgatory. An indulgence annuls this, and grants the full or partial remission of punishment for sins, but only after the sinner confesses and receives absolution. The Church's right to dispense such indulgences is based on Jesus's statement to Peter: "I tell you that you are Peter [the rock], and on this rock I will build my church, and the gates of Hades will not overcome it. I will give you the keys of the kingdom of heaven; whatever you bind on earth will be bound in heaven, and whatever you loose on earth will be loosed in heaven" (Matthew 16:18–19).

Protestant (and some Catholic) biblical scholars have contended that this statement does not give popes the power either to remit punishment or to cancel the need to make restitution for sins. But by the time they were writing, the dispensing of indulgences had been underway for five centuries. It began in 1095 when Pope Urban II remitted all penance of persons who participated in the Crusades and who confessed their sins. Later, the indulgences were also offered to those who couldn't go on the Crusades but offered cash contributions to support those campaigns instead. But this prepared the stage for possible abuse, which set in rather quickly. By the early 1200s, the Church, obviously influenced by evolving banking practices, began claiming that it had control of a "treasury of merit," a stash of indulgences paid for by the merits of Christ and the good deeds of the saints. Further, it could make withdrawals from this account for its own purposes and for other worthy persons. Technically, deserving penitents had first to confess, but then make an appropriate "contribution" to the church, with the amount usually stipulated by the presiding priest. Money and religion were being fused in a manner that did not bode well.

The system was obviously vulnerable to enormous corruption, and that is exactly what happened. When Luther posted his Ninety-Five Theses on the door of the castle church in Wittenberg in 1517, his main complaint was about indulgences. He also, of course, brought up other issues. If the pope did not have the authority to grant those, what others of the forms of authority claimed for him were also specious? Luther went on to question the whole institution of the papacy, and the Protestant Reformation was underway. But it had started with a spat about money.

For many artists and innkeepers, and for the church coffers, the Jubilee Years looked at the beginning of the sixteenth century to be a roaring success. In that moment, and in one city, the Christian God and the Market God appeared to be profiting in tandem. But the tidy arrangement was coming unglued. Luther as a young monk had visited the Holy City and been disgusted by its pomp and lascivious excesses. Back home, he inveighed against pilgrimages and advised people to stay put and read their Bibles rather than travel to Rome or the Holy Land or to any of the many pilgrimage sites that were thriving in Europe (usually built around the relics of a saint, which Luther also detested). Ironically, in the same year that Luther tacked his challenge to the door, Pope Leo X came to the conclusion that he needed a lot more money to complete his signature contribution to the skyline of Rome, Saint Peter's Basilica. Following a business model that has since then become commonplace—see, for example, McDonald's, 7-Eleven, and SuperCuts—he entered into an arrangement that essentially sold franchises. These allowed enterprising indulgence sellers to retain about half the funds they raised in return for sending the other half to Rome, which Leo could then pour into his ambitious construction project.

There is a downside, however, to franchising, as many licensors have discovered: it is often hard to control quality once the product is in someone else's hands. One such franchise holder, Albert of Brandenburg, attempted to get ahead of his competition by advertising indulgences (which he insisted were issued by the pope) that guaranteed a complete remission of sins, allowing escape from all the pains of purgatory. Sweetening the deal further with an appeal to family values, Albert claimed that purchasers of his brand of indulgences could use them to free already dead loved ones from the pains of purgatory they must certainly be suffering.

The sales pitch tugged at the heartstrings of potential customers. Who, having imagined their departed fathers and mothers pleading through flames, could refuse to release them from the torment? Albert also had a sliding scale. The going rate for an indulgence depended on one's station, and ranged from twenty-five gold florins for kings, queens, and archbishops down to three florins for merchants and just one-quarter florin for the poorest of believers.[4] It was a sales campaign worthy of the PowerPoint machinations of Madison Avenue, but it eventually became very costly indeed. Due in part to the venality of the indulgence trade, half of Europe joined in the Reformation, and the Catholic Church was left with only a portion of what today it seems fair to call its "customer base." I was reminded of this a few years ago when I visited Saint Peter's and was guided by a very knowledgeable Jesuit. One of the guests in our party asked him, "Father, how much did this whole place cost?" The priest smiled wryly. "It cost," he said, "northern Europe."

Still, despite the objections of the reformers, the succession of Jubilee Years rolled on, interrupted periodically by unsettled conditions in Rome. People still made their way there by the tens of thousands, received indulgences, and spent a lot of money. In 1575, at the time of

Pope Gregory XIII, as many as three hundred thousand people came to Rome from all over Europe. More than a half a million pilgrims made the journey to Rome for the Jubilee of 1825. Later in the nineteenth century it became difficult for the church to proclaim Holy Years because of the battles for the unification of Italy, the occupation of the city, and the abolition of the Papal state. But such celebrations do not die easily. The first Jubilee of the twentieth century was called by Pope Leo XIII for 1900 to mark the twentieth century of what he called "The Christian Era." This was followed by other twentieth-century Jubilees, proclaimed by Pope Pius XI in 1933 to mark the nineteen-hundredth anniversary of the Redemption carried out by Christ through his death and resurrection (presumably in the year 33); and by Pope Paul VI in 1975, who made a special call for reflection and action toward renewal and reconciliation.

Across all these occasions it seemed that the original redistributive intent of the biblical Jubilee had been lost. But in an indication that it had not been forgotten completely, when Pius XII called for a Holy Year in 1950, he said that, among other concerns, he wanted the year to call attention to the needs of the poor. It was during that year (on November 1, 1950) that the Pope defined the Assumption of Mary, Mother of Jesus, into Heaven as a dogma of the Catholic faith. Popes have almost always tied a Jubilee Year to some occasion in church history. In 1983 Pope John Paul II proclaimed one to mark another half-century, making it 1950 years, since the Redemption.

Meanwhile, it seems the initial cooperation of hoteliers and monsignors in sharing the yields of the Jubilee Years eventually skidded, but not completely off the road. A tone had been set. The Church no longer sells indulgences, although it does teach that a pilgrimage to Rome—or Lourdes or Compostela—will reduce the length of one's stay in purgatory. Many churches still display little cards indicating how many days this or that devotion will subtract from a period in purgatory. And the allure of these and many others of the old pilgrimage destinations, although it lagged for a while, now seems to be returning. Hundreds of thousands of people, not all of them Catholics or churchgoers, descend on Canterbury, Fatima, and other sites every year. They make their journeys, as did pilgrims of old, with varying motivations, but commonly claim to find a kind of spiritual atmosphere they do not encounter in their day-to-day lives.

What can be said about the possible future of Jubilee Years? Many people, myself included, were cheered when Pope Francis announced that 2016 was to be a "Jubilee of Mercy Year." Would that mean the pontiff would exhort Catholics and other people to forgive outstanding debts? Would nations, the IMF, and the World Bank be encouraged to engage in more massive debt relief? Would such disputes as the one between Greece and the Eurozone be left behind? In short, would the original intent of the Jubilee Year be resurrected?

It appears that the pope's goals were more modest. The Jubilee of Mercy Year was mainly a "religious" event, akin to many Holy Years (of which this one was the twenty-seventh) inaugurated by popes across several hundred years. Its timing, however, beginning on December 8, 2015, with the Feast of the Immaculate Conception and closing November 20, 2016, on the Feast of Christ the King, was intended to mark the fiftieth anniversary of the closing of the Second Vatican Council—which had not been held in such high regard by some previous popes, but which Francis clearly wanted to honor. It is notable that Francis, seen by many as an innovator, would follow such a very old custom as calling for a Jubilee Year. To explain why he had declared it more specifically to be a "mercy" jubilee, he wrote in his official proclamation, a document exceeding nine thousand words, that mercy was the key aspect of Jesus's ministry and work, and is the central function of the church.[5] In a subsequent letter, he addressed the question of how indulgences could be gained. "The experience of mercy, indeed, becomes visible," he explained, "in the witness of concrete signs as Jesus himself taught us. Each time that one of the faithful personally performs one or more of these actions, he or she shall surely obtain the Jubilee Indulgence."[6]

Pope Francis's Holy Year, like many predecessors, focused mainly on spiritual motifs and did not attempt to resuscitate any rules concerning debt and mortgage cancellation. Still, Pope Francis could honor the spirit of those biblical laws by other means. It is no secret that he is unhappy with the present situation at the Vatican Bank. Founded by Pius XII in 1942, the bank has by now, it is fair to say, acquired a somewhat unsavory reputation in financial circles. Because the Holy See is a sovereign state, it enjoys privileges like sovereign immunity and the bank pays no taxes. Its policies are also highly secretive, troubling in an institution with such global reach. Accusations fly that it has engaged in money laundering for drug cartels, the mafia, and high rollers looking for tax dodges. No wonder the pope is unhappy with it, and has begun to take action.

Recently, two American economists, James Henry and Laurence Kotlikoff, published some imaginative ideas for how the Vatican Bank could be not just cleaned up but also brought into line with the pope's well-known concern for the poor—and not incidentally, I would add, into line with the original vision of the Jubilee Year. Why could it not begin offering loans at very low interest rates to poor people all over the world? And why not, given its worldwide network, help hundreds of millions of low-paid international migrants transmit their earnings safely to loved ones in their home countries? According to the World Bank, such "remittances" amounted to $529 billion in 2012, and year after year provide a major portion of the foreign currency desperately needed by poor countries. Today, huge chunks are bitten off along the way by cartels and other exploitative intermediaries. The Vatican bank, under the new management Francis is installing, could be perfectly positioned to take on this Jubilee-like task.[7]

It has been rumored that Pope Francis may have more ideas in mind. Maybe transforming the Vatican Bank into a bank for the world's poor can happen. It may still happen that the pope will call for the forgiveness or sharp reduction of sovereign debt, especially the devastating debts of the world's poorest nations. If any of this happens, one hopes it could become an ecumenical, even interfaith, event and that creditor countries might join the jubilee. Perhaps the wave could extend to the millions of young people staggering under loads of student loans to repay, and the homeowners "under water" in mortgages they were made to believe they could manage, who now face the prospect of sleeping in church basements.

Would the prelates of the Market God in their Armani suits and Hermes ties go along with any such plan? What might they do when they hear the "jubel" blast? What would the establishment's economists think? It might require a miracle for them to get on board. But perhaps, too, the day will come when Jesus's advocacy of the forgiveness of debts will be seen as prescient. Witness the many reputable economists already arguing that forgiveness of sovereign debt is good for the global economy. It puts more money into the hands of people who will actually spend it, because they have no other choice. Increased spending on goods translates to companies' needing to produce more and thus creating jobs. Maybe those ancient Hebrews were onto something after all. Sound the jubel!

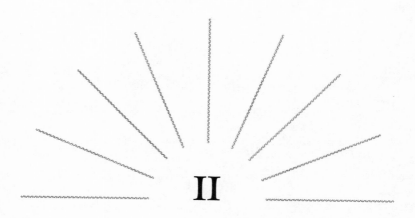

II

Disorders and Infirmities

7

Top-Heavy Short Circuits

Everyone who hears these words of mine and does not act on them, will be like a foolish man who built his house on the sand. The rain fell, and the floods came, and the winds blew and slammed against that house; and it fell—and great was its fall.

—Matthew 7:26–27

Speculation Never Creates Anything.

—Placard at Occupy Wall Street

Both the churches that claim to do the work of the biblical God and the financial institutions that serve the realm of The Market have a tendency to occasionally go haywire. In both cases what usually happens has the characteristics of an electrical short circuit. The energy that is supposed to flow back and forth enlivening the entire system begins to circulate only in one sector, in these instances at the top. The result, as in a short circuit in any home, is not only that the lights, the TV, and the toaster go off, but that sparks often fly and there is real danger of a destructive fire.

Both in religious history and in business, this buzzing and dimming is usually referred to as a "crisis." Thus we hear about the financial crises of 1929 and 2008, or the religious crisis that led to the Reformation of the sixteenth century. Note that during both these crises some participants interpreted them as mere passing glitches in an otherwise sound system; others viewed them as warnings that something was wrong with the underlying circuitry. Now let us look more closely at what has been happening in the realm of the Market God, and then see if recalling analogous events in religious history can help us understand these short circuits better.

In the past couple of decades, observers of The Market have noticed a dramatic change. The mature economies are not producing as many ships or as much structural steel as they once did. Instead, much of the energy has shifted from the manufacturing to the financial sector, which is now turning out more and more derivatives, options, futures, hedge funds, and a host of other paper documents and electronic impulses that some are still willing to call "products." Globally, the "financial economy" has grown so massively that the value of financial assets now exceeds the global output of all goods and services—the part that is called the "real economy"—by a factor of ten. This expansion has resulted in what some call an "inverted" or a "casino" economy. Whatever one calls it, the implications of the financial system's metastasizing are dramatic. But why did this recent metamorphosis set in just when it did? What factors at work in the past few decades resulted in such a drastic mutation?

Many economists link financialization to two other tendencies: globalization and growing inequality of wealth and income. Regarding globalization, in 1980, the value of nominal global financial assets was about equal to the global gross national product (GNP). In 2005 it had soared to three times the global GNP. From 1980 to 2007, derivative (financial) contracts increased from $1 trillion to $600 trillion.[1] Fees for managing money for mutual funds, hedge funds, and private equity skyrocketed. Over the same period that the proportion of financial assets was expanding, the values of foreign-exchange trading in finance also rose from eleven times the value of global trade in 1980 to seventy-three times in 2009. As the congressman Everett Dirkson once observed (adjusted for inflation), "a trillion here and trillion there, and pretty soon you're talking about real money." The transformation slowed down with the Great Recession that began in 2008, but now seems to be resuming.

What about the immense and growing inequality in wealth and income? How is it, for example, that the richest *tenth of a percent* of American households now control as much wealth as the bottom 90 percent combined—and the chasm widens every year? One visible outcome of the financialization of the economy has been the creation of a new, ultra-rich aristocracy. These are the people who prefer to invest their money, lots of it, in the money business. Thus the steady rise in financial profits as a percent of total domestic profits. These are also people who have no hesitation to move their assets to lower-tax states and foreign countries. The fact that some financial firms failed spectacularly did not seem to damage the incomes of the executives much. From 2000 to 2007, the top five executives at Bear Stearns received cash bonuses of over $300 million—and this was on top of the cash value of the shares of stock they held, valued at $2 billion. In the decade since then, despite a slight downturn after the recession of 2008, the same trend is underway again. Meanwhile, untold jobs at the middle-income level have disappeared, and the wages for the remaining ones have stagnated. In the past couple of years, some more jobs have been added, but mainly in low-paying sectors. The average take-home pay after taxes has scarcely budged.

What is the connection between financialization, wealth inequality, and the global economic crisis of 2008? Thomas Piketty, whose *Capital in the Twenty-first Century* was mentioned in the last chapter, is usually careful to hedge his assertions by acknowledging counterarguments and providing data-filled charts from which readers can draw their own conclusions. But in answering this question he does not. Here is what he asks: Is it possible that the increase of inequality in the United States helped to trigger the financial crisis of 2008? He points out that since the share of the upper decile of US national income peaked twice in the past century, once in 1928 (on the eve of the crash of 1929) and again in 2007 (on the eve of the near crash of 2008), the question is difficult to avoid. His answer: "In my view there is absolutely no doubt that the increase of inequality in the United States contributed to the nation's financial instability."[2] Indeed, he thinks it has done that and more.

The connection seems quite straightforward. The increasing inequality was the result of a huge siphoning-off of wealth from the lower- and middle-income ranges to those at the top. By slashing the purchasing capacity of those below the top ten percent, this led to both sluggish consumer demand and the assumption of more and more household debt in the forms of mortgages, credit cards, and student loans. As people turned to borrowing on a hitherto unknown scale, banks and lending institutions, many of them avaricious and not well endowed with moral scruples, were on the spot to take advantage of them. Recently freed from what they had decried as crippling regulations, these institutions often offered loans of different types with scant consideration for the borrowers' ability to repay. The result was that many thousands of people lost their homes as foreclosures multiplied, and new graduates entered a world with few career opportunities and therefore were unable to earn enough to make student loan payments. The fact that the debt burden fell disproportionately on young people was not only patently unfair but had an especially cruel twist. With ruined credit ratings, they were excluded from participating in an economy increasingly lubricated by borrowed money.

Eventually the circuits overloaded. Sparks flew, the lights dimmed, and the world experienced a monster blackout.

Globalization and inequality are closely related. And spectacular advances in technology have also played a role. Due in part to such changes, the economy can produce far more than people (except the very rich) have the means to buy. In their eternal quest for fresh opportunities to make money, companies first explored the far reaches of the globe for new markets to flood with the surfeit of goods they were churning out. When these emerging markets began to show signs of saturation, mature economies responded by creating "fictitious capital," the name given to debt claims that do not have counterparts in the "real world." The bundling of mortgages, some sound but many worthless, into saleable securities is a good example. They were nicely wrapped packages with nothing inside the box.

Still these empty—or nearly empty—packages did not have any difficulty finding buyers. Investors were already turning away from shares in goods-and-services corporations where profits were diminishing. They were seeking out financial "products" that promised quicker and larger returns—with the added advantage that investors felt they did not have to watch with bated breath to see how enterprises funded by their investments prospered, as they once did as shareholders in goods and services producers. There was no reason to bite their nails over merchandise that might or might not sell on the car lot or in the mall. They watched the financial section of the big board. Profit now came from the rise and fall of the value of their financial "products." There was plenty to be anxious about, but the angst over ups and downs now focused at a level above and beyond the production lines and the sales graphs.

Thus the world of finance took on a certain ethereal quality. It floated like a pristine penumbra over the gnarly arena of day-to-day building, shipping, and marketing. But as it happened, the relief investors felt in turning away from the numbers on the cash register to the balance sheets of the big banks turned out to be a grand illusion. Mortgage-backed securities and derivatives suddenly plummeted, and investing in this phantom biosphere was a decisive factor in bringing the world to the edge of an economic abyss. The Market God, like many divinities that had preceded it, came close to expiring. But it did not die, and has not died—at least not yet.

As long ago as the early 1980s, some leading economists, something like the Old Testament prophets, saw disaster coming and expressed their worries. James Tobin was a former member of John F. Kennedy's Council of Economic Advisors and he won the Nobel Memorial Prize in Economic Sciences in 1981. A few years later, in 1984, Tobin delivered a speech in which he confessed that he was "uneasy." He explained why: "We are throwing more and more of our resources . . . into financial activities remote from the production of goods and services, into activities that generate high private rewards disproportionate to their social productivity." He went on to say that he suspected computers were being "harnessed to this 'paper economy,' not to do the same transactions more economically but to balloon the quantity and variety of financial exchanges."[3]

But why would such a development worry Tobin? In short, the tremendously enlarged financial economy was, like a tumor, no longer serving the real economy but depriving it. And it deprived it not only of capital but also of talent. If more money could be made by investing in financial instruments or by getting a job in the financial sector, then why buy less valuable stocks or look for a job in a corporation that markets goods and services? Kevin Roose vividly portrays Wall Street's appeal to ambitious college graduates in his book *Young Money.* In the runup to the financial crisis, life on "the street," as he describes it, was antic and exhilarating, a heady cocktail of fast money and grueling hours but great parties.[4] It was like a "high." One of the young Wall Street traders Roose talked with confessed that, despite all the excitement, he was concerned that some of his colleagues were becoming "addicted to the money," and he was afraid the same thing could happen to him.[5]

Tobin, for his part, found all this both "short-sighted and inefficient." When he looked at the big picture, he saw the financial-sector tail beginning to wag the production dog—or, to revert to my earlier metaphor, a short circuit taking place. Energy that was supposed to be empowering the whole economy was doubling back and the financial sector was mainly enriching itself. But the toaster—and every other appliance in the house—was about to stop working.

These developments did not go unnoticed. The goal of the short-lived "Occupy" movement was not to advance plans for an alternative economy (although some of its supporters did try to do that) but to call public attention to growing wealth and income inequality and the danger it poses to our society. Its banners and slogans focused both on this inequality (by calling out the "One Percent") and on the hollowness of the casino economy ("Speculation Never Creates Anything").

But history moves on quickly. "Occupy" is now a fading memory. Opinion surveys indicate that inequality, although increasingly discussed, is for most voters still just one of many concerns, no matter how poor they are. Perhaps a certain kind of fatalism has set in. But business may be reconsidering its disproportionate investment in finance over production. The *New York Times* recently reported that GE was "substantially accelerating its retreat from finance to bet its future on its industrial business." This came as a surprise to some Wall Street insiders who were quick to point to risks. For example, with oil exploration generally scaling back, there would be less demand for the equipment needed to do it, which GE makes. But the company also builds jet engines, locomotives, power generators, and medical imaging equipment and it predicted robust demand for these. Indeed, the share of the company's earnings from its industrial division rose 14 percent on a per-share basis. This also prompted GE to shed its businesses in real estate and consumer finance, and its commercial lending and leasing assets. It will not be long before the company's income from its financial wing will account for only about 20 percent of the total.[6]

What is going on here? What GE has done seems counterintuitive to some analysts. Has its management taken the company out on a limb that might break off? Or are we witnessing the beginning of a broader readjustment, by which finance will start to play a diminished role in the global economy? Does The Market as God, and some of its oracles, see a dark cloud on the financial horizon that most mortals miss? There is a biblical adage that "God works in mysterious ways" to accomplish His purposes. Could the same be true of The Market?

As I read about the short-circuiting that took place in the institutions that administer the blessings of the Market God, I could not avoid thinking about a comparable disorder in the institutions that at least claim to perform the same service for the God of Christianity, namely the churches. I wondered whether the sudden rise and prospective waning of the financial economy might resemble the waves of revival and decline of religious enthusiasm that have periodically swept across America and other countries. One difference is that financialization is a recent phenomenon, while the analogous development in the church first set in at least fifteen centuries ago. Still, its consequences continue to pertain today.

It happened like this. In the early centuries after the earthly life of Christ, and as the faith he inspired spread over a decaying Roman Empire, many Christians worried about his unambiguous declaration that it would be "easier for a camel to go through the eye of a needle than for a rich man to enter the Kingdom of God." Some tried to soften these words by pointing out that just after he uttered them and the disciples seemed shocked, he had assured them that "with men it is impossible, but with God, all things are possible." But wealthy people continued to be uneasy. Some sincerely wanted to become his followers; if they took this saying seriously, along with his other warnings about the spiritual danger posed by wealth, were they in a spiritual no-fly zone? Was their salvation so unlikely? They no doubt enjoyed their affluence, but hated the thought it could jeopardize their eternal souls. What to do?

Some literally renounced their wealth, giving it to the poor as Jesus had admonished a rich young ruler to do (Matthew 10:17–27). But this could pose difficulties. Since most wealth was in the form of land, giving it to the poor meant breaking up large estates and handing over parcels to the people who tended them. In an age when landowning was an integral part of the larger political and social structure, this hacking up of property carried consequences. It fueled disputes and sometimes bloodletting among the intended recipients. It shook up the traditional power balance among local and imperial authorities. However intended to do good, it could inadvertently provoke serious disorder and trouble for everyone concerned.

Beginning in about the fourth century, the Catholic Church, growing in power and influence as the empire declined, advanced what seemed to many to be a reasonable solution. "Give us the wealth," said the abbots and the bishops, and "since we are the duly appointed successors of Christ, we will hold it in trust for the poor and distribute it in a careful way." Besides, they added, "we will send up continuous prayers and intercessions for you and your family both in this life and the next." It was an offer hard to turn down. It also had the result that in the ensuing centuries the Church, through its monasteries and dioceses, gradually became the richest institution in Europe. Donated wealth in the Church's care became known as "the patrimony of the poor." Therefore, to refuse to make a donation or leave a bequest to it was in effect to steal from the poor, an inexcusable sin.

This perception was grounded in the widespread conviction that Christ still appeared on earth at times in the person of the poor. In the sixth century, Gregory of Tours wrote glowingly about an obscure bishop of Rodez called Quintianus:

> This holy bishop was magnificent in his giving of alms. Indeed, when he heard poor men cry out he used to say: "Run, I beg you, run to that poor man.... Why are you so indifferent? How do you know that this poor person is not the very One [Christ Himself] Who ordained in his Gospel that one should feed Him in the person of the poor."[7]

In the centuries that followed, the ideal of the patrimony of the poor became the main rationale for the Church's growing affluence and the enhanced political and social power that wealth gave to the bishops. These prelates did not, like earthly kings, lead armies to war (although a few did), and they rarely held vast tracts of land in their own names. Their immense power stemmed, at least at first, from their claim that they were the representatives of the poorest peasants and burgers in Christendom, and that this meant they were protecting the unity of God's commonwealth.

The medieval historian Peter Brown reports that this idea was also reinforced by stern ethical injunctions and in liturgies. Those who in any way depleted church funds were called "necatores pauperum," murderers of the poor. The Council of Tours in 567 instructed bishops to assemble their clergy and chant together the malediction in Psalm

108 against such people: "Because he did not remember to show mercy but persecuted the poor and needy and sought to kill the broken hearted."

Brown also suggests that when the responsibility of the church to be the protector of the poor was interpreted in terms of the Hebrew prophets, it could impel the quest for justice and not just for charity. This, incidentally, is a reading of the idea that was brought forcibly back into circulation by the Latin American liberation theologians in the late twentieth century and is unambiguously evident in the teachings of Pope Francis.

Once this concept was duly inscribed into the mentality of early medieval people it was a hard argument to refute. It *was* hard, that is, until something began to happen that undermined the claim. What transpired, put shortly, was that church leaders in the upper echelons and even some of those in the lower rungs began to live rather lavishly, and quite openly, on the patrimony of the poor. Bishops moved into palace-like houses. Monastics consigned much of the labor they had previously undertaken to laypeople, and the monks ate well even when food was scarce outside the monastery walls. The image of the roly-poly Friar Tuck was more than a caricature. Contemporary anticlerical cartoons sometimes depicted monks gorging and gulping around heavily laden tables while poor people crouched at their feet and watched with hungry eyes.

As with the financial sector of the American and world economy, the growth in power of the clerical elite was not steady. It had its highs and lows. But as the centuries passed, the highs became higher and even more lavish and excessive. One particularly glaring and extravagant carousel was when the popes settled for almost a century in Avignon, but the parties roared on with the subsequent Renaissance papacies up until the early sixteenth century. As the infamous Medici pontiff Leo X told his brother, "God has given us the papacy. Now let us enjoy it."

The sleazy story began innocently enough. In 1309, the College of Cardinals, which was controlled at the time by a majority of French prelates, elected a French pope, who took the name Clement V. He never made it to Rome. Fearful of the turbulence and roiling anti-French sentiment in the Eternal City, he stopped at the village of Avignon in Provence near the mouth of the Rhone. It was a shrewd choice. The city clearly lay within the sphere of French influence and power, but it was technically not in France, since it was a fief of the Kingdom of Naples and Sicily. There, His Holiness Clement V planted the papal coat-of-arms, and the next five popes, all of them French, remained and ruled the universal church from Avignon.

The Avignonese papacy, which lasted until 1378, had a tumultuous history and led to divisions and scandals that culminated in the Reformation that took place 290 years later. As a distinct period, it presents a vivid example of the kind of short-circuiting that—along with many other factors—contributed to the protests of Jon Hus, Luther, Zwingli, and others. Avignon became the hub of a thriving international cartel in religious commodities that were distributed throughout Europe. This spiritual and ecclesial merchandise is not easy for modern people to understand, but it was vital to the late medieval customers to whom it was marketed. Its main products were ecclesial offices, paying positions or "preferments," or "benefices" as they were called in the vast hierarchy of the church. There was no shortage of these positions. At the time there were seven hundred bishops, and thousands of lesser offices. And since they all died regularly, there was a continuous renewal of slots to be filled. These appointments were often sinecures requiring little or no work, and sometimes not even the presence of the appointee. Hence they were eagerly sought, and they were openly and unashamedly sold—a practice called "simony," after the sorcerer Simon Magus who offered the apostles money for the spiritual power they demonstrated (Acts 8:9–24).

But appointments were only the beginning, and the appointees were often expected to turn over half of their first year's salary to the papal curia. When a bishop or an abbot died, his personal property reverted to the pope. The papacy also required its price for the dispensations that dissolved a marriage. Rich nobles could make a generous contribution to avoid the discomfort and inconvenience of trekking to the Holy Land on a crusade. The papacy also had its own highly effective method for collecting what was owed: threatening excommunication. A big enough donation could assure the legitimization of children born out of wedlock (and many of these were the children of priests). There was another price for permission to marry a cousin. As the historian Barbara Tuchman puts it, "Everything from the cardinal's hat to the pilgrim's relic was for sale."[8] Thus in one city in southern France, and then for a time in Rome, the Market deity was enjoying a heyday under the auspices of the Vicar of Christ.

Avignon was flooded with ducats, florins, and guilders. The popes and their retinues lived in a vast palace that still attracts tourists today. The city soon became not just the religious hub of Europe but its Las Vegas as well. Boisterous banquets lit up the sky night after night. One sumptuous feast was followed by another. Visitors from the provinces could look forward to barrels of fine wines, elaborate pastries, the best venison and beef, and fancy puddings and brandy. Plentiful entertainment was provided, and the services of prostitutes were readily available. But all the while, an inner decay was eating away the church's foundations. There can be no doubt that the excesses of Avignon contributed to what was to happen in Wittenberg, Geneva, and all over Christendom. It was a grand-scale short circuit.

Surveying the history of short-circuiting both in business and in religion, it can appear that the phenomenon is inevitable. Power, whether business or ecclesial, tends to corrupt. And the closer one comes to absolute power, the worse the corruption becomes. It almost looks like fate at work. I do not think it is. After all, the boundless corruption of the Avignonese and Renaissance church did finally come to an end. Although one could hardly claim that religion is totally free of all corruption today, the present pope lives in a small apartment and eats his simple meals with other guests. True, the Great Recession fired a warning shot over the bow of the finance industry, one that came close to sinking it. And if the news about GE recounted above means anything, maybe the lesson is being learned, however reluctantly, by the high priests who serve at the high altar of finance.

The quotation from the Gospel of Matthew at the head of this chapter about the foolish man who built his house on the sand is taken from Jesus's Sermon on the Mount. It comes just after the verses in which he asks, "Which of you, if your son asks for bread, will give him a stone? Or if he asks for a fish, will give him a snake? . . . So in everything, do to others what you would have them do to you, for this sums up the Law and the Prophets." This advice applies both to those who pander indulgences and those who market derivatives.

8

Big, Big Banks and Big, Big Churches

> They said to each other, "Come, let's make bricks and bake them thoroughly." They used brick instead of stone, and tar for mortar. Then they said, "Come, let us build ourselves a city, with a tower that reaches to the heavens, so that we may make a name for ourselves; otherwise we will be scattered over the face of the whole earth."
>
> —Tower of Babel Story, Genesis 11:3

Is bigger always better? The question is asked about both financial behemoths and megachurches. Does the gargantuan magnitude of big banking and trading institutions—we might call them "megabanks"—strengthen the rest of the economy? Or is it a drain? Does the fact that a single megachurch can attract five or ten thousand people on a given Sunday deprive smaller churches of worshippers, or does its activity contribute to the overall vitality of religious life and thus to all congregations, Lilliputian and Brobdingnagian? The fact that the same question needs to be asked about both sets of institutions shows how equally they have taken up Wall Street's sacred mantra: "grow or die." Both have in common a Market-defined ethos and conviction that growth is not only a worthy goal, but the driving *élan vital* of their existences.

Skeptical viewers see this preoccupation with growth more as a disease, which some call "growth-itis." Let us look at how these powerful assumptions and purposes function first in the temple of finance and then in the ecclesial realm.

Big Banks

First, a recent example: On June 16, 2015, the *New York Times* reported that Goldman Sachs planned to initiate a new program of lending money to consumers online. Because purely digital transactions would not require the Wall Street giant to open storefronts and staff them, costs would be low and loans could be made at lower than prevailing rates. Goldman would grow.[1] Naturally this news was not warmly welcomed by the thousands of small and medium-sized banks, the so-called "Main Street" banks, that planned to continue operating out of buildings, paying heating bills, and employing loan officers.

Early in 2015, economists Stephen G. Cecchetti and Enisses Kharroubi published a paper with the prestigious Bank for International Settlements on an ambitious study to determine the impact of growing financial sectors relative to "real" productive sectors in developed nations around the world. Do these increasingly dominant sectors benefit their economies or hinder them? To answer the question they analyzed data on thirty-three manufacturing industries in fifteen advanced economies. To sum up their finding, contrary to the claims of the managers and defenders of large banks, growing financial sectors act as a drag on overall productivity gains.[2]

Of course, one should not confuse the overall growth of financial sectors with the increasingly elephantine size of Big Banks, even though these colossi play an outsize role. Also, there are other voices among economists who insist that bigness, whether of Big Banks or of the financial sector, is nothing to be concerned about. Still, the findings

of the Cecchetti and Kharroubi study come as an unwelcome surprise to those who claim that a mushrooming finance sector stimu-
lates and lubricates overall production. It seems that is not the case.
Why not?

Banks are in business to lend money, yet businesses with good prospects in a wide range of industries often fail to get the funding they
need. This is not because banks, big or small or in between, do not want
to lend money. The problem is that they want collateral for their loans,
and the collateral they like best is owned by corporations with considerable real estate and by construction companies erecting new buildings.
These are assets which, if a loan goes sour, can be readily seized and
sold. By contrast, banks are not as favorably disposed to companies
whose assets take the form of knowledge or ideas. But start-ups, the
cutting edge of a vibrant economy, normally have more ideas than
real estate. Many have no real estate at all. Because it is hard for a bank
to repossess ideas, or to know what to do with them if it could, the
frequent result is that businesses with only so-so potential to produce
value get ample financial support while truly innovative companies
must scratch for it.

The news of Goldman's growth strategy was followed within a
month by an announcement by Janet Yellen, Chair of the Federal Reserve, that regulations mandating how much capital banks must keep
in reserve for financial emergencies (like the one that struck in 2008)
would be strenuously tightened. It seems the ruling was aimed especially at JPMorgan Chase & Co., the largest of the titans, but since
the policy sets the amount of capital required according to the size of
the bank, its effect is to encourage all large banks to come down in
size. Will we thus see the end of relentless enlargement by the big
banks? Given how these muscular corporations have pushed their way

around governmental restrictions in the past, it seems unlikely that they will waste away to ninety-seven-pound weaklings anytime soon.

There is another reason why an expanding financial sector is not good news for the rest of the economy: as we saw James Tobin worrying in the last chapter, it attracts to itself a lot of investments that might otherwise be drawn to the productive (or "real") economy. Finance also makes life harder for non-finance industries by drawing in intelligent, energetic workers who might have made other choices. It is hard for young people to resist the monetary lure of Wall Street, and it is true that wages in that sector are dramatically higher than in others. The amazing pecuniary grace of the Market God is showered on those it favors, with a little help from its prelates. Professor Cecchetti told the *New York Times'* Gretchen Morgensen: "When I was in college long ago, all my friends wanted to figure out how to cure cancer. But by the 1990s everyone wanted to become hedge fund managers."[3] Things may be changing a bit on this front; while 31 percent of the graduating class at Yale in 2000 was employed in the finance industry a year after graduation, that statistic for the graduates of 2014 went down to 17 percent. But 17 percent is still a significant portion of new diploma holders, and finance still ranked as their most popular choice (followed by education at 11.9 percent).

Professor Luigi Zingales of the University of Chicago's Booth School of Business, in his 2012 book *A Capitalism for the People,* says that "thanks to its resources and cleverness the financial sector has increasingly been able to rig the rules to its advantage."[4] Banks and trading companies, churches, and other religious institutions all inhabit the same Market-shaped culture. They breathe the same profit-seeking atmosphere. So it is fascinating to look at the houses of worship and note the analogies.

Big Churches

One of the most notable developments in Protestant Christianity in the past few decades, not only in America but also in Africa, Asia, and Latin America, has been the emergence of a new form of congregational life, the so-called "megachurch." This phenomenon is fascinating in its own right. But for our purposes, it is important to recognize megachurches as evidence that the geist of The Market and of consumer capitalism has spread into the religious sphere. It seems that the growth mania is contagious.

What is a megachurch? The term refers to churches with weekly Sunday attendance of over 2,000 people. More such churches are organized each year, but estimates indicate that in America there are probably only about 1,500 of them now—still a tiny percentage of the nation's roughly 335,000 churches. Of these megachurches, about 35 have grown to the point that they are labeled "gigachurches," meaning their attendance tops 10,000 people. These very large churches do not seem to conform to any single theological type. There are evangelical, Pentecostal, and charismatic ones. I know of no Unitarian megachurches. And while there are several large Roman Catholic parishes, they are not usually thought of as megachurches.

Megachurches have also been appearing in Africa, South America, and all around the globe. Indeed, five of the world's ten largest churches are located in South Korea. The biggest single Christian congregation in the world is the Yoido Full Gospel Church in Seoul. To serve its 800,000-plus members, it conducts six different services every Sunday in its mammoth edifice. Scores of shuttle buses pick up and drop off worshipers at skillfully calibrated times and places beneath its ground floor.

When I attended the Yoido church a few years ago, I was escorted along with a hundred other foreign guests to a balcony where installed headsets allowed us to hear the service translated into several different languages. By my estimation there were between ten and fifteen thousand people present in the main auditorium for that particular service, and I knew there were thousands more in other parts of the building watching on closed-circuit television. A full-size symphony orchestra played, as did a smaller ensemble. A hundred-voice choir sang. The faces of the ministers leading prayers and delivering the sermon were projected onto two jumbo monitors. The congregation belongs to the international organization of the Assemblies of God, a Pentecostal denomination, but the worship tends to be orderly, with little of the spontaneity one finds among many other Pentecostals. People seemed attentive and the music was well played. The sermon was mediocre.

The service ended after exactly one hour. The friend who escorted me had told me to expect a punctual conclusion; otherwise, the precisely orchestrated bus network would be hopelessly snarled. As we left, I tried to imagine what this experience had meant to the thousands of people who had attended. They live in one of the largest cities on earth, with an urban area population exceeding twenty million. They struggle with crowds and traffic every day. Given the compactness of most Korean homes, they do not enjoy much solitude. Do they really like being buffeted by swarms of people in church? Do they feel safer with so many fellow worshippers around them? Does being part of a well-known and prestigious church deepen their personal sense of dignity and significance in a faceless, fast-paced metropolis?

Later, when I reflected on my visit to the Yoido church I became aware that the impression I carried away was not so much that I had been inspired or touched, but that I had—if only temporarily—been awed to be part of something so big, and therefore maybe significant. And I suspected that this was what many of the other attendees were feeling, too. Size does seem to matter, at least for something, and scholars claim that the sheer size of these churches is indeed part of their appeal.

Back in America, one of the most prominent of the megachurches is the Saddleback Church in California. Its pastor, Rick Warren, delivered a prayer at the first inauguration of Barack Obama and is known for his bestseller, *The Purpose Driven Life*. Saddleback has a thirty-acre parking lot. Willow Creek Community Church in Illinois was one of the first such congregations. The Potter's House in Dallas, led by T. D. Jakes, is one of a growing number of predominantly African-American megachurches.

The churches vary widely in their theologies but tend toward evangelical and charismatic. One exception is Lakewood Church in Houston, led by Joel Osteen and his wife Victoria, which serves up a chirpy message reminiscent of *The Power of Positive Thinking*, by the late Norman Vincent Peale. Its congregation meets in a former basketball arena. Some of these churches started with extensive market surveys of their potential bases to determine what people like and don't like about attending church. The result is that many eschew traditional hymnbooks, and feature buoyant music delivered by guitars, keyboards, and trap drums, with the lyrics projected on large screens. Preachers often dress casually in jeans and open-collared shirts, and sit on stools. (The surveys of their target audience revealed little interest in hymnals or formality.) Many of these churches also sponsor television ministries that are viewed by many hundreds of thousands, possibly millions, of people at home.

We should be careful, however, as we try to understand these unusually large congregations, not to focus too much on their sheer bulk.

The most attentive scholars of the phenomenon insist on something else that should be noticed: megachurches represent a decidedly new form of religious organization, one that is unmistakably shaped by business models. Chief pastors function like CEOs, presiding over staffs attending to specialized responsibilities. They are acutely aware of their competition, and strive through various feedback mechanisms to be customer-centric. They devise strategic plans for next year and the one after that. They are happy, in their transactions with tithers, to honor major credit cards. Yet all of this is in service of size because it is continued growth that is the *sine qua non* of success. However big you were last year, you must get bigger this year or else enter your decline.

Indeed the most business-like feature of megachurches is their "relentless emphasis on growth," as one scholar puts it. Marion Maddox sees megachurches as products of what she calls, perhaps with an element of wishful thinking, "late capitalism."[5] As adherents to what other critics call "growthism," they focus their efforts on adding numbers of members and enhancing offerings, not caring that much of this activity is blatantly materialistic and devoid of real spiritual significance.

But perhaps this judgment is too harsh. I would suggest that the real meaning of the megachurches' emphasis on growth is more benign. Surely it is not a terrible thing to say, "look, this church is really going somewhere, and so can you." Such a message is a hopeful signal that orients a flock toward the future rather than the past. Often in sermons the expansion of a church is explicitly linked to the individual's own growth in grace. The danger arises when the metric becomes too arithmetical. This can give rise to a dodgy version of the "prosperity gospel," whose preachers emphasize the worldly, especially monetary, benefits of faith. As a favorite text to justify their lesson, they tend to brandish this one, from the last book in the Old Testament:

> "Bring the whole tithe into the storehouse, that there may be food in my house. Test me in this," says the Lord Almighty, "and see if I will not throw open the floodgates of heaven and pour out so much blessing that there will not be room enough to store it." (Malachi 3:10)

Prosperity preachers deploy this verse to suggest that those who are lacking in the material goods they need are evidently lacking in faith. They have not prayed hard enough or contributed enough to the church. Sometimes this style of preaching is called "name it and claim it." It teaches that God has clearly promised to pour out such rich blessings that the larder will not have room to contain them. So if your larder is not overflowing, it can only be your fault and not God's. You have not asked with sufficient confidence and ardor. Learn to do so, and you will soon be singing "Pennies from Heaven" as you reap your well-deserved reward.

This may sound cruel and malevolent. But nothing is simple, and even this seemingly despicable practice can have its benefits. A graduate student working with me found, when he got to know the members of a church in Boston made up of poor Brazilian immigrants, that "donating until it hurt" often gave them a sense of dignity and agency. They felt that they had become agents and not just bystanders or victims. Still, it is a sense of satisfaction that is all too easy to abuse.

Megachurches offer other ways to grow in the faith. Inviting someone to come to church with you both contributes to the congregation's enlargement and at the same time enhances your spirituality quotient—even if your personal attendance record is spotty. In this respect, the megachurches enjoy an ironic advantage. In a small, local church, if I fail to slide into a pew on a given Sunday, my absence will be noticed.

But a vast throng of congregants makes it hard to notice the absence of one stray sheep. No one can subtly admonish me by saying, "We missed you on Sunday," because who is to say I was not there, somewhere amidst the multitude? In this respect a megachurch can be a welcome relief for some urban dwellers who cherish at least a certain amount of anonymity. It should be added, however, that many megachurches also try to enlist those who attend into small study or ministry groups of perhaps a dozen people. The ministry groups carry on a range of worthwhile services like staffing soup kitchens, running shelters, and helping poor children with school problems. In this way, megachurches offer the option of ongoing face-to-face relationships as well as comfortable anonymity. In this respect, they seem to have hit on a winning combination.

The physical element of megachurches, the scale of their buildings, tells the same story of their linkage to The Market. A few years ago, I worked with a graduate student in the School of Design at our university. He had been sent to me by the dean of his school because he wanted to write about the architecture of megachurches, and apparently no one on that faculty knew anything about them. I agreed to help, and I am happy I did, because his work caused me to think about an important development in current religious life from a whole new angle. The student traveled all over the United States visiting megachurches and interviewing their staff and lay members. His conclusion was that, just as church buildings in previous eras echoed cultural and political signifiers of their times, megachurches mirror today's.

The basilica replicated the assembly halls of the Roman Empire. The Romanesque with its thick walls, and the Norman style with its ramparts, appeared in the age of feudalism. One can learn about the workers' guilds by visiting a Gothic cathedral. And what of megachurches? Some are built on sprawling campuses on which one can encounter multiple options in music. (Gospel? Soul? Or praise songs?) Many include gift shops and snack bars. Most have special sound-proofed areas for parents with crying babies and rowdy toddlers. Clearly, my student concluded, this was church architecture for the age of the shopping mall—and, I would add, of faith in The Market.

But precisely because religions and businesses are both built today in the shadow of The Market, the affinity between the two is not a one-way street. Influence flows in both directions. I first became aware of the dialectical exchange when I visited Milan, Italy, more than a decade ago. There on the pigeon-carpeted piazza in the center of the city stands its towering cathedral, the Duomo di Milano, one of the most beautiful Gothic churches in Europe. But just across the piazza stands one of the first shopping centers in the world—and it was clearly constructed to be the commercial replica of the cathedral. As you enter it, a long central nave-like corridor stretches before you, with side "altars" consisting of the many specialty shops and boutiques within the neo-Gothic structure. An acquaintance who lives in Milan once told me that whenever he steps into the shopping mall he wonders if he should reach for his wallet or cross himself. Not only do churches mimic the political or commercial buildings of their era, the relationship is complementary: The Market's edifices can also reflect those of religious culture.

The key ingredient that megachurches and large businesses share, however, is that their size is not just incidental; it is part of their essence. Research on the worshippers who attend megachurches has shown that such people are often initially attracted by the size. They notice the sheer mass of the building when they drive by. Since the congregation is so large, they sometimes know of an acquaintance who attends. There is also a name-recognition factor. They know if they begin to attend, they will never encounter blank looks when the subject of church comes up in conversation. All of their acquaintances will surely have heard of "that big church." In the business world, this is the value of branding.

Also, many people today have grown accustomed to large institutions. They may work in a towering office building. If they need medical attention, they might head to a hospital or clinic rather than a doctor's small office. They attend sports events and concerts with thousands of other people. The one-room schoolhouse is gone and schools have been consolidated. Big churches fit easily into this picture. Even more importantly, attendees share The Market's positive attitude toward success; size and growth obviously imply it. As we have seen, they often begin to conflate the church's numerical growth with their own spiritual growth.

There are many reasons for the impressive development of megachurches. Most such churches claim they are striving to be "seeker friendly." They conduct elaborate surveys of why people do and don't go to church and then trim the services accordingly. They try to make it easy to enter the premises, providing ample, convenient parking and eliminating the traditional, imposing red doors. I once visited a megachurch in Salvador, Brazil, which had eliminated doors altogether. It was ensconced in a shopping mall, and regular attenders as well as the merely curious could glide in and out easily. The conventional barriers between church and world, inside and outside, had been erased. People could stroll in, look around, listen for a while, then leave or stay, just as they might do in a Home Depot or Walmart.

Structurally, megachurches often mimic corporate organization with a head minister more attuned to modern management methods than to biblical exegesis. They project a strong image of being on the move, and therefore of the future: "This is not your grandfather's church." The fact that the churchgoing dress codes of a previous generation have largely been discarded and one can appear at a service in shorts, even cutoffs, strengthens this claim. However, it also underlines the fact, not always fully recognized by megachurch ministers, that their relaxed style conforms quite tidily to the current Market ethos. In the bygone time of grandfather's church, also a period when economies needed to build up capital reserves, the culture nurtured virtues like thrift, self-restraint, and delayed gratification. People were encouraged to save their money, not to spend it thoughtlessly. This provided a steady stream of capital for banks to lend. Today, however, what The Market needs is more, not less, impulse buying to increase revenues and profits. There was a time when stately hymns, chorales, and "Sunday-go-to-meeting" neckties and dresses all bespoke restraint and self-control. The modern turn to guitars, trap drums, rock music, jeans, and sweatshirts sends, if not always consciously, a very different message.[6]

But congregations often include more than one generation, with different preferences in music and dress. Therefore some megachurches, especially in America, cater to the specificity of people's tastes by offering different styles of worship at different hours: contemporary at 9 AM, traditional at 11 AM, "gospel" at 2 PM, and folk at 5 PM. One megachurch has refined this even farther by housing these niche preferences in separate buildings—to which the same sermon is projected as the one constant. Many now provide a parents-and-children area with large, soundproof windowpanes and, again, closed-circuit TV screens. Some also offer an area where one can savor a cappuccino and croissant while watching the service. Smaller churches have in some cases followed suit, but most cannot offer such amenities. Even at a time when niche marketing works for everything, including religion, they cannot compete with the big boxes.

So, does size matter, in businesses or in religion? My conclusion is that it does matter, but it matters in different and sometimes contradictory ways. Would breaking up the banks that are "too big to fail" or "too big to jail" prevent recurrences of the recent financial meltdown? No one can really predict, but some, including a growing chorus of voices within the world of finance, think it would help. It might well be that in a society split into niches, megachurches could become one more spiritual option among others—rather than put local congregations out of business. But insofar as both colossal trading houses and megachurches feed the feverish mindset of "growth-itis," they unwittingly pose a dangerous threat to our very finite planet. Nothing can grow forever. Even, or especially, in an age of mega-this and mega-that, small can still be beautiful.

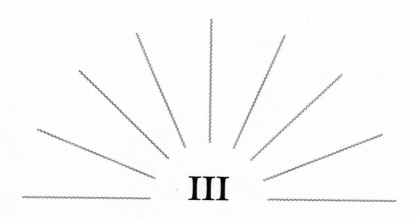

III

History: Following the Money

9

The Bishop and the Monk:
Augustine and Pelagius

> Do not store up for yourselves treasures on earth, where
> moth and rust destroy, and where thieves break in and steal.
> But store up for yourselves treasures in heaven, where nei-
> ther moth nor rust destroys, and where thieves do not break
> in or steal.
>
> —Matthew 6:19–20

No religion is immune from the spell of The Market or from
the persuasive influence of skillfully deployed wealth. From the
earliest years of Christianity, pecuniary values have affected its history in a variety of ways. "Follow the money" also obtains in the
realm of faith. It did in the early centuries of Christianity, and it still
does today.

Tracing some of the history of this semi-Faustian deal might help
us see how it persists in our own day. But the trail is often twisting
and overgrown. Official histories of doctrine have succeeded in ob-
scuring the monetary tracks involved in the controversies they describe
with layers of theological grandiloquence. For example, one of the
most famous disputes ever to have taken place in Christendom, at least
until the Reformation, was the prolonged altercation between Augustine, the bishop of Hippo in North Africa (later known as Saint

Augustine), and his principal adversary, the British-born monk Pelagius. Unknown by most people today, their long argument occupied center stage in the early decades of the fifth century. It focused on undeniably theological issues such as free will, original sin, and the nature of grace.[1] But the way in which the dispute was settled was the result of many factors that have little to do with the relative importance of faith and works or the inner life of the Trinity.

Few people today, including serious Christians, have even heard of the Augustine-Pelagius row, but its repercussions can still be felt in disputes—albeit using different language—on such topics as whether "biology is destiny" and "nature versus nurture." More significantly for our purposes, the role that money played in the way the quarrel ran its course provides a pertinent case study of how wealth and political power have often tipped the balance in what were cast as purely theological debates.

First, let's be acquainted with the principals. Augustine, the inquisitive and venturesome son of a middle-class family in Roman Africa, is well known as one of Christianity's most influential thinkers. But he earned that reputation, and his position as bishop of Hippo, only after a long period of searching and trying out the various philosophical options that were on offer during his youth. In this respect, he resembles many of the earnest students I have taught over the years. They are often in what one of them described to me as "search mode." Augustine was an ambitious student and his parents had to stretch to support his continuing education. But, even as he indulged in considerable partying and reveling in adolescent pleasures—this was the phase of his life to which his famous prayer, "Lord, make me chaste; but not yet," is attributed—he was also entranced by ideas. He read widely, captivated at one point by the poetic meditations of Cicero. This was followed by a period when he felt drawn to Manichaeism, and after that, to Neoplatonism. Both appealed to his reason while Christianity, at least at first, did not. All the while, however, his mother Monica, a Christian, exercised a quiet influence on her restless young intellectual. Finally, largely under the influence of Ambrose, the bishop of Milan, Augustine became a Christian, and was baptized on Easter Sunday of the year 387. The rest of Augustine's life is well documented. He became the bishop of Hippo in 391, but never laid aside his spiritual and philosophical endeavors. He wrote a number of books, such as his *Confessions*, *On the Trinity*, and *The City of God*, that became pillars of western theology. (Augustine was respected but never as revered in the Eastern Orthodox world.)[2]

Much less is known about Pelagius (circa 354–420) even though, during the years of his clash with Augustine, both were viewed as world-class theologians. This paucity of evidence on Pelagius can be put down to fact that he ultimately lost the argument. Many of the records of his life were not preserved, and even some of his key writings have not survived. We do know that he was a stocky, swarthy monk who lived simply and without ostentation, and that he came to Rome in the early fifth century. He was probably a Celt; Saint Jerome, one of his critics, once declared that his thinking had been dulled by too much Scottish porridge. But Pelagius was well educated, fluent in both Greek and Latin, and well versed in theology. For the most part, even his opponents admired him as an exemplary Christian, and in no way a grim one. Although he was shocked by the moral debauchery he found in the Eternal City, Pelagius still nourished a sunny and hopeful view of life. But this made him a severe critic of the theology of Augustine, which he viewed as pessimistic and even fatalistic.

Pelagius soon became well known throughout ancient Rome. An eloquent orator, he taught a robust version of human free will, and was an unyielding opponent of the idea of predestination he saw Augustine promoting. Augustine in turn accused him of denying the need for divine aid in performing good works. Other critics, too, understood him to have asserted that humans were not wounded by Adam's sin and were perfectly able to fulfill the law without divine assistance. It is true that Pelagius denied Augustine's theory of inherited original sin. In support of his position, he and other like-minded thinkers cited Deuteronomy 24:16, which says that children should not die for the crimes of their parents, and that "only for their own crimes may persons be put to death." Still Pelagius held that all people ultimately needed to be saved by God's grace.

He was well known in Rome for the self-denying quality of his public life as well as for the power and persuasiveness of his speech. His reputation earned him praise early in his career even from such pillars of the Church as Augustine, soon to become his nemesis, who referred to him as a "saintly man." However, he was later accused of lying about his own teachings in order to avoid public condemnation. He was questioned by the Synod of Diospolis in 415, but given a clean bill of theological rectitude. The Synod concluded:

> Now since we have received satisfaction in respect of the charges brought against the monk Pelagius in his presence and since he gives his assent to sound doctrines but condemns and anathematises those contrary to the faith of the Church, we adjudge him to belong to the communion of the Catholic Church.[3]

Thus it seems, at least on paper, that Pelagius had won. But his victory was short-lived. The battle was not over, and much of the quarrel involved not what the two men disagreed on, but on what they chose to emphasize, and—as it unfolded—what financial and political powers they could muster. On this front, Augustine held a distinct advantage. After a series of bitter disputes, in which Pelagius appeared to be prevailing, the tide turned. Eventually, at another Council of Carthage, organized by Augustine and his allies in 418, Pelagius was declared a heretic. He spent most of his later life defending his doctrine against Christian theologians who held that he was spreading novelties in the Faith that were unknown to the apostolic tradition.

Pelagius's ideas, however, continued to circulate. His interpretation of the doctrine of free will became known as Pelagianism and maintained a following—sometimes by people who were not aware of either the label or the source of their perspective. Even now, sixteen centuries later, some Baptists, many Methodists, a variety of liberal Christians, and of course religious humanists subscribe to his views on free will. On the opposing side, the ideas have been condemned by Calvinists and other Protestants. Perhaps somewhere between are Roman Catholics, who officially disapprove of his theology but are sometimes accused by Protestants of promulgating "semi-Pelagianism" because they do not fully embrace the Reformation doctrine of *sola fide*—that is, justification by grace through faith alone. Pelagius provides a poignant example of how a thinker can sometimes be defeated, yet continue, in his case for centuries, to be influential.

Although it took place long ago, the substance of the argument between Augustine and Pelagius remains intriguing. To what extent are human beings, caught as we all are in the currents of heredity, the negative pressures of society, cultural determinants, and our formidable capacity for self-deception, still capable of becoming truly moral beings? Pelagius thought we could. An illustration of his views on man's "moral ability" can be found in his "Letter to Demetrias." Pelagius was in the Holy Land when, in 413, he received a letter from a member of a renowned North African family in Rome. One of the aristocratic ladies who had been among his followers, Anicia Juliana, was also writing to a number of other eminent Western theologians, including

Jerome and possibly Augustine, for moral advice for her fourteen-year-old daughter Demetrias, who was already worried about whether being rich endangered her soul. She also fretted about whether as a sinner she could make worthy decisions about how to use the fortune she would inherit. Pelagius used his answer to the letter to argue his case for morality, stressing his views of natural sanctity and man's moral capacity to choose to live a holy life. He assured the girl that even though she—like every other person—was a sinner, she could still make sound moral choices. This letter is perhaps the only extant writing in Pelagius's own hand. Ironically, it was thought to be written by his detractor Jerome for centuries, even though Augustine himself references it in his work, *On the Grace of Christ*. It is a ringing affirmation of the inborn moral capacity of human beings.

No doubt thanks to his being labeled a heretic, little of Pelagius's work has come down to the present day, except in the quotations of his opponents—rarely a fully reliable source. However, more recently, some have defended Pelagius as having been badly misunderstood. His supporters argue that his thinking is in fact highly orthodox, following in the tradition established by the early fathers and in keeping with the teaching of the church in both the East and the West. As church historian Ian Bradley writes, "From what we are able to piece together from the few sources available . . . it seems that the Celtic monk held to an orthodox view of the prevenience of God's grace, and did not assert that individuals could achieve salvation purely by their own efforts."[4] His "heresy" had more to do with nuances and the way Pelagius was interpreted by his sometimes less precise disciples. But it also had much to do with the influence of his well-heeled enemies. Let us then now "follow the money" to see what roles they played in this dispute.

When Augustine and his followers finally vanquished Pelagius, despite the initial reluctance of the pope to support Augustine, it was not only theological ideas that won the day. Augustine needed funding to fight the battle. Fortunately for him his party had won an earlier struggle with a movement called the Donatists (purists who refused to accept fellowship with Christians they considered too willing to compromise). Augustine's people succeeded in having them officially labeled as heretics, which led to their estates being confiscated by the empire. Those Catholics who had followed Augustine then inherited those estates along with the revenues that went with them: the fruits of ecclesial victory. Consequently, they were able to draw on ample resources for the many expenses involved when they took their new case against Pelagius to the imperial court. The quiet whisper of cold cash spoke as persuasively there as it always has in politics, including the politics of religion. Despite the fact that Pelagius and the theologians who supported him had appeared to be winning the contest, the match was turned. As one historian with a proclivity for sports metaphors writes, it "may well have ended in a draw; instead, it went into 'extra' time and at the end of that, Augustine and his team won with the help of questionable decisions made by the referees and the touch judges."[5]

It seems that the pocketbooks of Augustine's followers were especially influential because of the financial disarray of many of the noble families. The latter might have been close to the imperial court, but their wealth had been decimated by the Vandal raiders who had only recently swept through their areas and devastated their properties. Moreover, the money Augustine's team was able to deploy was backed up by skillful politicking. Some of these families were in such reduced circumstances that they had refused to contribute to a common pot of funds being raised to buy off the barbarian intruders, and their reluctance had caused dissension and tension with the other nobles. Everyone shared an interest in reestablishing unity. Thus, while conflicting theological positions had been acceptable before the invasions, now any such discord was regarded as divisive and inadmissible. It was time to stick together, politically and religiously, against the plunderers from beyond the Alps. Augustine's depiction of Pelagius as a divider played into this prevailing sentiment. Division was bad, and money was welcome.

A timely death also helped their cause. The pope who had supported Pelagius died, and a new pope assumed the throne of Peter. Pope Zosimus was more amenable to the noble families—and more in need of their support. Thus the papacy, the nobles, and the emperor came into alignment. Pelagius and his thousands of supporters throughout the empire soon found themselves on the losing side. It is a chapter in Christian history that illustrates how much the weight of wealth can bear upon disputes which appear on the surface to be purely doctrinal. Perhaps any church rushing to point out The Market's hard-boiled pragmatism should not fail to see the beam that is in its own eye.

Being on the wrong side, however, did not by any means silence Pelagius or those who supported him. A new, young bishop of Eclanum named Julian, who was a brilliant thinker albeit one without many friends in high places, picked up where Pelagius left off. Unlike Augustine, who had never learned Greek, Julian knew both the language and the rich philosophy of the eastern part of the empire. He fought Augustine convincingly on the intellectual level. He detected (rightly, many think) traces of the Manichean dualism of Augustine's earlier philosophy in his Christian theology. The dualistic Manichaeists, for example, in their zealous rejection of all things fleshly and worldly, were deeply suspicious of sex, even within marriage. In many of his writings, Augustine, who had fathered a son by a mistress he later rejected, seemed to take a similar position. Since he taught that original sin was passed on from generation to generation through sexual intercourse, it seemed to some of his readers that avoiding sex altogether was the most prudent course.

Julian disagreed. He taught that sex was a gift of God for the propagation of the human race, and he warned any laypeople who might be tempted to take Augustine's side that, if they wanted to have a family, then supporting someone with such a negative view of sex and marriage was hardly a sensible choice. Also, Julian contended that Augustine's doctrine of original sin easily led to a destructive fatalism. He saw Augustine as a kind of Manichaen-dualist wolf in Christian sheep's clothing. This is surely something of a caricature. But the bishop of Hippo, for one, took him seriously, and wrote page after page of argument trying to refute Julian's views. This all went on many centuries ago, but it can hardly be said that spats about sex have been laid to rest in Christianity.

Augustine was not above deploying his theological opinions with political shrewdness. The same wealthy laymen who found Julian's position on marriage appealing also worried about Jesus's clear and repeated warnings about wealth. To ease their disquietude, Augustine advanced the idea that wealth was a "charisma," a mysterious gift of God, and that the real question was not whether you had it or how you had obtained it, but what you did with it. He taught that using wealth to extend the influence of the Catholic Church in the world trumped any consideration of whence it had come. There was no need to interrogate the sources of wealth, however questionable, and no need whatever to respond to such inquiries. It was a fifth-century monetary version of "don't ask, don't tell." Thus the tally in the sex and marriage column favored Julian, but on the vexed question of worldly goods, Augustine scored higher.

The skirmishes between these two thinkers were intellectually interesting, but in reality the substance of their arguments made up only part of the debate. The "commanding heights," as the military strategists say, were on Augustine's side. Julian, like Pelagius before him, was defeated in councils dominated by the emperor and the bishops loyal to the bishop of Hippo. Julian was eventually expelled from his diocese to live in exile in Cilicia, where he continued writing volume after volume attacking Augustine, mostly to little avail. When I was a seminarian, we studied Augustine for weeks. Whole seminars were devoted to his works. But I heard of Pelagius only as the heretic who was defeated by Augustine's brilliance and fidelity. And not a word was spoken of Julian. History, in theology as in other realms, is written by the victors.

The large role that wealth and worldly power played in the dispute between the party of Augustine and the party of Pelagius would be reprised in many subsequent disputes that were ostensibly solely theological. Resentment about the growing wealth of the church lies behind the rise of the monastic movement and the so-called "heretical" groups of the late medieval period. The Reformation originally exploded over a debate about the sale of indulgences. Mammon is never entirely absent even in the holy of holies. Reading church history through the lens of "following the money" does not explain everything. The force of ideas, arguments, and personalities also enters in. But since the cash-flow element is so often ignored or minimized in standard volumes about teachings and doctrines, it is critical to employ this lens to discern what is so often only said in fine print or between the lines.[6]

The same can be said for the history of western religion. Across its entire arc, Christian ideas and the values of The Market have both been present. But, like Augustine's famous two cities, they were never spatially divided, and are not today. Intermingled worldviews have thrived in all ages. They coexisted in the same movements and often in the same people. Merchants, as we will see in subsequent chapters, have often made use of religious motifs. Likewise, religious leaders have drawn freely on the devices of The Market. There are innumerable examples of this, but one writer in particular stands out as the classical embodiment of the straddling. It is Adam Smith, the eighteenth-century Scottish Protestant theologian and economist without whom any discussion of God and the Market would be sadly deficient. We turn to him in the next chapters.

10

Adam Smith: Founder and Patron Saint?

This disposition to admire, and almost to worship, the rich and the powerful, and to despise, or, at least, to neglect persons of poor and mean condition . . . is, at the same time, the great and most universal cause of the corruption of our moral sentiments.

—Adam Smith, *Theory of Moral Sentiments* (1759)

One has only to intone the name "Adam Smith" in the vestibules of the Market God to see people fall on their knees in reverence. This is an exaggeration, but only just. The eighteenth-century Scottish moral philosopher and professor of natural law is hailed by some economists as the founder of their discipline—the equivalent of their patron saint. He is also reverenced by some adepts as the authoritative oracle of the unencumbered market. In the very life of Adam Smith, the distance between the Cathedral and the Mall virtually disappears.

True, not many make pilgrimages to Incaldy, County Fife, where he was born in 1723, or clamor to watch a rib or knucklebone carried in procession. Indeed, neither pilgrimages nor relics would seem fitting for a lifelong Presbyterian like Smith. Still, his profile as sculpted on a medallion by Tassie has circulated throughout the world.[1] To mark the bicentennial of his birth, a pro-free-markets foundation turned out a hagiographic movie about his life. The economic historian Murray Rothbard reports that Adam Smith neckties were worn as a badge of honor in the upper echelons of the Reagan Administration.[2] But does any of this capture Adam Smith's real relationship to economics and to theology? I think not, and in the present chapter and the following one, I will show why.

First, in this chapter, I suggest that Smith is not really the founder of modern economics, and that his standing as its saint, the patron of the unfettered free market, is also dubious. In the following chapter I will propose that Smith might better be understood as a theologian (though this may surprise many readers) and as a prophet of economics. I do not use the term prophet in the sense of a soothsayer, but in its biblical sense: one who calls the powerful back to their fundamental obligations to the people and to the primal structure of the universe itself, understood to be God's creation and his covenant. The Hebrew prophets Amos and Jeremiah come to mind.

Was Adam Smith the founder of economics? Few serious students of the history of the field would now claim that he was. Rothbard speaks of the "enormous and unprecedented gap between Smith's exalted reputation and the reality of his dubious contribution to economic thought." It seems that this gap opened up shortly after Smith's death, and has been widening ever since. "Books on the history of economics," writes Rothbard, "after a few well-deserved sneers at the mercantilists and a nod to the physiocrats, would invariably start with Smith as the creator of the discipline of economics. Any errors he made were understandably excused as the inevitable flaws of any great pioneer." In truth, he insists, the field of economics has existed since the medieval scholastics. Decidedly not its founding father, Smith was a "shameless plagiarist" who appropriated earlier ideas without citation. Worse, says Rothbard, he introduced many mistaken ideas which continue to plague economics scholarship to this day.[3]

Others might argue with Rothbard's account of history, and it would be tempting to explore which purportedly wrongheaded notions he believes have warped current economic thinking. But from my point of view there is another and perhaps even deeper question that arises when we think theologically about faith in The Market. Suppose Smith's critics are right. The question remains: Why do people cling so fiercely to myths of founders—whether of schools of thought, or religions, or other collective endeavors—often long after those myths have been proven to be without substance?

The answer to this question, as we learn time after time in the study of religious history, is that traditions and compelling stories of founders endow enterprises with authenticity. Where they don't exist, they are invented or appropriated. Virgil wrote *The Aeneid* to enlist the history of classical Greece, including its religion, in the cause of the upstart Roman republic. One reason that the early Christians annexed the Jewish scriptures and included them in their Bible as the "Old Testament" was because, even then, everyone knew the Hebrew faith had a long history, while the nouveau Christian movement did not. When, after the fall of communism, the Russian Republic decided to remove many restrictions on religious freedom, the country's new law still favored those denominations with a long history in Russia, especially the Orthodox Church, while making things more difficult for Baptists and other, more recent movements. And in May 2015 it was announced that Moscow was preparing to build an eighty-foot statue of Saint Vladimir to mark one thousand years since his death. By erecting this very great Vladimir to tower over the city from a hill at its edge, Moscow essentially claims the legendary figure as its own— even though he lived in Kiev, in what is now the separate country of Ukraine. Given the tensions between the two countries, the political significance of this act of oversized piety was lost on no one.[4]

Founding myths are jealously protected and, regarding the mythic status of Adam Smith, it will be hard to convince his devotees to give up their devotion. Many point to his *Wealth of Nations* with the hushed reverence of those who consult *The Imitation of Christ*. Not unlike some Evangelicals, Smith's disciples love to cite isolated phrases from his works in a manner that borders on proof-texting. Their favorite, of course, is the one that seems to sanctify personal self-interest as the key to the common good. By now there is scarcely any educated person who has not encountered this well-worn quotation:

> It is not from the benevolence of the butcher, the brewer, or the baker that we expect our dinner, but from their regard to their own interest. We address ourselves, not to their humanity but to their self-love, and never talk to them of our necessities, but of their advantages.[5]

As a proverb, it is a mite too long to stitch onto a sampler, so other followers put the frame around Smith's shorter description of the "invisible hand" of The Market, perhaps seeing it as a more-than-worthy successor to the moth-eaten Christian doctrine of Providence.

Can Adam Smith be considered a saint of the Market Faith, invoked as, say "Saint Adam of Glasgow?" A careful reading of his works, avoiding selective cherry-picking, suggests otherwise. To pass muster for sanctification, he would need to be free of any taint of heresy or deviation from the free-market creed. As we will see below, he just is not. He is a serial backslider. But before turning to that evidence, let us consider the idea of sainthood and what the word "saint" means in Christianity.

Most Protestant churches consider all Christians, living and dead, to be saints. In doing so they claim to follow the New Testament's example, seen especially in the letters of Saint Paul consistently addressed to, for example, "the saints who are in Ephesus" or "all the saints who are in Philippi." These salutations seem to address whole populations, and that makes Protestants reluctant to set aside a special cohort of people for the title. This does not prevent them from calling a church "Saint Mark's Congregational" or "Saint Luke's Methodist." Yet the approach has a certain leveling effect: both Saint Matthew and the most diminutive choirboy are saints.

Roman Catholics have a different view of sainthood. Only certain people—and they have to be dead—are designated as "saints." Over many centuries the church has developed an elaborate system for choosing who qualifies, and who does not. Four steps must be followed in the Catholic process of canonization to sainthood, all of them demanding.

First, if someone, or preferably some large group, believes a person deserves to be elevated to sainthood, they must present a request for canonization to a local bishop. The bishop then begins an investigation of that person's life, looking for evidence of what is termed "heroic virtue." The information collected is forwarded to Rome for the next step, involving a determination by what is called the Congregation for the Causes of Saints. This group of cardinals, archbishops, and bishops combs through the information with the help of various consultors on aspects of verification. Usually one member of the panel is appointed to be a special advocate for the candidate. The discussion goes on for as long as it takes, and this can be a very long time indeed—although the pope has the authority to shorten the process, as Pope Francis did for Pope John XXIII and Pope John Paul II, both of whom were canonized at the same ceremony in Rome on April 27, 2014. If after due deliberation the panel approves the candidacy, then the pope proclaims that the person is "venerable" and can therefore serve as a role model in virtue. This is sometimes called the "first step" to sainthood, but many candidates never get any further. There is still a long way to go.

The next step is "beatification," an exalted state but still short of sainthood. As I was writing this book, a ceremony took place beatifying the late Archbishop Óscar Romero of San Salvador, a process which had been stalled since his assassination in 1980, but which was reactivated by Pope Francis.[6] To reach beatification, a candidate must be shown to have performed a miracle, almost always of healing, or to have died as a martyr. Then the person can be honored in a special way but usually only in a certain specified area or by a particular group. An example is Mother Teresa, who was beatified on October 20, 2003. She is now known as Blessed Mother Teresa of Kolkata.

Beatification does not confer sainthood; the final step of canonization requires proof of a second miracle. But note that a miracle can have been performed posthumously. In Mother Teresa's case, her supporters argued early that she had performed at least two posthumous miracles. In one case, a French woman in the United States broke several ribs in a car accident yet underwent a miraculous recovery. She was wearing a Mother Teresa medallion. Another possible miracle occurred when Mother Teresa appeared in the dreams of a Palestinian girl, and told the girl her cancer was cured. These claims were not sufficiently documented for the process to proceed. But in 2002, the Vatican recognized as a miracle the healing of a tumor in the abdomen of an Indian woman, Monica Besra, after the application of a medallion containing Mother Teresa's picture. The case is interesting, because various people close to the patient, including her husband and her physician, say the growth—which the doctor characterized as a cyst—was eradicated by medical science. "It was not a miracle,"

Dr. Ranjan Mustafi told a *New York Times* reporter. "She took medicines for nine months to one year."[7]

What makes this dispute so intriguing is that it raises the theological question of whether a miracle must always involve a suspension of the laws of nature. Can God work through standard medical procedures to effect healing? Current theological opinion on this subject is divided, but is trending toward the view that, given advances in the scientific view of "nature," disease often has a psycho-physical source, and also that medical treatment can be involved in a miraculous healing. When we think of theories of dark matter and the uncertainty principle, some conventional distinctions between what has been termed the "natural" and the "supernatural" might no longer obtain. We will return to this seemingly abstruse dispute below when we discuss the "miracles" claimed for The Market.

After the achievement of canonized status, some—but not all—saints are chosen to become the spiritual guardians of a country, a city, a profession, or almost anything. Some years ago, the idea was circulated that a patron saint might be named for the internet and its users. An ideal candidate, it was suggested, would be Saint Isidore of Seville, said to have written the first encyclopedia. If it happens, it is sure to bring some relief to many thousands who today resort to profanity when something goes awry online. They will have a conduit for intercessory prayer.[8]

With this brief tour of the steps toward sainthood in mind, now let us imagine ourselves privy to the chamber where the congress of the cause of one Adam Smith's proposed canonization is meeting. This time, the investigation proceeds not in an ornate gothic chapel adorned with the images of existing saints and a jeweled crucifix, but in a paneled boardroom with portraits of past CEOs on the walls and with the jury seated around a polished oak table. As in an ecclesial canonization hearing, consideration must be given to opposing views. A devil's advocate in the Vatican, for example, might have asserted that Mother Teresa had engaged in questionable pecuniary or sexual practices when not at work in her hostel, or that Pope John XXIII had uttered statements questioning the Virgin Birth. (No such accusations, of course, were made.) Any damning charges, if proven, slash the chances of advancing to sainthood to zero. Similarly for Smith, the evidence for and against must be examined with a fine-tooth search engine.

Say, then, that the case for the canonization of Smith has already been made (maybe by a committee of distinguished faculty from the University of Chicago), and we are now to hear from the other side, from the *advocatus diabolis*. Smith has been advanced for canonization and perhaps thought of as the possible patron of Wall Street or the stock market. But wait: the devil's advocate will now try to derail Smith's cause, with an argument based on three central points. The first has to do with Smith's dubious thinking, expressed in many places in his works, on the question of the overall goal of businesses and The Market. What is the "good" that they seek to fulfill? Admittedly, the celebrants of The Market are not always entirely forthcoming with an answer to this question. But their position seems clear to anyone listening carefully. The goal of a business is mainly to serve the monetary interests of its shareholders (with an occasional nod to other "stakeholders" like customers or the larger community). The goal of the economy is to maximize individuals' choices so that they can move toward whatever form of happiness or contentment they freely choose (because the economy itself should not impose or dictate what that expression of fulfillment should be).

The goal of maximizing individual choices obviously identifies ends with means. It is "procedural" and not substantive. The goal of the process and the means for achieving it appear identical. Both require the weakening or elimination of anything that diminishes the individual's autonomous choice. The Market supposedly does not dictate these choices (although the immense advertising industry seems to steer the invisible hand at times). Still its exponents insist The Market has no interest or competence in making distinctions between worthwhile and self-destructive goals. That should be left entirely up to the individual. Nor does The Market make any distinction between noble and ignoble desires, so long as the unimpeded freedom of the individual to select is preserved and enhanced. Theoretically, The Market as such is interested *that* you choose. The advertisers are concerned with *what* you choose.

So how faithfully does our candidate for canonization, Adam Smith, adhere to this decisive article of Market orthodoxy? Not too faithfully. Time after time he demonstrates that he does in fact have a substantive goal for the economy in his sights. Developing his theory of mankind's moral sentiments, for example, he states, in his lilting eighteenth-century prose, that "to feel much for others and little for ourselves . . . to restrain our selfish, and to indulge our benevolent, affections, constitutes the perfection of human nature."[9] Although, as a Calvinist of sorts, Smith sometimes rebukes "enthusiasm" in religion—a probable reference to Methodists—he has in fact borrowed a key idea from it. Human beings have the power to slip the leash of original sin and, as John Wesley put it, to "move on" toward the "perfection" for which God intended us. Therefore there are certainly both praiseworthy and base desires: those that contribute toward the progress of the race toward a genuine commonweal and those that do not, or that may even push us in the other direction. Here, candidate Smith is patently not the advocate of unlimited consumer sovereignty. He is teaching either sheer heresy or, at best, a doctrine that does not glorify the Market God. Score one against canonization.

Point two in the case against Smith as a saint of The Market is hinted at in the previous paragraph: he differs sharply from orthodoxy in his estimate of the human capacity actually to achieve the rather challenging goal set for us. The difference is important. In The Market's catechism, human beings do indeed have the power to select their own good from the myriad of possibilities presented to them, and when their choices turn out to disappoint them, it is not because of any inner weakness but for one of two reasons. Either too much regulation has skewed the range of choices, or the chooser has been provided with insufficient information to make a rational purchasing decision. Once again, any notion of a substantive good is eliminated: what is good is what is chosen, and it is chosen because it is good.

On this point, Smith, never a captive of a single theological tendency, seems to swing back toward the atmospheric Scottish Calvinism that he breathed in Glasgow. And in doing so he recalls the debate between Augustine and Pelagius discussed in the previous chapter. Siding with Augustine, Smith recognizes what classical theology calls *akrasia*, or a "weakness of the will." Because of this common human failing, emphasized especially by John Calvin himself, it is not necessarily true that every choice, even made with full information in hand, is good. As Saint Paul discerned within himself, even though he desired to do what was right, the evil he did not want is what he kept on doing (Romans 7:18–19). He concluded that it was only by God's grace that he could escape from his self-defeating impulses.

Smith sees the predicament too and his solution, though comparable to the Apostle's, sounds a little more like the venerable Jewish teaching that two wills constantly struggle within us. We must learn to heed what Lincoln called "the better angels of our nature" rather than give in to selfish motivations. Smith recognizes the same struggle between a higher and lower nature at war within us, and describes the higher nature as an "impartial spectator," a voice of conscience in our heads. Thus Smith departs again from the Market creed. It is "only by consulting this judge within," he writes, "that we can ever see what relates to ourselves in its proper shape and dimensions; or that we can ever make any proper comparison between our own interests and those of other people."[10] Plainly, Smith is advocating choices based not just one's own satisfaction but on one's perception of the common well-being. True, sentences can be found here and there in Smith's corpus that seem to contradict this assertion, like the oft-quoted one about the butcher, the brewer, and the baker. But the preponderance of evidence is on the side of those who oppose making Smith a saint in the firmament of The Market—especially considering that, in a canonization procedure, it does not take much to derail an ascent toward the halo.

But the *advocatus diabolis* still has one more argument to advance in order to nail down his negative case. It is one that is not ordinarily recognized, but that Paul Williams aptly points out in the concluding chapter of *Adam Smith as Theologian*. It concerns the ideas Smith has about place and the proximity people need to have to each other for an economy to fulfill its purpose. Contrast this with The Market's decree that people must be mobile. Attachment to a particular location is definitely not something to be cultivated; it should be discouraged. The Market requires a mobile workforce. President Lyndon Johnson is said to have remarked once that, when it comes to job-seeking, people should be "hunting dogs, not setters."

The logic of the Market's canon on this matter is obvious. To survive it needs to grow, and growth demands that inconvenient obstacles to the free flow of both capital and labor be eliminated. A rolling stone gathers no moss and, according to this doctrine, the freer a stone is to roll, the better. But human rootedness in a community, a neighborhood, or a landscape is just such a restriction, so The Market looks with disfavor on rootedness. The French philosopher Simone Weil lamented the increasing rootlessness of modern societies.[11] Other writers have suggested that it was the endless movement of peoples and the erosion of their connectedness to concrete places that made them vulnerable to the appeal of the totalitarian movements of the twentieth century, which promised them belonging and a pseudo-mystical bonding with blood and soil. Today, the same "distanciation" that pries people from their local habitats makes them susceptible to the pseudo communities they relate to through television and internet advertising—atomized groups who share their fleeting tastes in clothes, music, or beers. If there was never much substance to the "Pepsi generation" there is even less in its endless successors.

Adam Smith would not have approved of such a perpetual-motion culture. He wrote time and again that the virtues we need to live together in an economic system flourish when they are nourished by the people we live with on a day-to-day basis. Left on our own ("like a rolling stone," as the song goes) we do not develop these moral sentiments. We have, Smith writes, "a natural disposition to accommodate and to assimilate, as much as we can, our own sentiments, principles and feelings to those which we see fixed and rooted in the persons whom we are obliged to live and converse a great deal with." When it comes to choice between the limitless mobility of labor and rootedness, Smith comes down on the side of rootedness. This is why he has such favorable things to say about religious congregations in cities as centers of community. This view might have strengthened his case if he were being evaluated for sainthood by the Church. But it is not an opinion that would permit him to take his place on the iconostasis with the other saints of the Market.[12]

Can we attribute any miracles—meaning secular and economic ones, of course—to Smith or even to his teachings? (We'll stop short of expecting anything of his bones.) Some readers might shake their heads and smile at a question they believe extends the analogy of The Market as religion too far. Businesspeople are too logical and calculating, they might insist, to expect or hope for the miraculous. But look again. In the decades after World War II there was much talk about what was called the German *Wirtschaftswunder*, the "economic miracle" that took place in a country where the infrastructure had been pounded, often into smoking ruins, by Allied bombing. As Germany recovered with surprising alacrity, the language of miracle was used almost immediately to describe the transformation. Some attributed the miracle to the faithful application of free-market principles, and liked to contrast West Germany's recovery with the very different experience of the command economy of East Germany. But skeptics immediately retorted that such pious embellishment was misplaced. There were other reasons, they pointed out, why West Germany had recovered so quickly. First, there was the Marshall Plan, a massive infusion of funds into Europe to allow for the purchase of equipment. There was also the onset of the Cold War in which the United States enlisted West Germany as an ally and stationed thousands of troops there. East Germany, later the German Democratic Republic, did not have any such sources of revenue. Indeed, trainloads of manufacturing equipment had been removed by the Soviet Union for use by its own people.

I lived in Berlin in the early 1960s when the glittering luxury of the Kurfürstendamm in the west in contrast to the dingy greyness of Alexanderplatz in the east was constantly held up as proof of the superiority of the western system. It was clear to most Germans then, however, that although the western economic arrangement might indeed be better, the comparison was not a fair one. The "miracle" had benefited from a host of very worldly assets.

Whichever side is right regarding the German economic miracle, the debate echoes in some ways the arguments over the healing miracles claimed in Catholic sainthood causes. Again, we are forced to consider: must a "miracle" always be devoid of any human intervention? If doctors treated the woman reportedly healed by the intervention of Mother Teresa, even as she also clutched a rosary to her breast, can her surprising recovery count as a miracle? Adam Smith, by the way, as a practitioner of the "natural theology" that was so popular at his time, always insisted that God worked *through* the natural laws he had established at creation, not in spite of them. But miracle or no, Adam Smith could not make it past the examining committee or the onslaught of the *advocatus diabolis*. He uttered and wrote too many words counter to the sacred creed of Market orthodoxy.

So much, then, for Adam Smith's standing as the founder or the patron saint of economists. But then how should we understand his place in our economic and religious history? I think the answer is that we have to see Adam Smith as a moral theologian and maybe as a kind of prophet. I will go on to present this case in the next chapter.

II

Adam Smith: Theologian and Prophet?

> Then you shall see and be radiant; your heart shall thrill
> and exult, because the abundance of the sea shall be turned
> to you, the wealth of the nations shall come to you.
>
> —Isaiah 60:5

As mentioned in the previous chapter, any discussion of The Market as a religious phenomenon must come to terms with the sublime aura of Adam Smith. I examined the claim that Smith is the founder of economics and also the proposition that he could be the patron saint of free markets, and found them both unconvincing. In this chapter I will assert that Smith is best understood as an eighteenth-century Protestant theologian in the Scottish Calvinist school. I will also argue that he can be considered a prophet.

Let us begin with Adam Smith as a theologian. Doubtless because of the profession of the present writer, this assertion may sound far-fetched, if not a case of special pleading. But there is mounting evidence of its accuracy, and as I have examined that evidence, I have become convinced not only that reading Smith as a theologian makes sense but that it clarifies much about him that other readings do not. In fact, as the economist Jacob Viner once observed, "Adam Smith's system of thought, including his economics, is not intelligible if one disregards the role he assigns in it to theological sentiments."[1]

Adam Smith lived and wrote before what we now call economics and theology were put asunder and went their own separate ways. His work bears little or no resemblance to what either economists or theologians in the twenty-first century tend to publish. His writing, however, does follow a pattern of reasoning analogous to that of many classical and contemporary theologians. He draws on the streams of religious and philosophical traditions that informed the Scottish intellectual culture of his era. These included biblical studies. Notice from the epigraph to this chapter, for example, that Smith borrows the title of his most famous book, *The Wealth of Nations*, from the Bible.

It is true, of course, that many writers have appropriated scriptural phrases for the titles of their books with no theological intent. But Smith is different; he did have a theological intent. Perhaps this is more evident to those who have studied the history of theology than to those unfamiliar with that history. Still, only by reading him with willful ignorance can one can miss Smith's continued references to "the Author of nature," or simply "the Deity." Throughout the nineteenth century, Smith was read by theologians as one of their own and, as we shall see below, the Calvinist doctrine of Providence played a key role in his thinking. Take this sentence, for example: "Every part of Nature, when attentively surveyed, equally demonstrates the providential care of its Author, and we may admire the wisdom and goodness of God even in the weakness and folly of men."[2]

In addition to the Bible, the theologians of Smith's time delved into the history of doctrine, but they also interested themselves in what were termed "natural theology" and "revealed theology," in the philosophy of religion, and in what we call today "philosophical theology." They tried to hone their familiarity with all these pursuits which today, regrettably, are disconnected into discrete sub-disciplines. Taken together, as they were in Smith's time, they constituted a field that was called "Divinity." That name migrated to North America along with our Puritan founders, and is still used to designate graduate schools where these disciplines are pursued, such as at Harvard, Yale, Chicago, Duke, and elsewhere. Smith did not command all the fields subsumed in Divinity, but they constituted the stream in which he swam. In Glasgow he lectured on natural theology among other subjects. It is important to remember that before he wrote *The Wealth of Nations*, Smith had published, in 1759, his widely admired *Theory of Moral Sentiments*—which can be read as a text in psychology or theology or ethics, or all of these. I would agree with those who claim that *The Wealth of Nations* cannot be understood without seeing it as the heir of the earlier work. The first book lays the groundwork for the second.

As an eighteenth-century theologian, Smith worked, as have theologians before and since, with both the classical and the contemporary currents that were available to him at the time. Why would an eighteenth-century Protestant theologian involve himself with Stoicism? Like some of his peers, Smith was attracted to this ancient movement in part because of its emphasis on simplicity and on being in command of oneself. The Stoics must have seemed to him to be the forerunners of the down-to-earth and no-nonsense burghers of Edinburgh, Aberdeen, and Dundee. He also leaned toward Stoicism because of his dislike for the more aristocratic Aristotelean thinking that was so popular at the time among Catholics. But the question remains: as a theologian, why would he delve into any non-Christian philosophy?

The answer, of course, is that this is exactly what theologians always do. They try to reinterpret Christianity in dialogue with the intellectual and cultural trends of their era. The entire *Summa Theologica* of Thomas Aquinas consists of an elaborate reworking of the philosophy of Aristotle, whose thought had recently been rediscovered. And Aquinas is still the official philosopher of Roman Catholicism. Nineteenth-century German Protestant theology made use of the categories of Hegel and Kant and others. In the twentieth-century, the religious thinkers responding to the challenge of existentialism included Protestants (such as Paul Tillich), Catholics (Gabriel Marcel), and Jews (Martin Buber) and Darwinian ideas of evolution were addressed by still others (such as Pierre Teilhard de Chardin). Liberation theologians have struggled with various expressions of Marxism. As for Stoicism, many historians have remarked on its similarity to Christianity and biblical scholars suggest that it is noticeable in the writings of Saint Paul. It was in no way an odd choice for Smith.

The second influence on Smith's theology was the moderate Calvinism that was dominant in Scotland in his time. "Moderate Calvinism" might sound like an oxymoron for those who can summon up a mental picture of the steely, sixteenth-century Geneva reformer, or of the theologically strict Calvinist founders of New England, such as John Winthrop and later Jonathan Edwards. But Smith lived two hundred years after Calvin, and the version of Calvinism that reigned in his time did not put much emphasis on human depravity. Rather, as we have noted, it emphasized other ideas vital to Calvin: the providential presence of God in the world, the beneficial contribution of religion in society, the important role of reason in establishing divine truths, and a blissful future for humanity under God's benevolent guidance.

This does not mean that Smith harbored a naive or saccharine view of human nature. He was well aware of human sin and folly, which he found especially evident in our unwillingness or inability to notice the complex interconnection of things. But he believed that what he called "the benevolent and all-wise Being . . . can admit into system of his government no partial evil which is not necessary for the universal good."[3]

Another important source of Smith's theology was what was then called natural theology, the premise of which was that God had composed "two books" for the benefit of humanity. One was the Bible and the other was Nature, usually spelled with a capital "N." The best-known practitioner of this discipline was Isaac Newton, whose magisterial *Principia* (formally titled *Philosophiæ Naturalis Principia Mathematica*) promised to lay out the mathematical principles of natural philosophy. Few today know that Newton also wrote several volumes of commentaries on the Bible, with a special interest in the book of Revelation. He was strong believer in the "two books."

Finally, a dominant influence on Smith's thinking was the tradition of natural law, which he was familiar with especially in its German expression. This school of thought was more concerned about ethics and morality than about the natural universe as such. It played a key role in Smith's teaching of "moral philosophy" at Glasgow. Believers in natural law contend that human beings are naturally endowed with the capacity to discern right from wrong; those explicitly addressing the theological implications teach that this capacity is instilled by God. At times the objection has been raised that this idea goes against the Protestant, and especially Calvinist, idea that human reason is so distorted by sin that such moral discernment is virtually impossible without the help of grace. Smith had to contend with this apparent contradiction. But the notion that a theologian might want to engage in such a lively intellectual current should not be surprising. Even in the twentieth and twenty-first centuries, both philosophers and theologians still work with one or another version of natural law. Much of Roman Catholic social teaching (that is, the church's doctrine on social justice) is based on it.

Adam Smith, I conclude, counts as a theologian. The assertion is not only historically accurate, but enormously helpful in wrestling with some of the problems that beset both economics and theology today—the very issues that are central to this book on the religion of The Market. For example, many economists complain that their discipline is reaching a kind of stalemate, in that the most pressing issues cannot be addressed within the boundaries of their field as it is now defined. They realize that insistent questions about moral values and life meaning defy the measurement and quantification that have become so integral to their work. Asked to weigh in on policy options having to do with employment, product pricing, investment, advertising, and organizational behavior, they find even the latest econometrics and most complex algorithms not up to the job. Another dimension is needed. But not many have any idea what that dimension is or how to access it—and so far, Adam Smith, in his reduced (and mistaken) status as the icon of unregulated market capitalism, has not offered much help. Maybe a new conversation with the "real Adam Smith," the theologian and moral philosopher, would help.

For theologians, a similar dead end is looming. After generations in which so many of their number (with important exceptions) have expended so much effort honing the fine points of doctrine, and comparing the intricacies of the various world religious traditions with each other, many theologians today sense a mounting impatience among laypeople who wish they would do and say something about the gross injustices that threaten the world such as persistent poverty and disastrous climate change. But because of their divorce from economics, theologians often lack the conceptual apparatus to address these threats effectively, and are therefore sometimes dismissed as well-intentioned but inept do-gooders. What might constitute a first step toward reconciliation of these two artificially separated fields of inquiry?

Both parties might begin by listening in to the conversation of what Robert Heilbroner calls the "worldly philosophers"—the thinkers, past and present, who ponder the meaning of a life increasingly defined by the categories of economics.[4] As we begin to take that first step toward a détente, there is one element in religion that commends itself as a promising point of convergence. As it happens, it is also a feature with which a more fully understood and appreciated Adam Smith might offer some insight. I refer to Smith not as a saint, but as a prophet.

What is a prophet? And how might the characteristically religious institution of prophecy facilitate a rapprochement between religion and economics? The most important characteristic of the Hebrew prophets was that, while they were deeply embedded in the political and cultural life of ancient Israel, they were never totally defined by it. They had another perspective, a transcendent point of reference which enabled them to be critical, sometimes severely critical, of their own society and especially of its leaders. They could be "in but not of" their world.

Prophets therefore stand out even when they have established roles in the world as it is. Consider Saul, who gained this perspective late in life. "And when all who knew him before saw how he prophesied with the prophets, the people said to one another, 'What has come over the son of Kish? Is Saul among the prophets?'" (I Samuel 10:11). Saul was a king, but he also functioned as a prophet. Can an economist also be "among the prophets"?

Most students of history recognize prophecy as the most distinctive and important feature of Hebrew faith. Some Jewish scholars, however, express ambivalence about this judgment because they feel that Christians have overrated the prophets, seeing them as significant because they have often read the prophets mainly as predictors of Jesus Christ. But one of the greatest Jewish scholars of the twentieth century, Rabbi Abraham Joshua Heschel, insists that the prophets were and are indeed central to Jewish life, and that they should not be devalued just because Christians have made use of them for their own purposes. In his famous book on the prophets, Heschel advances an idea that can be seen as the keystone of his thinking. He contends that Amos and Isaiah and the other prophets dramatize the central tenet of Jewish faith: that God is best understood not as anthropomorphic (that God takes human form) but rather as "anthropopathic"—that God has human feelings. Heschel calls it "divine pathos." In this view, prophets do not speak for God so much as they remind their audience of God's voice among the voiceless, the poor, and the forgotten.[5]

These observations also apply to the Christian idea of a God as one who suffers the pain and anguish of humanity. Jesus places himself clearly in this tradition. It is how he introduces himself in his inaugural message in his hometown, sometimes called his "Nazareth Manifesto" (Luke 4:14–19). Here, he declares that God's coming kingdom has a special place for the poor, the prisoners, the blind, and the oppressed. He later exhorts his followers to demonstrate mercy and justice to "the least of these among you."

Like the prophets, Jesus is not particularly concerned with "religious" issues. One of the most overlooked features of Jesus as a prophet is that in his principal form of teaching, the parables, he focuses almost entirely on "worldly" (including economic) issues and the moral challenges they present. Any random sampling drawn from the thirty-five parables recounted in the New Testament will demonstrate this worldly language. Each of them resembles a miniature "case study" like those used in a school of business administration. "The sower and the seeds" (Mark 4:3–9) and "the weeds in the garden" (Matthew 13:24) are based on agricultural practices, as is the parable of the fig tree (Matthew 24:32). Drawn from viniculture, but concerned more with employment practices, is the story of "the laborers in the vineyard" (Matthew 20:1–6).

The puzzling story of the dishonest steward who cheats his employer but is commended by Jesus for his daring and originality (Luke 16:1–12) comes from the world of trade. The famous anecdote about the master who entrusts sums of money ("talents") with his servants who either boldly invest them or stash them away takes the reader (or listener, in Jesus's time) into the sphere of banking and finance. The parable of the good Samaritan offers a peek into the sometimes perilous life of merchants and how wayside inns operated. The story of the "prodigal son" and his lavishly forgiving father relies on the often tricky dynamics of family inheritance for its material. It is also worth mentioning that, in all these teachings, the prophet Jesus only mentions God once. He noticeably wants his listeners' attention centered on the moral dimensions of everyday commerce and family life, or what we call the secular world.

What does it take to qualify as a prophet? The Bible endows a range of people with this designation, beginning with Moses and continuing through Samuel, Elijah, Amos, Isaiah, Jeremiah, Ezekiel, and a host of "minor prophets" such as Habakkuk, Zechariah, and Malachi. In common usage today, the word is also applied to inspiring moral leaders such as Martin Luther King, Jr., Nelson Mandela, and others who address burning issues not just in religious communities but in the larger world, especially the economic realm. Here is an example of this kind of prophetic critique from the eighth-century prophet Amos:

Thus says the Lord: "For three transgressions of Israel, and for four, I will not revoke the punishment, because they sell the righteous for silver, and the needy for a pair of shoes—they that trample the head of the poor into the dust of the earth, and turn aside the way of the afflicted." (Amos 2:6–7)

For Biblical scholars, Hebrew prophecy may be the most important feature of Jewish faith, but like many other features, it was not without precedent. The prophets emerged from an earlier group called "seers" who, like today's fortune-tellers and writers of zodiac columns, purported to have knowledge of future events. "Seer" is not a word in the lexicon of The Market. But the arena of finance is graced with cadres of people who perform a very similar function. Where would the world of investment be were it not for the folks who, if we cross their palms with silver, tell us in which stocks or bonds to entrust our shekels? Indeed, the world of Wall Street might well be thought of as a vast assembly of people anxiously trying to peer into the future, frequently with quite limited success. There is, after all, even a lively market for "futures."

Still, a prophet is not just a seer. The word "prophet" derives from an earlier Canaanite word meaning "announcer," a forth-teller rather than a foreteller, as the textbooks have it. But setting aside for the moment the fact that Jeremiah, Isaiah, and the other prophets also sometimes engage in some foretelling, the Bible itself makes clear that although the prophets developed out of the seers, there are important differences. To complicate the picture even more, something similar to Hebrew prophecy also emerged in non-Hebrew cultures, including ancient China and Greece.[6]

The thing to notice relevant to the concerns in this book is that the prophets constituted an internal, loyal, but self-critical community within Israel. Unlike the religious functionaries of other near-eastern societies, they did not serve as obsequious lackeys of the divine king, transmitting his dicta to the masses. Although the Hebrews had kings at times in their history, they always claimed that their real king was God. Few of the prophets hovered near the throne of the earthly sovereign; rather, they stood among the masses and, when necessary, confronted the earthly king in the name of the heavenly one. The most poignant example is Nathan's confrontation of King David, who had just sent Uriah—one of his warriors—to his death in battle so that he could snatch his wife. Bathsheba was a beauty he had glimpsed on a rooftop while she was bathing. When Nathan goes to David, he tells him the story of a man who despite owning many animals, took a poor neighbor's only, and beloved, little lamb to slaughter for a meal. He then points his finger at King David: "Thou art the man!"

The prophets were also willing to issue blistering reproaches against the religious practices of their day if they sensed that these rituals had lost their essential moral content. Consider these words of Amos:

> I hate, I despise your feasts, and I take no delight in your solemn assemblies. Even though you offer me your burnt offerings and cereal offerings, I will not accept them, and the peace offerings of your fatted beasts I will not look upon. Take away from me the noise of your songs; to the melody of your harps I will not listen. But let justice roll down like waters, and righteousness like an ever-flowing stream. (Amos 5:21–24)

Another prophet, Isaiah, sounds a sharp attack, not on religious rituals as such but, again, on spiritual practices that seem to have lost their ethical imperative:

> "The multitude of your sacrifices—what are they to me?" says the Lord. "I have more than enough of burnt offerings, of rams and the

fat of fattened animals; I have no pleasure in the blood of bulls and lambs and goats. When you come to appear before me, who has asked this of you, this trampling of my courts?" (Isaiah 1:11–12, NIV)

The prophets of Israel lived in a different age, but they were like us in at least one respect. They did not inhabit a monochrome religious culture. They existed both in continuity and discontinuity with a spiritually hybrid world. Historians now recognize that different religions held sway not just around the outside borders of the two Jewish kingdoms of Israel and Judah, but within their borders as well. When David conquered the Canaanite city of Jerusalem and made it his capital, he retained the services of its resident Jebusite priests for whom it was already a holy site, and they conducted their worship side by side with the priests of Yahweh, David's favorite God.

David's successor King Solomon not only had many, many wives (though the reputed one thousand might be a stretch) but also had many "foreign" gods and goddesses in his Temple. In this piebald context, the prophets created what one historian has called a "Yahweh only" theology. But it was not monotheism as we understand the term today. They never insisted that the foreign gods did not exist; they only said the Israelites should not worship or serve them. This idea is stated in a straightforward manner in the first Commandment: "Thou shall have no other gods before me." The prophets did indeed often rail against the worship of Baal and other deities of the time, but their main concern was not the Baal cult itself. It was aimed at the Israelites who slid into it. Again, this is an important insight today for Christians, Muslims, or Jews, all of whom consider themselves to be "monotheists" living on a spiritually pluralistic planet. We need not confute or seek to invalidate the values of other faiths in order to be faithful in our own.

The prophets are most relevant to us today not because they tore down other people's altars but because they spelled out what it meant to mete out justice to the disinherited, and to be faithful to the Covenant. To be more specific, prophetic faith lived in continuous tension with the various powerful religious, economic, and political institutions of their time. The prophets' calling was to "speak truth to power." No wonder, then, that the people were astonished to see King Saul, at least momentarily, among the prophets. That was an unusual (though not impossible) combination.

Like the other distinctive features of Israelite faith, such as the Sabbath and the Covenant, the prophets emerged gradually out of something that preceded them. In their case, it was the old tradition of the seers. Often in religious history such developments are hard to locate. But in this case, the Bible itself makes it plain. In the book of Samuel we learn: "Formerly in Israel, anyone who went to inquire of God would say, 'Come, let us go to the seer'; for one who is now called a prophet was formerly called a seer" (I Samuel 9:9).

The seers often went into states of ecstasy or alternative consciousness, which frequently took place during hectic gatherings at holy sites. After these episodes, the seers claimed to have had encounters with the holy and to be able to discern what the future would bring. Is there any equivalent to these overwrought occasions or the feverish tone they evoke among The Market faithful today? I think there is. Many television watchers who have surfed from channel to channel with remote control in hand will have noticed the striking similarity in voice, tone, and fervor between the evangelists and the sales pitches for diet aids or kitchen implements. Both hold forth in urgent, hurried voices. Both emphasize the necessity of acting now. They do not counsel quiet reflection on whether to send in a contribution or dial the number on the screen. Billy Graham called his famous program

"The Hour of Decision." Skin-cream hucksters inform you that their offers will soon expire. You are at risk of losing a shot at eternal life or a blemish-free complexion.

For centuries, religious people have danced themselves into frenzies or fasted into altered states of consciousness, and we have not left that stage entirely behind. Anyone who has attended a tent revival or a praise meeting of Pentecostal worshippers, or watched footage of the pandemonium on a stock-market floor, will recognize a comparable level of commotion. Again, much is at stake, in terms of salvation or opulence. The agitated state seems to induce decision-making. The arms waving in the air at the revival are raised in prayer and supplication; those at the stock market to make bids on securities whose values are changing by the second. In both cases, the period of heightened elation may not end when today's benediction is pronounced or trading-floor bell rings. Periods of revival have gone on for months, and economists have charted long outbreaks of "unwarranted enthusiasm," like the notorious clamor over flower bulbs that induced the "tulip mania" of 1637.[7] Traditional religions do not have a monopoly on ecstasy. The cult of the Market has its share, too.

After the prophets emerged as an identifiable movement, the main powers to whom they tried to speak their truth were the kings. The Hebrews were relatively late in establishing the institution of kingship, and did so with considerable reluctance, as is made clear by the prophet Samuel's ominous warning to them when they asked for a king. When "the people" (or probably, just some of them) asked him to give them a king, so they could be "like the other nations," this was his answer:

> These will be the ways of the king who will reign over you: he will take your sons and appoint them to his chariots and to be his horsemen and to run before his chariots. And he will appoint for himself com-

manders of thousands and commanders of fifties, and some to plow his ground and to reap his harvest, and to make his implements of war and the equipment of his chariots. He will take your daughters to be perfumers and cooks and bakers. He will take the best of your fields and vineyards and olive orchards and give them to his servants. He will take the tenth of your grain and of your vineyards and give it to his officers and to his servants. He will take your male servants and female servants and the best of your young men and your don-keys, and put them to his work. He will take the tenth of your flocks, and you shall be his slaves. And in that day you will cry out because of your king, whom you have chosen for yourselves, but the Lord will not answer you in that day. (I Samuel 8:10–18, ESV)

In any investigation of the fraught relations between religious voices and economic power, this is a highly significant passage. The proph-et's warning against having a king is phrased almost entirely in terms of the economic injustice it is sure to create. The king will take com-mand of virtually every aspect of economic life, and the result will be disastrous for the common people. Once established, the kings would become the constituted governing authority. And since, at this period of history, the economic structures had not yet been clearly differ-entiated, the kings controlled the power those structures would one day hold. When the prophets challenged rulers, as they did continu-ously, they were threatening not only the throne, but also the treasury, the land tenure structure, and the taxing system.

In confronting the kings, the prophets drew on a religious tradi-tion they both shared. True, sometimes their fiery denunciations of rituals make the prophets appear to be iconoclasts who did not want to have anything to do with the holidays, festivals, and sacrifices that reenacted and celebrated the symbolic worldview of ancient Israel. But that would be a mistaken impression. Without these rites and symbols, Israel would not have been Israel. Through them, the people recalled their deliverance from Egypt in the Passover. They told and retold the stories of the Patriarchs, and they marked their continuity with them in the custom of circumcision. After the Temple in Jerusalem was built, they gathered there for the annual New Year's Enthronement of God. It was through these cultic activities that they remembered what God had done for them in the past, and this both located them in the present and gave them hope—even in the worst of times—for the future.

Why, then, did the prophets fire off such polemics against what they knew quite well were rituals essential to the well-being of the people? The answer to this question can be discerned by a close reading of Isaiah 1:13: "I cannot endure iniquity and solemn assemblies." The word "and" in this short verse supplies the clue. The prophets attacked the hypocritical inconsistency of rituals that had become disconnected from, even contradictory to, the moral imperative they symbolized. They were in danger of atrophying into form without substance.

In some key figures, the prophet and the priest even overlapped. In Exodus 2:11, Moses is referred to as a Levite, or priest. We are informed by I Kings 18:32 that the great prophet Elijah offered sacrifices. Ordinarily, however, the prophets were not priests. The two followed separate vocations. Sometimes there were tensions, but they relied on each other. The prophets often borrowed the language of the priestly rituals for their prophetic utterances. Studies of later prophets including Habakkuk, Nahum, and Joel show that their writings rely heavily on liturgical rituals.

The prophets were not religious mavericks chafing under the stifling constrictions of the ceremonies and holidays of their people. They fed on these celebrations, which in turn shaped their messages. But they wanted them to be coherent with God's call to his people to "let justice roll down like waters and righteousness like a mighty stream." Jesus, who continued the prophetic tradition into another era, struck this balance when, in one of his best-known teachings, he told his followers that, if they were on the way to the Temple to make a sacrifice and remembered a wrong they had done to a neighbor, they should first repair that rift, then proceed to the Temple and make the sacrifice. It was not an anti-priestly gesture when he chased the money changers out of the Temple; it was his effort to cleanse it of the racketeers who were gouging the poor pilgrims.

This critical but appreciative rapport between the prophets with the "religious establishment" of their day enables us to understand our present-day prophets better. Two prophets of the American civil rights movement and anti-Vietnam War protests, Father Dan Berrigan and Rev. William Sloan Coffin, combined their priestly and ministerial roles with their activism. Berrigan, a Jesuit, continued to say mass and lead prayer retreats while he and his associates burned draft records and nonviolently opposed nuclear weapons. Coffin occupied the pulpit of one of America's leading congregations, the Riverside Church in New York City. Dr. Martin Luther King, Jr., while leading protest marches and demonstrations against racial and economic injustice all over the country, insisted on returning to his pulpit on Sunday mornings. Nuns, priests, and one bishop lost their lives in Latin America during struggles against military dictatorships. And in recent years, Pope Francis manages to sit at the pinnacle of ecclesial authority as Bishop of Rome and Pontiff of the Universal Catholic Church while he speaks in clarion tones against poverty and inequality. Obviously, some clergy have faced demotion and dismissal when authorities considered their activities too disturbing of the status quo. The lively synergetic relationship between prophecy and the religious establishment, which first appeared among the Hebrews twenty-five hundred years ago, is still in force.

The net result of the radical demotion of absolute royal power to relative authority passed through many ups and downs in world history. The early Christians found themselves in deep trouble when they refused to accept the divinity of the emperors. The popes and the later emperors fought out their jurisdictional disputes for centuries. The battle reached a boiling point in the eleventh century when Pope Gregory VII deposed and excommunicated the sitting Emperor, Henry IV. The clever monarch, however, journeyed to Canossa in Tuscany, where he stood barefoot in the snow in a theatrical plea for clemency. The pope had little choice. How could he refuse absolution to such a demonstrably humble supplicant? He granted it. But Henry had barely arrived home before he convened a synod that deposed the pope and installed another one: Clement III (later declared "antipope" in official Catholic annals). The seesaw contest went on for centuries. It continued until the nineteenth century, when, finally deprived of all its real estate except for the miniscule Vatican State, the papacy began to turn its attention to the spiritual and moral realm where it could still lay claim to some authority.

The Protestant reformers differed on just how the spiritual and the secular spheres should be delineated, but all agreed that they must be separate. The idea of the "divine right" of kings made a short-lived return in early modern Europe, but some of its major royal protagonists literally lost their heads defending it. Today, even in modern democracies, religion still commands significant symbolic authority. To this day, the monarch of England is crowned in Westminster Abbey by the Archbishop of Canterbury, and the president of the United States, taking the oath of office with one hand on a Bible, concludes with the words "so help me God."

Still, the prophetic breakthrough marks a critical point in the history of Hebrew monarchy, the importance of which cannot be exaggerated. It resulted in the Jewish version of what historians Karl Jaspers, Eric Voegelin, and more recently Robert Bellah refer to as "the axial age," the point in the long saga of human evolution at which "man as we know him today" appeared.[8] In that age, they argue, since a divine king was no longer the conduit between a transcendent God and the people, a space was opened up for criticism and reflection, a transcendent point of reference by which people could envision political, cultural, and religious change at the most fundamental level. Not only had the "archaic myth" of a flawless connection between divine and human rule now been questioned, but human beings began to see that they were responsible for the construction and correction of their values and institutions. The valuable tension between prophets and kings in ancient Israel provides an indispensable model for those Jews and Christians who see themselves as perpetuating the prophetic tradition. The relationship between our communities of faith and governments should never sour into automatic antipathy but neither should it become too cozy. Prophets would make bad kings, and kings should not be expected to be prophets. Maybe the real answer to the people's question about whether Saul was among the prophets should have been, "maybe, but not for long." There needs to be a creative tension, the shape of which changes as history moves on. No formula can prescribe exactly what it should be at any moment.

The Hebrew prophets appeared at a moment in history far removed from ours, but what they say is not bound to their time. Their voices confront us unsparingly with the rank injustice of the vast inequality and unnecessary suffering that distort our world today. Speaking to us from a distant past, they are as relevant as this morning's headlines As Rabbi Heschel says, "Prophecy is the voice that God has lent to the silent agony, a voice to the plundered poor, to the profaned riches of the world. It is a form of living, a crossing point of God and man. God is raging in the prophet's words."[9]

So how does this exploration help us to understand the so often misunderstood Adam Smith? As a theologian, he definitely qualifies. He worked faithfully in his time at the same task theologians have worked at before and since: relating the timeless Gospel to the highly particular challenges of their times. But Smith as a prophet? Given the demanding standards of the predecessors in that guild, it is hard to think of him as filling the bill completely. He was no Amos and no Isaiah. But in reading him, it is also impossible not to detect some of the prophetic spirit that, originating in ancient Israel, found its way into that assiduous student of the Bible John Calvin, and then to Smith. Recall the words from his lectures noted at the beginning of the previous chapter:

> This disposition to admire, and almost to worship, the rich and the powerful, and to despise, or, at least to neglect persons of poor and mean condition . . . is, at the same time, the great and most universal cause of the corruption of our moral sentiments."[10]

Do these words not seem akin to the ones Pope Francis has been using? If not an Amos, one can discern in Smith an embryonic prophet struggling to delineate, within an emerging business civilization, the justice that God requires and how it might be advanced. Living in a severely anti-Catholic time and place, he might even be surprised and pleased by what Francis is saying about the "wealth of nations" and how it should be shared among all the children of the earth.

12

Banker, Philosopher, Trickster, Writer

> The social imaginary ... [is] the creative and symbolic dimension of the social world, the dimension through which human beings create their ways of living together and their ways of representing their collective life.
>
> —John Thompson

As The Market has emerged in the past few centuries to become both the summit and the hub of society, it has in no way restricted itself to the "economic" realm. Its language, images, values, and assumptions have seeped throughout the entire culture to permeate the ways we think and live. It has begun to shape us in ways that elude our awareness. A useful way to think about this saturation is by means of what historians of culture and religion call the "social imaginary."[1] As briefly described in Chapter 3, this consists of the cluster of patterns through which people envision their collective existence. A social imaginary functions largely on the pre-reflective level, and therefore differs from a "worldview" which informs a more cognitive awareness. My point here is that what might be characterized as a market-shaped social imaginary has grown and enlarged its scope during the past three centuries, especially but not exclusively in America. In this chapter we will chart its progress from banking to philosophizing to literature.

Philosophy

In the early nineteenth century there lived and thrived in upstate New York a small-scale banker named Alexander Bryan Johnson. Born in England in 1786, he immigrated with his mother to the United States when he was fifteen years old, following his father who had arrived four years earlier and who had established a successful general store in Utica. Young Alexander was fully aware of his newcomer status, and strove to improve himself through wide reading as he worked first in the family store, then as a lawyer, and finally as a banker.

Johnson's life would not merit a single paragraph in an American history text based on his banking career. He was successful at it, but only moderately in comparison to the financial titans, like Andrew Carnegie and John D. Rockefeller, who would rise with the Gilded Age. Johnson, however, displayed a singular quality that makes his story a unique one. In addition to his assiduous attention to his ledgers and his clients, he nourished an avid interest in philosophy and wrote three books on the subject. These books, which attracted rather little interest at the time, provide us two hundred years later with invaluable evidence of how a "banking mentality" had already begun to leach into and shape the everyday life of the young republic.

In terms of his formal religious affiliation, Johnson was at first, like Adam Smith, a Presbyterian. It was the denomination of his wife Abigail, who as it happens, was the granddaughter of President John Adams. Later, however, when the local Presbyterian fathers and brethren censured him for using the mail on Sunday, in violation of their strict Sabbath observance principles, he joined the more forbearing Episcopal Church. But Johnson's real outlook on life was derived from neither latter-day Calvinism nor low-church Anglicanism.

It was shaped by his extensive experience with checks, mortgages, and currency. He held forth on these views as a frequent lecturer participating in an active lyceum movement. These discourses and his philosophical writings display a mindset that was soon to become the unofficial but operational "religion" of the modern market society. Johnson was both its harbinger and an early champion.

There is another feature of Johnson's thinking which, after so many years of obscurity, has made him interesting to the current generation of philosophers: the avid attention, indeed almost obsessive at times, which he devoted to language. From the middle of the twentieth century, American and Continental philosophers, from the logical positivists to Ludwig Wittgenstein, have been engaged in what has been termed "the linguistic turn." And in this respect Johnson can resemble a long-forgotten, faded family photograph discovered in an attic—a forgotten ancestor who suddenly seems to have said something important and relevant after all.

Johnson was fully aware of the admixture of categories that characterized his lectures and writings. Yale historian Jean-Christophe Agnew, in an excellent article on Johnson, quotes the Utica banker as saying of himself, "The labors of the counting room and the study were constantly intermingled and often the sheet of a treatise in hand and a current balance sheet might be seen on the table together." As Agnew quips, "Johnson's writings were nothing if not inter-textual," and then goes on to conclude that this intertextuality foreshadowed a central aspect of American market culture.[2]

So, just what is it about Johnson's homespun philosophy that proves so prognostic? Handling so much paper money and so many bonds in his banker's office, Brown was struck by the fact that currency has almost no intrinsic value at all. Take it to a bank for exchange, and all you get is more paper, or at best coins, whose inherent worth is a fraction of the numbers stamped on them. The value of any form of money is entirely projected on it by those who accept it for payment for real physical goods and services—for land or horses or restaurant meals. The worth of money, he decided, is wholly a function of its usefulness. Absent the willingness of human beings to attribute real value to it, it is not worth the paper it is printed on, so to speak.

So far we can easily follow the course of Brown's thinking. It is probably ingrained in the mental habits of those who routinely handle large amounts of money. Who has not watched with at least temporary fascination as a bank clerk shuffles through stacks of twenties, or even hundred-dollar bills, with indifference? It is when Brown makes his next move that we have to observe carefully, as we might watch a seasoned cardsharp flip over jacks and aces, or a magician shift the shells under which a bean is hidden. Brown now suggests that in all important respects, words are like money. They have no intrinsic value or significance, only that which custom and everyday use allots them. As Agnew characterizes Brown's view, "Words were like mirrors: social conventions that were empty in themselves but that possessed as many potential meanings as the objects placed before them."[3]

From this premise it was only one short step for Brown to deduce his conclusions. First, that since language was so chimerical; it was a mistake to look to words to help us understand ourselves or our world. But second, and also because words are so devoid of substantive significance, we may deploy them to charm, persuade, even flatter people without any sense of guilt. Words are there to be used.

Can we not see in Brown's down-home ruminations a portent not only of William James's truth-is-what-works pragmatism, but of the consummate adroitness with which Madison Avenue employs symbols, words, and images to cajole prospective customers into parting with their coins? At an even deeper level, can we not also see the beginnings of a culture in which, by this point, the relentless metrics of the monetary have filtered into our thinking about virtually everything, from family life to politics and from education to spirituality and art?

In retrospect, it can be seen that Johnson was not a mere flash in the American philosophical pan. It was not long after he died that William James, sometimes considered the greatest American philosopher, devised his enduring contribution of "pragmatism"—in simple terms, the argument that ideas are true insofar as they are useful. In his many writings on this subject, James often employed the metaphor of "cash-value" to make the idea clear to the ordinary reader. James was strongly criticized by his contemporary thinkers for injecting this crass note into philosophical thinking. Some contended that the "cash-value" concept not only trivialized his ideas but was not suited to the essence of pragmatism. The debate has continued in our own day. The British philosopher A. J. Ayer sardonically called the cash-value metaphor "more vivid than precise."[4] Although James was aware that his metaphor troubled many, he continued to use it. His point, not too different from Johnson's, was that ideas as such have no inherent truth or value. They reveal their value only in the realm of experience.

My point here is not to make a judgment on whether James's metaphor was helpful or not in illuminating his philosophy, but to suggest that Johnson's ideas, although they were peripheral in his time, still reverberate today. William James is no minor figure in our intellectual history. The underlying social imaginary of the market has shaped even the core tradition of American thought.

Enter the Trickster

Consider the sales strategies of a Madison Avenue branding wizard, the great showman P. T. Barnum, or a TV revivalist who instructs viewers to place their hands on their screens to be cured of ailments like backache. Is there an essential difference? The overlapping tactics employed by the ingenious priests of The Market, by showbiz hucksters, and by Elmer Gantry-like hawkers of religion have intrigued observers of American culture for a long time. In the field of religious studies, the figure of the "trickster" provides an inviting vehicle for comparing them. Jokes, pranks, cunning, playful deceits: these are some of the artifices in the well-stocked bag that students of mythology and folk religion uncover in the trickster, an archetype to be found in virtually every known religion, whether high or low. The trickster can be a god or demi-god, an animal, or a human being. Specific characteristics vary from one tradition to the next, but the trickster is always smart, cagey, and creative—and a source of jokes and ruses that flout convention and normal rules of decorum. Examples of this character range from Loki of Norse folklore to the coyote of Native American stories. The slick gambits of Reynaud the Fox gave the word "foxy" its meaning in English as guileful and cunning. Some tricksters have been plucked from popular yarns and cast into more formal roles. Shakespeare put one, Puck or Robin Goodfellow, in *A Midsummer Night's Dream*. The composer Richard Strauss celebrated another in his tone poem *Till Eulenspiegel's Merry Pranks*.

Some biblical scholars assert that the Hebrew patriarch Jacob is best understood as a trickster.[5] He cheats his brother Esau out of his legitimate heritage by taking advantage of their blind father, Isaac. Later he hoodwinks his father-in-law Laban—who has already tricked him into working for seven years to win the hand of Rachel, only to end up with her older sister Leah, whom the Bible describes as cross-eyed. Tricksters delight in tricking other tricksters.

Jacob is a particularly good example of the trickster type because, even though he lies and swindles, we are clearly meant to esteem him for his spunk and inventiveness. And this is true of nearly all tricksters. We may shake our heads at their unseemly antics, but we smile and indulge them, maybe even admire them. This may be because the trickster is often, if not always, serving some good purpose. Or more likely it is because, given the unfairness and uncertainty of life, he exhibits at least one way of beating misfortune at its own game.

American literature has produced more than one world-class trickster. At about the same time that Alexander Bryan Johnson was thumbing through account books and ruminating on the pecuniary nature of language, someone else in that same burned-over region of upstate New York was pondering a closely related subject. The man who would become America's greatest novelist, Herman Melville, moved with his family to Lansingburgh, a few miles north of Troy, in 1830. He wrote short stories and novels, some successful, some not. His *Moby Dick*, although not a smash hit at the time of its publication in 1851, is now viewed by many critics as the prototypical American saga and a perceptive parable of the American spirit.

A few years later, in 1857, Melville published another novelistic probe into the soul of his native land. *The Confidence Man: His Masquerade* is set, like *Moby Dick*, on a ship—this time not a whaler but a Mississippi riverboat. It includes an oddball who clumps about on a wooden leg like Ahab, the obsessed captain of the *Pequod*, and a congeries of other characters meant to represent a motley, cosmopolitan culture. Melville christens the lumbering side-wheeler *Fidele*, a none-too-subtle hint of the book's theme—the persistence of trust and indeed credulity in his fellow citizens of the new republic, and perhaps of the whole world. The author is similarly not-too-subtle in naming his characters; they include a Frank Goodman, a Charlie Noble, and even a Pitch. The names suggest a medieval morality play. At one point, his peg-legged character refers to the vessel as a "ship of fools." Later, another character described only as a philanthropist says that "life is a pic-nic *en costume;* one must take a part, assume a character, stand ready in a sensible way to play the fool."[6]

The Confidence Man unfolds a satirical series of incidents in which passenger after passenger is fleeced by one smooth swindler after another. Melville, who, like Dostoyevsky, got some of his ideas from reading newspapers and magazines, had seen the accounts of a well-dressed gentleman named William Thompson, who was arrested in 1849 and eventually shipped to Sing Sing for a series of petty thefts—mostly of watches willingly handed to him by strangers after he asked for their confidence. His escapades were even the basis of a farce called *The Confidence Man,* staged by theater owner William Burton. A commentator at the time wrote in the *Weekly Herald* that Thompson was no worse a con man than the financiers on Wall Street, who were pulling off their con "on a large scale."[7] The novel Melville published (hardly accidentally) on April Fools' Day of 1857 more than hints at exactly the same point.

But the novel is much more layered, and as the story blossoms the reader begins to ask, "exactly who is conning whom?" Eventually, in an ingenious feat of literary legerdemain, Melville causes readers to perceive that, throughout the yarn, we too have been taken in. Indeed our whole lives are spent in a big, carnival sideshow tent, or a Wall Street, that stretches from coast to coast, where everyone seems, just as on the *Fidele,* to be hoodwinking everyone else.

No one knew this better than P. T. Barnum, who was thriving then as a showman, a business man, and one of the smoothest confidence men who ever turned a trick. He did so well at all of these callings because he saw clearly what most people discern only through a glass darkly; namely, that at some level people know they are being tricked, and even enjoy it. The mark who pays good money to squeeze into a sideshow to gawk at a dog-headed boy or to watch a woman being sawed in half either knows or suspects he is being taken in. But he enters willingly into the charade.

We are all actors in the costume picnic and passengers on the ship of fools. And Melville does not exempt himself from this floating festival of knavery. He is, after all, a writer of fiction, and fiction is at one level a tissue of lies, with its reader a willing accomplice. Yet in a chapter written as an aside to the reader, he explains how fiction can satisfy readers looking not only for more entertainment, but even "for more reality, than real life itself can show." In real life, people mask their authentic selves for the sake of propriety, but characters in a novel are not so constrained. He then makes the connection to religion, which is just as much a web of falsehoods, perhaps, but performs the function of revealing truths that are not apparent to human eyes. "It is with fiction as with religion," Melville concludes: "it should present another world, and yet one to which we feel the tie."[8] One is reminded of Saint Paul's observation that "we are regarded as deceivers, yet true" (2 Corinthians 6:8).

Here then is a book about something that The Market and biblical religion share, and that Melville with impressive sensitivity saw. A superficial reading of *The Confidence Man* might easily suggest a sour and even cynical view of human nature. But Melville is going much deeper. Raised in a Presbyterian family and never too far from a Calvinist view of human nature, he was aware of the capacity for self-deception that lurks stubbornly in the heart of human beings. In *Moby Dick*, Ahab's fatal flaw is that he sees all evil incarnate in the white whale that has robbed him of his leg. Striving to eradicate it in its cosmic entirety, he sends his whole ship to the bottom. But Melville is also mindful of the enduring, if sometimes dim, hope for redemption. He believes that all of us on the global *Fidele* need faith, and that, one way or another, we will find it.

Melville severely qualifies his Calvinism, however. His point is that, instead of ignoring or denying the savage within us, we need to be aware of it and in touch with it. He also speculates about an understanding of God that Calvin would have found totally unacceptable. Researchers have found a manuscript version of a chapter in *The Confidence Man* that Melville eventually did not include. In it, the novelist speculates that even God, whom he calls "the author of authors," cannot escape the contradictions and conundrums of the human condition. We are all in this together. Successive drafts show that Melville kept revising the wording of this idea but eventually discarded it altogether, perhaps concluding that it would offend the devout and damage sales of the book. Like a skilled trickster and confidence man, he kept a high card tucked inside his vest.

I am sorry Melville consigned this chapter to the scrap can. It might indeed have seemed impious to some readers in his day. But many more recent schools of religious thought would not have reacted so negatively. "Process theology," for example, the movement based on the philosophy of Alfred North Whitehead, teaches that God has not yet reached—and may not even want—the perfections attributed to him by classical theologians. This would mean that God shares some of the limitations of finitude with which humans struggle. In an earlier chapter, we explored the argument advanced by Abraham Joshua Heschel, in *The Prophets*, that the biblical God is not anthropomorphic but anthropo*pathic*—meaning that God shares the feelings, both joyful and painful, of human beings. Some Christian theologians suggest that Christ's self-emptying, or *kenosis*, described by Paul (Philippians 2:6–7), is evidence that God, although he possesses all the divine perfections, sets them aside in the Incarnation and fully shares the restrictions that finitude imposes on human beings. I think Melville would have agreed.

13

The Breath of God and
The Market Geist

The wind bloweth where it listeth, and thou hearest the
sound thereof, but canst not tell whence it cometh, and
whither it goeth: so is every one that is born of the Spirit.

—John 4:8

In the last days it will be, God declares, that I will pour out
my Spirit upon all flesh, And your sons and your daughters
shall prophecy, And your young men shall see visions, and
your old men shall dream dreams.

—Saint Peter in Jerusalem on the Day of Pentecost, Acts 2:17

In Christianity, the term "Holy Spirit" refers to the presence of God
within—"closer . . . than breathing, and nearer than hands or feet,"
as Tennyson phrases it—but also in the waters, the forests, and the
mountains, and for some theologies in all sentient beings. The concept
is not uniquely Christian. The idea of such an immanent divinity can
be found in almost every religion. It also has its counterpart in the
religion of The Market, whose spirit was classically analyzed by Max
Weber in his *Protestant Ethic and the Spirit of Capitalism*. Weber published
his book in German, and since the word he uses for spirit (*geist*) is the
same as that used for the Holy Spirit (*Heilige Geist*) the kinship of the
two could not be mistaken.[1]

But in the century since Weber wrote, this capitalist geist has spread all over the world and to an extent he could not have imagined. The nature of capitalism, too, has changed quite radically. Weber wrote when the accumulative stage of the economic system was in full bloom, and certain "Protestant" virtues such as thrift and delayed gratification were needed. Now, however, in the market-consumer stage, not only are these qualities no longer needed, they have become hindrances. People must be inspired not to save for a rainy day, but to buy now while the sale lasts. The same geist must inspire different mindsets.

Many will remember when, in English, the Holy Spirit used to be called the "Holy Ghost." It still occasionally is, when the poetic line calls for it, as in the widely used Doxology (the beloved "Old Hundredth" hymn) where a rhyme is required with "heavenly host." The word "ghost" is derived from the old English *gast*, akin to the German geist. But in recent decades, biblical translators have almost completely eliminated it because in common parlance it calls to mind a Halloween spook, or the apparition of a dead person. In any case, the Holy Spirit, whether referred to as "the Spirit of God," or "the Spirit of Truth," or simply as "the Spirit," is mentioned throughout the Bible. In the Hebrew Scripture it is the *ruach*, the breath of God. In the Genesis creation narrative, it is the spirit hovering over primal waters. In many accounts of events, we learn that the spirit "came upon" key figures such as Joshua, Saul, and David. In the New Testament, the spirit is portrayed as especially active during the entire life of Jesus. He is described as "conceived by the Holy Spirit" at the Annunciation to Mary. The spirit descends in the form of a dove when he is baptized by John in the Jordan—making the dove the main artistic symbol of the spirit for centuries. The spirit leads Jesus into the wilderness where he struggles with the temptations of power and fame. Near the end of his life, Jesus promises his followers that he will send the spirit after he has gone to comfort them.

Saint Paul appeals to the widely shared idea of the near-universal presence of a divine spirit when he addresses the crowd on the Areopagus in Athens (Acts 17:15–34). The rhetorical pattern of his famous discourse suggests that when he starts to speak, the Apostle to the Gentiles is not in a good mood. When he arrived in Athens, that ancient Greek capital had left its glory days behind but was still a must-see site for cultural tourists. As a Jew with a strong bias against "idols," and a first-time visitor, Paul was apparently vexed by the many statues of divinities he saw as he walked through the city. So he begins by roundly scolding, apparently unbidden, the people he encounters. He pointedly asserts to them that God does not need such man-made artifices. Then in a change of tone, and in an effort to bridge a cultural gap, he continues. "God is not far from each of us, for in him we live and move and have our being, as even some of your poets have said" (Acts 17:28).

By this point in The Acts of the Apostles, the part of the Bible immediately following the four Gospels, the spirit has been invoked many times. In the first chapter, the resurrected Christ tells the confused and anguished disciples, "You will receive power when the Holy Spirit has come upon you, and you shall be witnesses to me in Jerusalem, and in all Judea and Samaria, and to the end of the earth" (Acts 1:8). Shortly thereafter, the spirit does in fact descend on them. In Acts 2, we find the distraught followers of the nascent Jesus movement gathered from far and near in Jerusalem for the festival of Pentecost (marking, as the word implies, fifty days since Passover). Suddenly a tumult erupts. The roar of a mighty wind sweeps through the room. Tongues of fire rest over each of the followers' heads, and even though they speak a hodgepodge of languages, somehow they all understand one another. All this must create a considerable rumpus, because passersby mistake what is happening for a drunken revel. Peter, however, reassures everyone: "these people are not intoxicated, as you suppose, for it is only nine o'clock in the morning." Rather, what is going on, he says, is no less than the fulfillment of the prediction of the Hebrew prophet Joel—that one day the spirit will be "poured out on all flesh."

Peter's statement signals a breakthrough. The key words "all flesh" suggest that the spirit will now make its presence felt not just in kings and prophets, and not just on pivotal occasions such as conceptions and baptisms, but in all people, whether believers or not, and at all times. This makes the indwelling spirit akin to the image of God in human beings, an idea that is traceable to the creation stories. It also calls to mind the Quakers' conviction that there is "that of God in every man." Saint Paul frequently mentions the activity of this spirit. It is not only the interior connecting point that provides the opening for God's grace, it is also the source of the spiritual gifts of love, joy, peace, kindness, and the rest. As Jesus says, the spirit "will guide you into all truth" (John 16:13).

This spirit within, it would seem, is indispensable to God's connection with human beings. But Christians have not always recognized this and, operationally, the Trinity has often been reduced to a two-party collaboration. But this is changing. One of the most fascinating features of the course of Christianity over the past hundred years is the explosive growth of Pentecostalism, which strongly emphasizes the personal experience of the spirit. In one brief century, this movement has burgeoned from a tiny group meeting for prayer in a renovated livery stable on Azusa Street in Los Angeles to a global torrent whose adherents number in the hundreds of millions, representing perhaps a quarter of all Christians in the world. And it is still growing, especially in Latin America, Africa, mainland China, and the Asian rim. (Recall the Pentecostal Yoido Full Gospel Church described in a previous chapter—the largest single Christian congregation in the world, located in Seoul, Korea.)

The Bible says different things about the exact nature of the relationship between the God within and the God without. Sometimes humans are described as "in God" but at other times we hear of the God within us. Saint Paul makes the relationship highly intimate. He writes that "it is no longer I who live, but Christ lives in me" (Galatians 2:20). The mystical paths in all religious traditions have focused on the inner way. In Islam, for example, Sufis maintain that one does not need to travel all the way to the Mecca on earth (in Saudi Arabia) to complete the obligatory *haj* because the vital thing is to undertake the arduous journey to the "Mecca within." The Spanish mystic Saint Teresa of Avila described the approach to God's presence as entering the rooms of an "interior castle."

But the sequencing of the descriptions of the spirit in chapters one and two of Acts of the Apostles sets up a tension that has remained with Christianity ever since. The problem is that there seem to be two different "sendings." If, as the second chapter says, the spirit is sent (poured out) on "all flesh," then why does Jesus find it necessary to send his followers to spread this message "to the ends of the earth" (Acts 1:8)? What is the purpose of evangelism and missionary work if God's spirit is already present in all people? Is the spirit present but unrecognized? Is the Spirit only potentially present? Does the same spirit express itself in different ways in different cultures and perhaps even in different religions?

Christians have fought titanic battles over these dilemmas for centuries. Those who emphasize the already-present spirit (sometimes referred to as "universalists") regard sending missionaries as a waste of time and even as an unwarranted intrusion. Those who take the other position insist that Jesus's "great commission" to "go ye into all the world and proclaim the Gospel to the whole creation" (Mark 16:15) must be obeyed. The latter belief is what compelled Christian evangelists, by the twentieth century, to reach out to nearly every tribe and tongue on earth. Indeed, there are some fundamentalist missionaries who believe that Christ will delay his Second Coming until the Gospel is preached in every language and dialect; they relentlessly search out even the tiniest and most remote tribes in the upper Amazon.

The other dilemma raised by these accounts of the spirit concerns the tension between universality and uniformity. Again, if we follow Peter's description of the Pentecost, we understand that what was once a somewhat episodic presence of the spirit has now become universal. That is the significance of the words "all flesh." But does the presence of the spirit everywhere imply or require that it be everywhere the *same*, distributed with uniformity? This is another dispute over which much ink and no little blood has been spilled for hundreds of years. It is, as we shall see in a moment, also a quandary that has troubled the religion of The Market, in which it assumes a similar profile. Can we locate a Market equivalent to Pentecost or to the sending forth of the apostles to all the world? Why do the missionaries of the Market feel compelled to carry its message to every last village and hamlet? Must the golden arches rise across from every mosque, temple, church, and pagoda? Must Audis be sold in Tbilisi and Google Androids in Tashkent? Must there be a Starbucks on every third block in Buenos Aires as well as in Kyoto? How much uniformity must be evident in the architecture, the design of the chassis, or the mix of the brew?

In the rest of this chapter we will consider the parallel between the Holy Spirit and what I would call "The Market Geist" or in more psychological terms, "the market mentality." In the next chapter, we will turn to the similarity between the ways Christianity and The Market have coped with the contradiction between uniformity and particularity.

Does the Market God, a recently ascendant deity, include a counterpart to the Holy Spirit, a coequal collaborator interior to human beings? I think the answer is yes. When Max Weber wrote *The Protestant Ethic and the Spirit of Capitalism*, the original word for "spirit" was, as noted, the German *geist*. Scholars have debated Weber's thesis for decades, but few disagree with the core of his argument: in order to succeed, capitalism needs more than just an infrastructure of institutions. It also requires a new mentality, one that in its early stages has to embody such habits as thrift, diligence, and delayed gratification. But there is something Weber did not foresee—namely, that capitalism would at a later stage need to stimulate consumption more than thrift. Weber had industrial capitalism in mind. In our age of consumer capitalism, this interior geist is not so much what William James called the "will to believe" as the will to purchase. Weber's argument stands nevertheless. There is an all-important dimension of The Market that is not "out there" but gets under our skin and into our synapses. Without this internal partner, the external Market God would not be able to connect. In order to work its will, it must render people receptive to its message and susceptible to its bidding. It is imperative, therefore, to understand the Market God both as something around and above us, and as something "nearer than hands or feet." How does The Market "pour out its spirit on all flesh"? How does it instill its geist within? The answer involves both an external and an internal process.

Let us begin with the exterior landscape. The Market abhors anything uneven or asymmetrical. Marketing, production, and distribution all go more efficiently when the social environment is uniform; it is costly to bother about constantly rewriting advertising copy and adjusting sales techniques for varying cultural landscapes, social institutions, local tastes, and traditional practices. The Market, like the Psalmist, wants hills and valleys made smooth and "the rough places plain." It is true that important innovation occurs only when the mold is broken; this is what the economist Schumpeter called the "creative destruction" of capitalism. But The Market resents these disruptions and yearns for as much consistency and predictability as possible. Consequently, it relentlessly erases these irksome asymmetries. This is why, wherever we travel in the world today, every place begins to look like every other place. What used to be indigenous architecture, local foods, and "native" dress are fading as indistinguishable housing blocks (or worse still, architects' contemporary facsimiles of traditional buildings) spring up. Clothes from Walmart and The Gap and prepared foods in celluloid wrappers from supermarket shelves homogenize couture and cuisines.

Next comes the interior landscape. The Market calls not just for a monochrome outer topography. It needs an internal predictability as well. It needs people open to conversion. The Market mentality within us must match The Market that surrounds us, or else the vital connection will misfire. The gospel of The Market is not a complicated one. True, it may be delivered in a staggering number of ways, but underneath, the content is the same. It says, simply: "buy this and you will be happy." But because profit derives from the mass production of countless identical blouses, cars, and wristwatches, a certain interior uniformity of taste must be generated. The problem is that human beings are not the same. They reflect—or once did—a mishmash of wildly disparate preferences and desires. So the Market God needs to transform people from what they once were into people prepared to receive and act on its message. They have to be born again.

They have to be reconfigured to want the same thing, with only manageable variations in packaging, color, or flavor.

Intellectual advocates of global markets are fully aware of the subversion of local and regional diversity and the leveling of interior human sensibilities The Market causes. In fact they applaud it. Michael Novak is a lay Catholic who once studied for the priesthood, and enjoyed a long tenure as George Frederick Jewett Scholar in Religion, Philosophy, and Public Policy at the American Enterprise Institute. He brings a sharp intelligence and considerable philosophical sophistication to his attempt to establish nothing less than a metaphysical foundation for the age of The Market. He is also sensitive to the dangers of both the individualistic ("cowboy") entrepreneurial spirit and the threat of crony capitalism. He may be the best theologian The Market faith has produced.

Novak premises his case on the observation that God is, above all his other attributes, the Creator. In making man from dust "in his own image," he therefore made a creature with the capacity and the responsibility to create. Man continues the work of God beyond the initial six days by creating things of value. The entrepreneur and by extension the corporation are literally God's agents on earth. The next logical step after this theological foundation is laid is to recognize that whatever impedes this divinely initiated activity—and this would include crippling regulations and burdensome taxes—obviously frustrates God's will. The best way to eradicate poverty anywhere in the world is to get these obstacles out of the way and allow the Market to fulfill its manifest destiny.

Novak is no novice. He has crafted a formidable theological *Summa* for the age of The Market. And like his redoubtable predecessor, Thomas Aquinas, he does not hesitate to spell out its ethical, political, and societal implications. "Clearly," he states, "the exercise of personal economic enterprise is close to the moral center of the human person."[2] At the societal level, this requires entrepreneurs to become actively involved in reshaping the cultural and political institutions, and thus the spiritual mindsets, of countries in which they do business. The objective must be to remove the stubborn, traditional obstacles to the God-given imperative to create wealth. In what may be an unconscious echo of the French colonial-era belief in a *mission civilisatrice*, Novak calls it "the civilizing practices of the market."[3]

Novak realizes, of course, that this rationale for not only extending the gospel of The Market but replacing the cultural and religious barriers that obstruct it could be seen as a kind of imperialism. In particular, the people whose customary way of life it threatens might level that charge. They might even recall those heavy-handed Christian missionaries who chopped down totem poles, burned pagan temples, and insisted that bare-breasted African women wear Mother Hubbard dresses. Novak insists we cannot be deterred by that risk. His reasoning is itself creative. As one who started his career with a large measure of sympathy for liberation theology and its "preferential option for the poor," Novak asserts that alleviating poverty is a prime duty of religiously committed people, and to do so obviously necessitates generating wealth. This is the way we advance the Kingdom of God in earth. It is not all that complicated.[4]

There was a time when any such sweeping away of cultural obstacles to achieve a degree of sameness posed a daunting challenge. The Market's first missionaries who tried to preach their message and vend their wares in Asia, Africa, or Latin America were repeatedly frustrated by so many potential customers inclined to stick with their chapattis and tortillas and their loose-fitting robes and sandals instead of reaching for Big Macs, blue jeans, and Reeboks. The Market's pioneers were a bit like those luckless Christian missionaries who, having been dispatched to Muslim countries, had to write back to supporters after ten years of labor in the vineyards that they had not converted anyone yet.

The problem for The Market was that it had not yet created the all-important interior dimension. In the old days, people undoubtedly got excited when they strolled through the souk or traveled to a trade fair. But buying things was not always on their minds and it was certainly not the secret to the fulfilled life. The billboard had not yet appeared, much less the animated popup on an internet browser. This was before "Born to Shop" T-shirts became the rage. But now things are changing. Blue jeans are becoming the authentic native costume from Tokyo to Timbuktu. So the question now is: how and when did this change occur? When did what we call the "market mentality" cease to be merely episodic? When did it begin to pervade the mindset of whole cultures? When did its divine presence move from being mainly external to inhabiting our inward parts? Is it possible to specify the Market God's "Day of Pentecost?" If the message of the Market God, like the Christian Gospel, must be carried to every people and place, how can its apostles cultivate a fruitful reception? We turn to these questions in the next chapter.

14

"Go Ye into All the World"

> But you shall receive power when the Holy Spirit has come
> upon you; and you shall be witnesses to Me in Jerusalem,
> and in all Judea and Samaria, and to the end of the earth.

> —Jesus, to the disciples, Acts of the Apostles 1:4–6

We have already seen the tension inherent in the two different "sendings" of the Spirit described in the early chapters of The Acts of the Apostles, one for the world and one for the disciples. First God sends the Holy Spirit, poured out "upon all flesh." Second, Jesus tells his followers to expect the spirit to come upon them, which will give them the power to spread the word to all the nations, "to the ends of the earth." In this chapter we will explore the relationship between these two pourings, or sendings, and look at their equivalents in the Market religion.

Even the briefest of glances at the history of the expansion of The Market and its message during the last few centuries suggests a striking resemblance to the spread of the Christian movement. There is little doubt about what impels the managers of The Market to go "into all the world." The Market has no choice. Unless it constantly expands, it stagnates, and as soon as it stagnates it begins to die. This is the inner logic of the capitalist system. Growth is not optional. But there is a tougher question: When the marketing gospel arrives on far-flung shores, why and how does it "connect"? It could be argued that until relatively recently, the promulgation of the Market Gospel has been a hit-or-miss affair. Some people have been reached by the message, but many remain unsaved. But in the last few decades, a decisive change has taken place. A new age has opened—a Market equivalent to the Day of Pentecost with its tongues of fire and descent of the Spirit upon all flesh.

Let us date the beginning of this epochal internalization, this pivotal change for the Market mentality, to the advent of the pixel. Used in this context, a pixel is the tiniest element in the electronically generated images that cluster together to form what we see on, for example, a handheld device or television screen. It is by the grace of these flickering icons that the spirit of The Market "descends." It pours into us a flood of signs that easily slip into our brains without our having to think. A pixel image not only imprints the brain but alters it, leaving a memory trail. It takes only about three-tenths of a second for a visual image to pass from the eye to the cerebral cortex. But it is vital to notice that its receptors in the brain are not the ones that handle logical or rational messages. The pixel connects directly to the circuits that convey emotions. Pixel images also bypass our language grid and, once established, these neuro-chemical imprints are virtually impossible to erase. Once the pixel Pentecost has come, its impress remains with us, world without end. But how do the pixels get into you? Behold the age of electronic images, first with television, and then with smartphones.

Often, schoolteachers, therapists, and religious thinkers bewail the loss of reflection and deliberation in modern life. But not the moguls of the television industry, who look upon it as a stroke of luck. Roger Ailes, the CEO of Fox News, is an evangelist for the pixel and unabashed celebrator of the emotion-over-reflection wave. Sometimes referred to as "the master image maker," Mr. Ailes was one of the first to recognize our culture-wide attention deficit disorder, the ever-diminishing ability to focus on anything for more than a blink of an eye. But rather than decrying the syndrome, he decided to cash in on it. As one reviewer put it, even as early as the 1980s in his book *You Are The Message*, Mr. Ailes talked frankly and presciently "about the efficacy of appealing to an audience's emotions, staying on offence and embracing television's love of brevity, speed and colorful language."[1] In order to hold people's attention, he maintained, one has to be punchy and graphic.

Roger Ailes did not invent the pixel, much less attention deficit disorder. Both are products of the breakneck tempo of technology and its alliance with The Market. The descent of the pixel was both a prerequisite and consequence of the spread of The Market's presence unto the ends of the earth. But did the pixel descend upon all flesh? Well, almost. The breakthrough moment came first with television. Nielsen, a company famous for its ratings of audience sizes, reports that television is watched in fully 99 percent of American households, and that 95 percent of Americans spend some time watching every day. Americans watch, on average, over five hours of programming a day, and among people over sixty-five, that rises to over seven hours.[2] To be sure, these statistics might overstate things a bit since it is hard to say for how much of the time a television is on, no one is actually watching. (I know people who leave their televisions on when they are away to fool potential burglars into thinking someone is at home.) Still, the reach of the pixel is obviously extraordinary, and it is hard to imagine anyone but cloistered monks spending equivalent amounts of time in prayer, meditation, or Bible reading. The matchup of the Biblical God and The Market appears to be a particularly uneven one.

In the television context, the gospel of The Market is proclaimed mainly, but not exclusively, through the commercials that consume more than a third of total air time. As Jerry Mander writes: "The average television viewer watching television for four-plus hours per day is hit with about twenty-five thousand commercials per year, and by age sixty-five, that number exceeds two million. That would be twenty-five thousand annual repetitions of basically the same message: *You will be happier if you buy something.*"[3] The statistics in the rest of the world are not much different. Now, since the advent of the pixel, more up-to-date impressions of what one should wear or eat can be transmitted directly into billions of people's heads, bypassing not only custom and tradition, but reflection and conscious evaluation. Is there a remote village in Nigeria or a favela outside Rio de Janiero where the telltale TV antenna has not replaced the once omnipresent crucifix on even the poorest hovel? The Market spirit is far outpacing the religious missionaries in reaching the most remote corners of the earth.

Jesus once said, "Let the little ones come unto me," and The Market does not neglect the children, either. A University of Washington study found that 40 percent of three-month-olds and 90 percent of two-year-olds watch (or are at least exposed to) television regularly. Many parents place sets in their children's rooms, even in infants' rooms. For busy parents, the pixels become surrogate babysitters. Children from two to eleven watch an average of four hours a day, and much of the advertising is designed to get them to urge their parents to buy one or another product.[4] In the face of intense lobbying by the advertising industry, efforts to legislate against targeting young children with television ads have not gained much traction. And what parent can resist the pleading of a five-year-old to buy Tasty-Crunchy breakfast cereal or that toy Navy Seal?

The descent of the Spirit at Pentecost and the advent of the pixel are alike in some respects, but they are importantly different in others. The similarity lies in the fact that neither was or is a rational process.

The first Pentecost was lit up by tongues of flame. So, too, the passage of the pixel from the screen to the cerebral cortex is not a logical one. Like with the Pentecost experience of the disciples in Jerusalem, pixels communicate directly. They speak in all tongues. The words are secondary. True, the pixel flames that hover overhead today are invisible electronic impulses, and the roar we hear may just be the volume on our television receivers, but the net result is uncannily analogous.

However, although the coming of the Spirit and the arrival of the pixel are structurally parallel, their consequences are radically different. The distinction has to do with the tension between universality and particularity discussed above. Biblical scholars interpret Pentecost as a ringing celebration of diversity. The text says that there were in the room "Parthians, Medes, Elamites and residents of Mesopotamia, Judea, Cappadocia, Pontus and Asia, Phrygia and Pamphylia, Egypt and parts of Libya . . ." (Acts 2:8–10). Although they all spoke different languages, the Spirit enabled them to understand each other. Notice, however, that they did not all speak Greek or Latin or Hebrew. They were not subjected to a linguistic uniformity. Rather, they spoke in their own languages, and were understood. This means they were able to maintain their cultural distinctions, since languages provide the fabric of cultures. The event of Pentecost is a reversal of the Tower of Babel story, in which people were made to speak different languages and suddenly could not understand each other. The first Pentecost made a more inclusive community possible without erasing cultural particularities. The pixel Pentecost creates a new conglomerate by expunging such differences. On Super Bowl Sunday, a single commercial imprints itself on a hundred million people at once.

Any salesman or missionary knows that the best way to get a signature on the bottom line is to demonstrate the wares, to display what the vendor is trying to get the potential customer to buy or the potential convert to accept. The devotees of The Market know this all too well. In some cases it is not hard to do. They can invite you to sip the coffee, examine the model house, test drive the new Camry. In other cases it is not. Who knows how to sample a securitized package of mortgages?

In the historic religions, it is also not so easy to do. The Bible says, "Taste and see that the Lord is good" (Psalm 34:8), and some small groups have offered themselves as living illustrations of what life in that faith would be. But theologians have had their doubts about this strategy. Still, human beings have rarely been willing to consent to the partition completely. Mere earthlings, we all crave to taste, smell, or see at least a hint of what the Heavenly City might be like.

Consequently time and again in religious history the promoters of various faiths have tried to provide an earthly mock-up, a demonstration model, of the heavenly city. The main purpose of these showcase displays has been to flesh out the message so that it was not conveyed in mere words, but incarnated. "If you want to find out what it would be like to become an adherent of this way of life," they offered, "just look here." They were the equivalent of a test-drive or a stroll through the pristine bedroom and spotless kitchen of the demonstration house in a new real-estate development.

But these earthy outposts of the celestial realm had another purpose, as well. They provided a place to escape, if only in part, the temptations and allurements of the fallen world. Here, at least in theory, one could live out the ideals of the creed without being distracted by the Vanity Fair of the quotidian world. The best known example of this combination of evangelizing the outsiders and sheltering the insiders is the Christian monastic movement. True, it began when, after their once-outlawed religion became the ideology of an empire, some Christians who refused to accept such a compromise with worldly power fled to hills and deserts. At first they lived in isolation or in small bands, but gradually they gathered in larger communities to share prayer and work in common. It was Saint Benedict who, in the fifth century, formulated a code for living this common life in his famous Rule, which is still followed by Benedictine monks fifteen hundred years later. But the brothers saw themselves as more than just a shelter from the wicked world and an aberrant church. They viewed their enterprise as a sort of counterculture and as a visible embodiment of what being a Christian should mean.

Of course, men being human, the monastic enterprise inevitably developed flaws and blemishes. Some monasteries acquired wealth and vast acres of land, often from the last testaments of people who in life had besought their prayers and intercessions. With these holdings, they also acquired power. The monastery at Monte Cassino in Italy and the huge monastery at Cluny in southern France rivaled, and some said even surpassed, the papacy itself in pomp and influence. Some abbots began to live very much like the worldly lords they had first implicitly (and sometimes explicitly) rebuked, and many monks followed their example, if at a lower level of self-indulgence. Nonetheless, however monastic practice fell short in reality, the monastic ideal remained. Against the spirit of a sordid world of lust, greed, and violence, members of orders strove to demonstrate the life of simplicity, brotherhood, and discipline.

America boasts a rich and varied history of religious demonstration colonies. Indeed this demonstration impulse was there at the outset and remains in the American DNA. The Puritans believed they were building a "city upon a hill" which would allow the whole world to witness a living paradigm of a people ruled by the Word of God. But just how such a people should actually live was never fully clear. In the nineteenth century, John Humphrey Noyes founded a controversial colony of heaven in Oneida, New York, in which not only work and physical goods were shared but also sexual favors. Residents of the communal Oneida Community believed they were demonstrating a kind of Christian "perfection" in which possessiveness and jealousy would give way to a pooling of goods and affections.[5]

The most striking quality about these different attempts to establish religious "demonstration colonies" is how much they differed from each other. Quakers in Pennsylvania, Shakers in Massachusetts, the Oneida Community, and Benedictine monasteries anywhere—all displayed a strikingly different take on what a life of faith could or should be.

In contrast, The Market has a difficult time with variety. Its inner logic drives toward uniformity. A good example is McDonald's, which in its relatively short history has burgeoned from a drive-in eatery in Pasadena in 1940 to a global restaurant empire with 36,000 locations in 119 countries staffed by 1.9 million employees in 2015. The Big Mac's leap to such unprecedented success began in 1948 when it hit upon The Market's charmed talisman of conquest—namely, standardization. That year, McDonald's decided to institute the restaurant equivalent of the potent technique that had made Henry Ford and his plain black automobiles such a phenomenal triumph: the production line. Trained cooks became as unnecessary as china plates and silver cutlery. Instead, teenagers could be hired to perform simple tasks over which they had no discretion—flipping a burger, putting it on a roll, slathering it with special sauce, and placing it in a disposable cardboard box. Very little training was needed, so lower wages could be paid.

All this made for speedy service, a uniform product, and low prices, and therefore sales multiplied. The standardization of ingredients and preparation had another result. It meant that wherever you bought a Big Mac, whether in Poland or Japan or Uruguay, you knew just what you would get. "If you visit a McDonald's anywhere in the world, the great taste of our world famous French fries and Big Mac is the same" their website announced. The byword was "One Taste Worldwide."[6] The problem with this one-flavor-fits-all formula was that, when it ran into local food taboos, a certain culinary creativity was called for. In Tel Aviv, the meat had to be kosher. In Muslim countries, it had to meet the standards of Halāl. In India, where cows cannot be slain, Big Macs had to be made from goat meat. Despite all this, McDonald's management strove, with mixed success, to keep the taste as identical as possible.

Once the impulse to enforce uniformity sets in, it often establishes its own momentum. McDonald's decided early on that not only should its every hamburger taste the same, its every restaurant should look the same. Searching for an appropriate iconic symbol, it introduced what are now the familiar golden arches. Later, a psychology-trained marketing consultant named Louis Cheskin persuaded managers not to change the logo because it evoked the subconscious memory of a mother's breasts.[7] Whatever truth there may be to this Freudian possibility, something was working, and in 1969, McDonald's sold its four-billionth burger. By 1976, the count had reached twenty billion. Another four decades later, restaurants no longer display the billions; the digits rise too quickly. McDonald's restaurants became one of the fastest-growing architectural features of the century.

The spread of McDonald's into nearly nook and cranny of the known world mirrors in some ways the explosive expansion of early Christianity. Less than two centuries after the life of Jesus, the new faith had reached Britain and Spain, raced across North Africa, and penetrated to Afghanistan and India. Shortly after that, Nestorian Christian congregations appeared in China. Divisions over theology, liturgy, and governance among the geographically scattered and culturally different wings and branches of Christianity soon appeared. Distinct varieties grew up in Persia, Abyssinia, Egypt, and India, and despite the effort of the bishop of Rome (only later called the "pope") to hold it all together, splits occurred—many of which remain to this day. A major schism took place in 1054, when what we now call the Eastern Orthodox Church separated from Rome. Contacts remained hostile for centuries, especially after Western Christians sacked Constantinople during the Fourth Crusade in 1204. Even in recent times, relations continued to be chilly. Only in 2013 did the Orthodox patriarch, who still resides in what is now called Istanbul, attend the consecration of a pope; he did this for Pope Francis in March of that year. The year 2016 brought the first meeting of a pope and a patriarch of the Russian Orthodox Church in nearly a thousand years.

One of the most fascinating and fateful of many attempts to enforce a spiritual uniformity on a sprawling Christian world was the so-called Chinese rites controversy. It happened in the early eighteenth century, when the famous Jesuit missionary to China, Matteo Ricci, who had become a trusted advisor in the Emperor's court, decided that certain ceremonial rites of Confucianism and ancestor veneration were basically civic in nature, and that Chinese converts to Catholicism should be allowed to continue practicing them.

However, representatives of another religious order, the Dominicans, insisted that these rites were pagan and that Christians should be forbidden to take part. The argument dragged on for years until finally the Emperor expelled the missionaries who did not support Ricci's position. Then, however, the Spanish Franciscans jumped into the fray. They persuaded Pope Clement XI that the Jesuits were, in effect, going native. They were watering down the Gospel to squeeze it into Chinese cultural patterns. For example, the Franciscans decreed that the Chinese word *Shang Di* (supreme emperor) could not be used for "God," and that *Tien* (heaven) did not mean what Christians meant by heaven. The Jesuits refused to accept this judgment and the case continued to drag on. At last, in 1742, Pope Benedict XIV took sides against the Jesuits, banned the use of Chinese cultural categories in Christian worship, and ended all further discussion of the issue.

For many years after this, Matteo Ricci lingered in bad odor in the Catholic Church. Further, the chance for an indigenous Catholic community in China that was both authentically Christian and genuinely Chinese seemed to be lost. Eventually, in 1958, in an encyclical entitled *Princeps Pastorum*, Pope John XXIII decreed that Matteo Ricci should be honored as a model missionary.[8] But by that time, it was too late. The possibility of a bona fide Chinese Christianity has recently been revived, but not by Catholics. Today it is Pentecostals who are growing rapidly in China—precisely by admixing Christianity with Chinese culture. Variety trumps uniformity.[9]

The same kind of dispute, however, continues to rage over other issues and other areas. In 1997, the Vatican took the radical step of excommunicating Tissa Balasuriya, a Sri Lankan priest who was trying to reformulate Christianity in the cultural idiom of his homeland. When he was Prefect of the Congregation for the Doctrine of the Faith, Joseph Ratzinger, later Pope Benedict XVI, was more concerned about the mingling of Catholic and indigenous practices than he was even about the danger of liberation theology. But Balasuriya was eventually readmitted, suggesting that "Catholic" need not always mean Roman.

The history of the global church of The Market follows a somewhat different trajectory. The biggest problem it has faced is that its lightning growth, its planetary reach, and its effort to impose a common pattern everywhere make it increasingly difficult to reconcile variety with its need to standardize.

Again, McDonald's provides a useful example. Faced with such global sprawl, in 1997 the company's CEO did what the Emperor Diocletian did nearly two thousand years ago when the Roman Empire became too large. He divided it into two semi-autonomous, self-managing sub-empires. The tension between universality and uniformity seems to be built in. The bigger something gets, the harder it is to enforce sameness, or perhaps to enforce anything.

But this could turn out to be a sign of hope. The tension, which has so often been seen as a challenge for both traditional religion and The Market, might even save both from the dreariness and monotony of endless reiteration. Agronomists say that crop diversity is a necessity for human survival on the planet. An orchestra constituted of strings, percussion, and woodwinds delights the ear better than one made of forty tubas or fifty clarinets. In recent years, through innumerable ecumenical and interfaith movements, most of the religions and denominations of the world have begun to affirm and appreciate the diversity of faith rather than lament it.

Some "big picture" observers have noted that the two most dramatic and visible movements of the century have been the unexpected resurgence (for bane and for blessing) of religion, and the expansion from pole to pole of the institutions and values of the Market. Throughout this book, we have been examining the changing connections between religion and commerce. But in our time, we are witnessing a special instance of this long interaction since both are growing. What, if anything is the link, if any, between these two movements?

Early in the new century, the Theology Department of the University of Oslo, Norway, launched a long-term study to address this question. One result of this project was the publication in 2006 of a volume significantly entitled *Spirits of Globalisation*, which included contributions by a wide variety of scholars. But there was little agreement on what the correlation is. Some thought that the new religious surge might feed and support the mentality of The Market. Especially in its Pentecostal expression, it could, for example, encourage the impulse away from reflection and toward immediate gratification which The Market needs to fuel sales. Others thought, however, that vigorous religious movements could question the greed and acquisitiveness The Market inspires. The conclusion, as happens in many such academic ventures, was that the relationship between God and Mammon remains a highly complex one, and that it undoubtedly differs from region to region.[10]

Still, even though the scholars barely discuss it, the decision to include the word "spirits" *(Geisten)* in the title of such a study of globalization was accurate and illuminating. Two powerful impulses, often at odds but sometimes overlapping, are at work in our time, and both are, in the largest and most significant sense of the term, "spiritual." These conclusions, though modest, inspired me to look more carefully into The Market as a religious phenomenon, which is what this book is about.

15

The Liturgical Year of The Market

From its earliest stages, The Market has appropriated words and symbols from the spiritual realm. This shouldn't surprise us. From the dim past in which they first emerged, religions have always borrowed, stolen, and recast aspects of previous religions. The writers of the Bible, for example, lifted stories about the creation of the world and a great primeval flood and reworked them for their own purposes. The Christian rite of baptism is an adaptation of an ancient Jewish practice called the *mikvah*. Stories from the Hebrew Scriptures and the New Testament are folded into the Koran. Buddhism carries within itself elements of the Hindu milieu from which it emerged in 500 BC. The Market faith is simply repeating this age-old practice.

For example, when the beauty brand Philosophy, owned by Coty, looked for names for its original products, it came up with "Hope in a Jar" for a moisturizer, "Hands of Hope" for a hand cream, and "Amazing Grace" for a fragrance. Of course, "hope" (*elpidis* in Greek) is a key term in the New Testament. It is said by Saint Paul to be, along with faith and love, one of the three most abiding virtues (I Corinthians 13). And "Amazing Grace" may be the most familiar of all Protestant hymns. Composed by the converted slave-dealer-turned-abolitionist John Newton, it rose even higher in popularity when President Barack Obama sang it from the pulpit of the Emanuel African Methodist Episcopal Church in Charleston, South Carolina, in June 2015.

A *New York Times* story about a philanthropic initiative by the Coty brand quotes the inspirational sermonette printed on its hand cream container: "Hands of Hope are the hands that help, heal, protect and comfort.... Use your hands to give hope, and you will have hope to hold."[1] As that *Times* piece went to press, the company had arranged for singer-songwriter Natasha Bedingfield to compose a new song entitled "Hope" and release a music video, with 20 percent of the iTunes proceeds going to mental-health charities. The company has its own hopes that the promotion will generate sales. Now customers can enjoy both exuding a better aroma and performing a work of mercy at the same time.

But the more The Market assumes the mantle of religion, the more its advocates discover that there is both an upside and a downside to having a spiritual aura. A good example of the uncertainty of this strategy is The Market God's liturgical year, with its succession of festivals and holy days. Every faith tradition has such an almanac of special celebrative occasions—various feasts and fasts that punctuate the months with their different customs and stories. But Holy Days are not decreed by heaven. They are created by the priests and prophets of one religion or another, often to mark the birth, death, or significant event in the life of a founder or saint, or an important occurrence in the saga of the tradition.

The history of any religion also reveals the story of how certain holidays rise, but also fall, as these religions develop, divide, spread, and decline. It is also a well-known feature of red-letter days and seasons that their meanings do not remain constant. It seems that people become accustomed to marking off a particular time as special, and if certain foods are associated with the day, they continue to prepare and eat them. At the same time, the content and significance of the day can metamorphose depending in part on changes in the environing culture. In his classic work *The Ancient City*, the French historian Numa Denis Fustel de Coulanges documents how the civic festivals of Rome mutated from the earliest years through the republic and the empire, often with the outward forms remaining while the inner substance was fundamentally altered.[2]

Plainly, as we will see below, the significance of the religious and civic holidays we celebrate in America has not been static through the years, and we can see parallel changes going on in the high holidays of The Market. Also, the relative importance of holidays in the minds of a populace can rise and fall. A fete that was widely popular a few decades or a couple centuries ago can become peripheral, and holidays that once seemed minor sometimes acquire more popularity. Often such changes are not the result of different thinking on the part of the adherents of the faith in question, and can even annoy them. Thus Chanukah, for centuries a distinctly minor Jewish holiday, gradually acquired more importance because it falls so near Christmas, the major celebration of the environing majority culture. Jewish leaders have fought a noble but largely losing battle to put Chanukah back in its traditional niche. No holiday is exempt from the larger society within which it operates. Now Chanukah cards are stocked next to the Christmas cards in the local drugstore.

The religion of The Market constructs its liturgical calendar in two ways. Sometimes it invents its own holidays. But more often it latches onto the sentiments and practices generated by existing festivals, most often religious ones, and makes use of these feelings for its own purposes, which are not always commensurate with those of the holiday in question. By and large, The Market prefers the latching-on strategy. This is entirely understandable. Capitalizing on the élan of a religious holiday is easier than trying to create your own, *ex nihilo.*

No holiday is exempt from being enlisted as an opportunity for expanding sales, although the special day needs to be well enough known to attract a sufficiently large number of potential customers to make it worth the effort. The latest example I've seen of this very old story is a vigorous campaign by Tommy Hilfiger to enlist the Muslim holy month of Ramadan as an additional Christmas season. The move was almost inevitable. Ramadan, which marks the first revelation of the Koran to the Prophet Mohamet, lasts a whole month, and it ends with three days of feasting called Eid al-Fitr at which families gather and consume a lot of food, and women are expected to look their best. To take advantage of this enticing market, Hilfiger has introduced a line of women's clothes including caftans and a cowl-neck black satin evening dress and a long-sleeve teal gown (with a somewhat un-Muslim slit from knee to instep.) So far, the strategy seems to have been a success. An analyst with market research firm Euromonitor International predicted that "a typical 'Ramadan consumer' is likely to emerge in the same way as the Christmas shopper as a global phenomenon."[3]

Of course Tommy Hilfiger is not the only player in this game. Many people who celebrate Ramadan have more than ample financial resources, and an embroidered Oscar de la Renta caftan that sold for $2,890 also became a favorite, but was challenged by a bib-front silk Valentino midi-dress which went for $3,790. And this is in no way a shopper pool confined to the Middle East. The American Muslim Consumer Consortium points out that of the nearly two billion Muslims in the world, about nine million live in North America. One of the founders of this consortium, Sabiha Ansari, estimates annual Muslim spending power in the United States to be about $100 billion.

It is fascinating to observe not only the various ways in which the religion of The Market has constructed its sacred calendar, but also how that calendar has been undergoing changes caused by both internal factors in The Market faith itself and by shifts in the culture in which it lives. In the following discussion of The Market religion's liturgical calendar we will focus on what might be called the "major feasts," in each case showing how the holiday originated and how it has evolved or devolved.

The Rise and Fall of Black Friday

We begin with the day of frantic selling and frenzied shopping which bursts on us in the United States each year on the day after Thanksgiving. Black Friday, so called because it is traditionally the day when many retailers cross over from being "in the red" (unprofitable for the year) to "in the black" (enjoying revenues in excess of expenses), kicks off The Market's most important sacred season, one that continues for five weeks until after Christmas. The fervor it generates can be glimpsed in some recent melees. In 2008, a security guard was trampled to death when he opened the doors at a Walmart in New York City. In 2013, a woman pulled out a stun gun and aimed it at another shopper at Franklin Mills Mall in Philadelphia. In Los Angeles, a woman used pepper spray to get past fellow shoppers in order to lay her hands on an Xbox video game console she obviously wanted very badly. She completed her purchase and left before police arrived, but thanks to the ruckus she caused, CNN reported, twenty people were treated for minor injuries. In a New Jersey Walmart, it was the police who used pepper spray, to subdue an especially disruptive shopper.

John Roberts, a security consultant, told a Boston newspaper that the situation "seems to be escalating every year." Many of the violent encounters take place in the parking lots as zealous shoppers vie for spaces close to the doors so they will not have to struggle very far under the piles of items they buy. In 2013 a man was stabbed outside a Virginia Walmart. All told, at least eight people have died from injuries sustained on this festival of consumer fervor.[4]

All of these incidents took place on one of the principal holy days of The Market because the throngs that converge on its holy places, the high-end boutiques and bargain basements, easily exceed those that flock into Lourdes or Fatima. Nor does unfriendly weather dull their ardor. In November of 2014, eight inches of snow blanketed parts of the northeast and temperatures dipped below zero, but eager pilgrims were not slowed down. They appear in the freezing darkness wrapped in blankets and wearing ski togs, waiting for store openings at five and six o'clock in the morning so they can be first to scoop up what the stores call their "door buster" sale items. In 2013, twenty-two million people pushed and elbowed their way through Walmart stores alone on Black Friday, more than visited Disney's Magic Kingdom during the whole year. And those people were not just window shopping.

They bought things. Lots of them. Target reported that it sold eighteen hundred televisions and two thousand video games every minute in the first hour of the opening of its stores.[5]

It would be easy simply to blame this sometimes fatal devotion on greed, or as the classical theologians called it, "the sin of avarice." But on further scrutiny, it appears to be not that simple. John Roberts, the retail security expert who sees the situation getting worse, believes there is another motive also at work. People seem actually to enjoy the thrill and even the danger of the experience itself. Maybe what happens is a resurgence of primitive drives from the hunting and gathering phase of human history. "Shoppers like the adrenaline rush of pushing through the door, grabbing things, and getting deals. It is a climate of apprehension and excitement," Roberts says.[6]

To many it would seem that store owners have tapped into a primal stratum of the human psyche, and are on a roll that will last forever. But will it? Even as the hour of some store openings was moved up from early Friday morning to late Thanksgiving night, the crush began to thin a little. Lines shortened and fewer injuries were reported. What happened was yet another way in which a holiday of The Market is replicating the history of the holidays of other religions.

History is scattered with the desiccated remains of once prominent holidays. Several that used to be celebrated in America have gradually been watered down by various cultural trends. One such diluting force is the popular demand for the "long weekend" in a society that values leisure and consumption. When the dates for marking holidays are intentionally set on Fridays or Mondays, people get seventy-two hours off instead of twenty-four. The result has often been the loss of the symbolic significance they were once intended to have. This is especially true for the holidays of our American civil religion. Presidents' Day, Independence Day, Veterans' Day, and Labor Day are all now located within a three-day time span that allows for travel and mini-vacations. This is undoubtedly to the benefit of hard-pressed and often overworked families, as well as to the growing leisure industry. But the result is that the original purpose for creating these holidays is often lost. Who, except a few veterans, now pays much attention to the ceremonies on the day dedicated to them? Do vacationers at the beach, or setting off fireworks on the long holiday over what we now simply call "The Fourth," give much thought to the colonies' battle for independence from Great Britain? How many people think about laborers on Labor Day? Who now even remembers some holidays that were marked when I was a youngster, like Flag Day and Decoration Day?

So where does Black Friday now stand on the standard arise-thrive-fall arc of traditional religious holidays? It appears that its heyday is over, and that its period of waning has set in. This decline became especially evident in 2014. One effect was that the above-mentioned extension of post-Thanksgiving Day sales into Thanksgiving itself, which had previously been spotty, became a general practice. Sales for the whole weekend, which had been $57.4 billion the previous year, dipped to $50.9 billion, a greater than twelve percent drop. That weekend, 133.7 million people shopped, 5.2 percent fewer than the previous year, and the shoppers spent 6.4 percent less. Black Friday was not what it once was. Ken Perkins, the founder of Retail Metrics, suggested to the *New York Times* that Black Friday was becoming a thing of the past.[7] In 2015, the retail researcher ShopperTrak told *Time* magazine that, focusing on Black Friday alone, sales in brick-and-mortar stores fell from $11.6 billion in 2014 to $10.4 billion in 2015.[8]

But why? One reason for the decline is that a nascent popular protest against its spirit and its excesses is already underway among customers and even some merchants. In October 2015, the sporting-goods chain Recreational Equipment, Inc., known as REI, made the startling announcement that its 143 outlets would not be open for business on Black Friday, and that it would pay its employees to spend time outdoors instead. The following letter, published online and in newspapers, could not have been welcome news for the curates who tend the altars on this sacred day:

REI is closing on Black Friday. You read that correctly. On November 27, we'll be closing all 143 of our stores and paying our employees to head outside. Here's why we're doing it.

For 76 years, our co-op has been dedicated to one thing and one thing only: a life outdoors. We believe that being outside makes our lives better. And Black Friday is the perfect time to remind ourselves of this essential truth.

We're a different kind of company—and while the rest of the world is fighting it out in the aisles, we'll be spending our day a little differently. We're choosing to opt outside, and want you to come with us. (Jerry Stritzke, President, CEO)

This is a remarkable note. In religious history, when it is merely the folks in the pews who object to a given practice, their complaints can be safely ignored, at least for a while. But when the minor clergy and then even the higher-ranking ones begin to chafe, change will probably come soon. When an angry woman of the sixteenth-century hurled a bench at a minister in Scotland for "praying out of a book," the now-famous incident might have been overlooked as an isolated case of questionable manners, but when higher church officials joined in the growing dissent against sterile formalism in worship, the result was the Scottish Reformation. Perhaps most importantly, REI's decision, although it attracted much favorable notice, does not appear to have been based solely on a bid for publicity. Other values—shared by employees and customers—led it to encourage fresh air and exercise, and to emphasize its dedication to quality and service over bargains. This demonstrates that, despite The Market's strenuous effort to attain omnipotence, it is not quite there yet. Other centers of value are still operative in its realm. Stritzke may be only one CEO, but REI's refreshing new policy casts an ominous shadow on the future of one of The Market's red-letter days. Was that a small bench we just saw flying through the air?

Undoubtedly, another reason we are witnessing the twilight of Black Friday is that extending the bacchanalia of spending earlier and earlier into November inevitably diluted its intensity. Customers have begun to feel that if they wait a few more days, prices will drop even more. Thus Black Friday is placed within a longer period of buying fervor and consigned to a fate similar to the holidays, like Presidents' Day or Independence Day, now attached to long weekends. Another reason for its shrinking is the expanded opportunity that shoppers have to make their purchases online. Each year, the percentage of sales accomplished through electronic screens grows. And the brick-and-mortar stores' share goes down. Already in 2014 the somewhat thinner crowds and the slightly shorter lines signaled that the salad days of Black Friday might be passing.

But even the vicars of the merchandising church were not sure of the answer. One possibility was that the gradual economic recovery of 2014 had cut two ways. The still unemployed or under-employed people, who had yet to taste its benefits, just did not have the money to do much purchasing, even with many prices slashed. Meanwhile, those who were feeling the wave of recovery, and had a bit more money, were not as motivated to brave the crowds in search of bargains. It may be too early to hang the crepe, but marketing experts are talking about the erosion of Black Friday. (*Sic transit Gloria mundi.*)

Christmas: Jesus, Santa, Tiny Tim, and Rudolph

No one knows either the date or the year of the birth of Jesus. In part for this reason, the early Christians did not celebrate his birthday for many years, concentrating instead on Easter, the Feast of the Resurrection, which they understood to be the much more important holiday. When they eventually did decide to mark his birthday, they were still suspected and sometimes persecuted by the Roman authorities, so they cleverly chose the day of the raucous pagan festival of Saturn

(Saturnalia). Amidst its feasting and carousing, their own modest celebrations would not be noticeable to authorities. For the first centuries
of Christian history, Easter remained the preeminent holiday.

Christmas, dated differently in the Eastern Church, gained importance in the medieval period. It continued to do so into the Reformation. Martin Luther famously dragged an evergreen tree in from the
forest and lit it with candles. But the more Calvinistic Puritans who
settled New England would have none of it. To them, it seemed both
pagan and popish. After all, the word "Christmas" does contain the
word "mass," and pine trees exude a whiff of sprites and wood spirits,
redolent of paganism. They ignored Christmas completely and trudged
off to work in their frozen fields on the twenty-fifth of December. It
was only the arrival of Rhineland Pietists, and later of Lutherans and
Catholics, that eventually made Christmas so central to American culture. But is Christmas, like Black Friday, already in decline?

Many have been the loud laments about the commercialization and
even the ruination of Christmas. It is certainly true that the day was
originally conceived by the early Christians as a time to celebrate the
birth of the baby Jesus, and that focus has often been lost as Santa Claus,
Tiny Tim, and Rudolph dominate the stage. But as today's Christians
bemoan the excessive drinking, garish materialism, and revelry that
now surges during the last two weeks of December (in the West), it
is well to remind ourselves of that sly co-opting of Saturnalia—which
was characterized by, yes, excessive drinking and revelry.

In modern history, certain features of the Christmas story have
undergone a kind of translation to bring them into conformity with
the marketing ethos the season has acquired. The story of the three
"wise men" is a good example. They came "from the East," and the
narrative was originally intended to suggest that the birth of Christ
was God's act of mercy not just for the Jews but for all humankind.

As the centuries passed and monarchies gained power, to the point that the Catholic Church even considered making coronation a sacrament, the three camel riders found themselves transmogrified into "kings."

More recently it is not so much as Gentiles or as crowned heads that they are remembered, but as the bearers of gifts: gold, frankincense, and myrrh. They are seen to have initiated the practice that has morphed into an avalanche of gaily festooned packages, the lifeblood of The Market. According to cultural historians, this latest manifestation of the turbaned Big Three began in America in the nineteenth century, as an industrial economy took hold and marketers had to stimulate consumer spending. The wise men did their job well. Before the nineteenth century, Americans preferred to give and receive homemade baked and knitted gifts, and they considered giving "store bought" presents tasteless and impersonal. But by the end of the century, thanks to immense efforts by advertisers, tastes had been redirected to manufactured items. The switchover was vital to business. One suspects at this point that, if in one year in the United States no one bought Christmas presents, the entire economy would collapse in chaos.

Those three robed figures led by the star to the manger in Bethlehem are not the only religious figures that have undergone reconstructive surgery over the years. Think, for example, of the third-century bishop of Myra (now in modern Turkey) named Nicholas. He is recorded as having attended the Council of Nicaea in 330 CE, but went on to become the patron saint of children and sailors. No one describes him as "jolly" or records his ever saying, "ho, ho, ho"; nor was he ever spoken of as an elf. Bishop Nicholas, however, eventually became the most widely known prelate in history—albeit in a role he would hardly have recognized. He has become, of course, the plump, white-bearded, and red-suited Santa Claus, now the patron of gift-giving and, of course, gift buying.[9]

Doubtless, the most important boon to Santa Claus's reputation was the publication in 1820 of Clement Moore's "A Visit from Saint Nicholas," which has been constantly republished with added illustrations throughout the ensuing years, and is now more than ever integral to Christmas lore. But this piece of doggerel did more than catapult Santa to fame and to teach us the names of the reindeer. It also helped transform the holiday from what in the nineteenth century had been a time of "wassailing," with bands of youths and poor people roving the streets and pounding on the doors of their wealthier neighbors demanding drinks, gifts, and sometimes money. It helped "domesticate" Christmas. As the historian Stephen Nissenbaum writes, the evolving Santa story was fused with the gift-giving cult, and it served to move Christmas from the street and into the family parlor. And now the gift giving was changed: instead of the well-to-do giving to the poor, now it became the older generation giving to their own children and grandchildren.[10]

Some concern for the poor has remained, represented by the baskets of food that churches deliver to families who cannot afford turkey and cranberry sauce, and in the "Remember the Neediest" campaigns that newspapers wage around the holidays (although some critics point out that these efforts, however honestly motivated, obscure the distasteful fact that poor people prefer justice to charity and are likely to resent being the objects of even the most generous Lady Bountiful's succor).

"Do you believe in Santa Claus?" At a more explicitly theological level, the verdict on Santa is mixed. Some church leaders complain that placing him in the realm of faith and belief confuses toddlers.

Still, he often appears with his sack of goodies in Sunday School Christmas events.[II] Others criticize him as the main culprit responsible for the debasement of Christmas into an orgy of consumption, which confuses spiritual with material well-being. Santa, they say, subtly perpetuates the idea that God rewards those he favors with wealth and prosperity—and that, therefore, those who have neither must somehow not be in a state of grace. This in turn feeds the idea that the poor have only themselves to blame for finding their stockings filled with coal. With a little more industriousness, perseverance, hard work, and thrift, they might be in the circle of God's favor.

Central to the Santa myth is that the white-bearded senior citizen is enshrouded in mystery. For young children, it is not their parents who stuff the stockings tacked on the mantel, it is Santa. But since in the Santa fable these presents all come from a North Pole workshop staffed by cheerful elves, some note that this also obscures the uncomfortable reality that people somewhere do in fact make the toys. We are thus shielded from looking further into the wages or working conditions of those actual human being workers. At a time when consumers increasingly demand to know where and how the products they buy were made, and consumer campaigns against sweatshops are appearing, the Santa story thus serves a questionable purpose. It mystifies the corporate system and the real employment practices involved.

The donnybrook over Saint Nick can become heated. When his supporters say that teaching children to "believe" in him instills the value of faith, some critics reply that that is just the problem. Implanting this kind of uncritical credulity is exactly what is wrong with religion, and is not an appropriate attitude in a democracy. Santa's fans respond by echoing a familiar argument used to minimize the "belief in" dimension of religion in order to defend its moral importance. They say that, by modeling for children the virtues of generosity, charity, and even cheerfulness, Santa makes an invaluable contribution to the common good. One writer, Steven Hales, contends that as a paradigm of these qualities Santa is an even better exemplar than Jesus.[12]

Is Christmas in decline? It seems not. Macy's famous Thanksgiving Day parade, which has always climaxed with the appearance of Santa, has now become almost entirely a Christmas parade. In 2015, not a single Plymouth pilgrim was to be seen in its procession, but the world's largest elf hovered as a huge balloon overhead.

As a holiday marking the birth of a child in a stable, the meaning of Christmas seems to have been overshadowed by Santa, Scrooge, and the Sugar Plum Fairy. Yet hundreds of millions of people still celebrate it in one way or another as the natal day of the Prince of Peace. Untold thousands who do not set foot in a church any other day of the year attend on Christmas Eve. Millions watch the pope celebrate the Mass of the Nativity at Saint Peter's in Rome on television.

It would be ironic if the original spiritual meaning of Christmas and the "happy holidays" acquisitiveness of The Market were able to coexist for a long time to come, and thus unintentionally replicate the early Christian experience of quiet gratitude for the coming of the Savior, surrounded by the blare and commotion of a postmodern debauch. But that cheery compromise seems improbable. After all, the roisterers quaffing their drinks on the Roman Saturnalia did not try to co-opt the infant Jesus as one of *their* symbols. Today, as we have seen above, so many of the elements of the Christian holiday have been blended into its commercial parody that the compound seems unstable. Only time will tell whether the infant in the manger or the gnome in the sleigh will prevail.

Mother's Day: Return of the Female Divinity?

On what day of the year are more phone calls made than on any other? It is not hard to guess. The huge spike in jingling or beeping telephones, up 37 percent in a recent year, takes place on the second Sunday in May, which, at least in the United States, is celebrated as Mother's Day. But Mother's Day provides a particularly dramatic example of how a single holiday can go through a series of transitions, in this case within a very short time. It is also a vivid instance of how the religion of The Market can co-opt a holiday and imbue it with its own pecuniary meaning.

Mother's Day can lay claim to the oldest lineage of any holiday in the world. The only picture of a human being scratched on the wall in the Lascaux cave is that of a woman who is clearly pregnant. After that came a succession of mother goddess cults, including those of the Romans and the Greeks who set aside special times to honor Rhea and Cybele. Ceremonies honoring motherhood were often mixed with celebrations of fecundity or sexuality, and sometimes both.

As Christianity spread, these practices were often fused with the growing veneration of the Virgin Mary. When the Council of Ephesus was convened in 431 CE, one of the controversial questions on the table was how Mary was to be understood. Should she be honored simply as the mother of Jesus? Or as the mother of Christ? Or should she be venerated as *Theotokos*, the mother of God? The council fathers decided on the latter designation, and historians have speculated for centuries on whether the venue of the council—which had been the main location for the worship of "Diana of the Ephesians" and therefore a center for the worship of a powerful and divine woman—played any role. I once asked a historian of Catholicism why she thought the council fathers had come to the "Mother of God" decision, and she answered without hesitation: "They wanted a female divinity."

This may not be the case, but clearly as the medieval period set in, a flowering (some would even call it an excrescence) of Marian piety took hold. She became a powerful spiritual and cultural force. Henry Adams once wrote that it was Mary who built Chartres Cathedral. Then, however, the sixteenth-century Protestant reformers moved in a different direction. They thought of Mary as another saint, albeit a very important one, and they were firmly opposed to prayers to saints. Mary was marginalized. It is understandable, therefore, that during the Counter-Reformation and the centuries that followed, in pushing back against the Reformation, Catholics placed an increased importance on Marian devotion.

The nineteenth and twentieth centuries saw this escalation of Mary's place in Catholic devotion continue in different ways. In 1854, Pope Pius IX proclaimed the doctrine of the Immaculate Conception (not to be confused with the Virgin Birth of Christ), which states that the sexual intercourse between Mary's parents was preserved by God from transmitting original sin, so that Jesus himself, the offspring of Mary and the Holy Spirit, could be born free of the stain. Then, in 1950, Pope Pius XII took another step and promulgated the doctrine of the Assumption of Mary. It affirmed something that was already widespread popular belief—that the Virgin was taken bodily to heaven in the flesh without passing through the portal of death. Some Catholic theologians urged that Mary should be seen as "Co-Redemptrix" with Christ. Meanwhile, as the doctrines were being introduced at the theological level, a parallel development was underway in popular religiosity. Time after time, apparitions of Mary—at Lourdes and Fatima and in many other places—were reported, often by children, with the result that pilgrims then poured to these sites. It seemed that Christianity was edging ever closer to having a female divinity.

Protestants were not at all pleased with these developments either in doctrine or in popular piety. Some saw them as serious barriers to any reunification of the separated denominations.

But Carl Jung, the son of a Swiss Protestant pastor, hailed the doctrine of the Assumption as the most important development in Christianity since the Reformation, since it symbolized a female aspect to the divinity.[13] In any case, when our current Mother's Day was introduced in the nineteenth century, it echoed a long history of religious celebration of motherhood.

How did the latest iteration of this primal human reality begin? As with other holidays, the why and when of the founding of the modern Mother's Day are disputed questions. One credible account claims it was created by Julia Ward Howe when, in 1870, she issued a "Mother's Day Proclamation." Her idea for a "mothers' peace day" was that mothers would rally to call for world peace (a somewhat ironic project for the author of "The Battle Hymn of the Republic.") Another founding theory attributes the holiday to Ann Reeves Jarvis of West Virginia, who in 1865 organized something she called "Mothers' Friendship Day," at which mothers invited veterans of the Union and Confederate armies to meet together and work toward reconciliation. These efforts are now usually seen as predecessors of the work of Anna Jarvis, the daughter of Ann Reeves Jarvis. After her mother died in 1905, she dedicated herself to making Mother's Day an official American holiday, as a memorial to her own mother and to honor the sacrifices all mothers make for their children.

But here is where the acolytes of The Market enter the picture. Anna Jarvis, eager to get her project moving, sought and won support from a famous Philadelphia department store magnate. John Wanamaker might have been inspired by her vision (who can resist the magic of motherhood?), but he also had a vision of his own: just think of the business this new holiday could engender! But the entente between God and Mammon soon became problematical, and it soured into a partnership Anna Jarvis would come to regret. In May 1908 she arranged for the first recorded Mother's Day service at a Methodist Church in Grafton, West Virginia. But on the very same day, Mr. Wanamaker held an immensely successful Mother's Day event at his store in Philadelphia. This was a first step in co-opting of Mother's Day into one of the principal red-letter days in the liturgical year of The Market.

Still, building on the partnership with Wanamaker, Jarvis set out to make Mother's Day an officially recognized national holiday. She detested the fact that all the American holidays that focused on individuals were designed to honor men. She launched letter-writing campaigns and lobbied politicians. She established a Mother's Day International Association. Finally, she attained her goal when, in 1914, President Woodrow Wilson signed a law officially establishing the second Sunday in May as Mother's Day.

Almost immediately, the battle for the control of Mother's Day erupted in earnest. Ann Reeves Jarvis had wanted it to be day of reconciliation between Civil War veterans who had fought on different sides. Julia Ward Howe had envisioned a day for promoting peace. Anna Jarvis saw it as a time to wear a white carnation and visit one's mother. But the florists and restaurateurs and gift shop proprietors had other ideas. Maybe it was the carnations that were the opening wedge. Mother's Day soon became a banner day for greeting card and knickknack makers. Restaurants urged customers to save Mama some work and treat her to dinner out. Catching on to the possibilities some decades later, the automat restaurant chain Horn and Hardart added a whole line of pre-cooked, take-home foods and marketed them as "less work for mother" meals.

Meanwhile, seeing how the marketers had seized on her idea, Anna Jarvis became frustrated with what she took to be the co-optation and cheapening of her vision. Admittedly, at first, she had worked with the floral industry to make Mother's Day more visible, but by 1920 she had become appalled by the blatant commercialization. She began by denouncing what she took to be the despoiling of the holiday, then moved to actually urging people not to buy the cards and flowers being pushed by stores. But the genie was out of the bottle and even the holiday's founder could not stuff it back in. Growing angrier and more desperate, Jarvis introduced legal suits against companies that used the word "Mother's Day." She poured out most of her personal wealth on endless legal fees. Nothing worked. By 1948, she not only completely disowned the holiday she had helped to create, but tried to persuade the federal government get it erased from the national calendar.[14] This effort failed too. Mother's Day had escaped its inventor's purpose and taken on a meaning more amenable, and profitable, to The Market.

But there is another complex twist in the story. Although it did indeed become a huge commercial success, Mother's Day, born in a Methodist church in Grafton, West Virginia, never completely disappeared from the churches. It is marked in nearly every denomination on the second Sunday in May. Ushers often distribute flowers to mothers. Ministers and priests preach on motherhood. Choirs sing anthems about mothers to mothers who have sometimes been served breakfast in bed by their children and husbands.

Recently, another subtle spin on Mother's Day has begun to appear in many Protestant churches. Mary is back. Along with the mothers in the congregation, and significant mothers in history, some

Protestant churches have begun to take special notice of the mother of Jesus. On Mother's Day of 2015, I found myself in The Riverside Church in Manhattan, sometimes considered the "cathedral of liberal Protestantism" in America. There on that day, Mary occupied a prominent place in the hymns, prayers, and sermon. I immediately asked around, and found that a similar thing was happening in many other churches. Mary has never disappeared from Christmas cards or lawn crèches, of course, but now she has begun to appear in Protestant liturgies. Gounod's setting for "Ave Maria" is now heard in Presbyterian churches.

One cannot claim a return of *Theotokos*. Still, this is a change that might well have shocked the Calvinist founders of New England or the exclusively Jesus-centered Baptists and Methodists of a previous era, who did not want anyone else, even his mother, crowding Jesus for center stage. Drawing from the examples I have just mentioned, it now appears that the Protestant aversion to Marian piety is receding. Mother's Day may be best understood not as a nineteenth-century invention but as the latest manifestation of a very old, indeed ancient, tradition.

This brief survey of the history of mother veneration, and its relationship to both the religious and the commercial incarnation in Mother's Day, serves to illustrate a point that also applies to many holidays people celebrate. Market forces love to draw on the energies generated by religious holidays for their own purposes. This is entirely understandable. Latching on to a religious holiday is easier than trying to create your own, ex nihilo. No holiday is exempt, as we saw in the fashion industry's effort to capitalize on Ramadan.

Will we now begin to witness tensions between the traditional meaning of Ramadan and the "Ramadan consumer?" Will pious Muslims begin to demand that we "put the prophet back into Ramadan?"

More basically, how does the fact that the spiritual and the commercial dimensions of any holiday are so closely linked influence either or both of them? If the business side of the relationship draws much of its energy from the religious side, can it continue to do so without diminishing its original spiritual capital? If, for example, more of the traditional qualities associated with the Virgin Mary—like simplicity, humility, and self-sacrifice—surface even more in future years, will that dampen any of the enthusiasm for excessive consumption? Can Christmas as a traditional religious holiday continue to be closely interwoven with the shopping spree of The Market without its core spiritual message being decimated?

These questions focus in a particularly sharp way on the ongoing problem of how religion should relate to culture. Should it accommodate, criticize, flee, or just ignore the values and worldviews of the culture in which it finds itself? The question has been around at least since the ancient Hebrews crossed the Jordan and had to decide how to respond to the customs of their neighbors in Canaan. Later it arose when someone asked Jesus whether or not to pay taxes to Caesar. In each case, it was necessary for the parties concerned to uncover the often-hidden religious dimensions of the surrounding culture, and to decide if those conflicted with their own aspirations. This is why it matters that we expose the implicit religious aspects of our market-oriented society and weigh them in the light of the spiritual tradition we continue to claim as our own. The day may come when our present, market-suffused culture will pass, just as the Persian and Roman Empires did. But that will not solve the Christ and Culture conundrum. It is perennial, and will have to be tackled time and again, no matter what follows the eventual but inevitable death of The Market God.

16

All Desires Known

> Almighty God, unto whom all hearts are open, all desires known, and from whom no secrets are hid, cleanse the thoughts of our hearts that we may perfectly love thee and worthily magnify thy holy name.
>
> —Book of Common Prayer

> We have become a singularly confessing society. The confession has spread its effects far and wide.
>
> —Michel Foucault

God, says the traditional prayer, already knows the desires of our hearts. But The Market wants to know them, too. God's purpose is to make us capable of love, for him and for our fellow creatures. The Market's purpose is a little different. It is to multiply sales. It is important to recognize that, although it is said that God already has this deep knowledge, God's representatives on earth do not. But they want to gain it. In Christianity, over many centuries, the church has devised highly effective ways of learning the secrets of the heart. The main technique of course is the sacrament of Confession, the history and significance of which the French philosopher Michel Foucault has studied at length.[1]

The practice began as the way a priest could enable penitent persons to unburden themselves of guilt by bringing their sins to light and then being absolved. But as the years went by, priests were instructed by their manuals to go beyond merely uncovering the transgressions that the person confessing could recall. Priests were now expected to suggest other vagrant thoughts and deeds that might have been overlooked. But, given the highly suggestible character of human beings, this procedure many times also had the effect of implanting desires the confessing person might not have thought of. No one knows how many new, previously unrecognized desires were invented in this way. But there must have been many.

As a young Augustinian monk, Martin Luther was caught in this penitential crossfire. He recounts how, whenever he went to Confession, as soon as he got up off his knees and walked away from the booth, he would remember some other misdeed or impure thought and would have to return. It became torture for him until it came to him, while he was reading Saint Paul's Epistle to the Romans, that God had already forgiven him of all his sins. In the reforming church he started, Luther cut the seven sacraments down to two, eliminating individual confession.

The Market, too, needs to know our inner desires so it can link them in our psyches to the commodities it wants to sell. Likewise, it has elaborated ingenious schemes of discovering them. One of the best known and widely employed of these methods is the "focus group." Michael Schudson in his informative book on the history of advertising describes how, in the 1980s, the Leo Burnett Company, which handled the United Airlines account, discovered that fully a quarter of the passengers on its planes were women, and the proportion was increasing as more women entered the workforce.[2] The company assembled small groups of these travelers and encouraged them to talk about what they liked and did not like about air travel and also how it was promoted and advertised. It was an early triumph of the new method. Schudson quotes marketing scholar Karen Shapiro: "The words of the target audience as spoken in these research sessions provide the most valued information for creatives who are trying to learn how people should sound in the commercial."[3]

The "creatives" mentioned here are, of course, the people who create the advertising for the airline, not the people who manage the business, much less the workforce of pilots, terminal personnel, and flight attendants. There is little suggestion that the results of the focus groups changed the nature of air travel itself, which in the opinion of most observers has gotten progressively worse over the decades, whether on United or any other airline. Seats are squeezed closer together and meals are either skimpier or nonexistent. The focus groups changed only one thing: the manner in which travel by plane was marketed. As Schudson comments about the information gleaned from focus groups, it keeps the ad agencies "in some kind of personal touch with the man and woman on the street, provides a source of ideas and even offers a reservoir of words, phrases and colloquialisms to inspire the creation of ads."[4] In other words, the packaging was changed—not the contents.

In recent years, focus groups have not played as important a role because marketers have learned to use data to locate niches—that is, clusters of like-buying customers identified by their postal zip codes or other markers of probable tastes and preferences. Corporations began building gigantic databases linked to what are called "data mining" enterprises. The amount of data collected on prospective customers, clients, and voters is staggering. The largest data broker in the United States is Acxiom. According to a recent report, it has 23,000 computer servers processing 50 trillion data transactions annually. It stores an average of 2,500 data points in "digital dossiers" on 200 million Americans, each of whom is tagged with a thirteen-digit code. This means these individuals can be tracked wherever they go. Much of the data Acxiom amasses can be harvested from social media such as Facebook. Each person is also placed in one of seventy "lifestyle clusters," the better to facilitate targeted marketing. Acxiom, of course, sells this invaluable data to its customers, which include the top credit-card companies, insurance firms, retail banks, global automakers, and pharmaceutical corporations. Overall, its client list includes about half of the hundred largest corporations in America.[5]

Whatever the specifics of their surveying, like the traditional confessional, marketers go far beyond discovering the secret desires of the heart. They do everything they can to create them. Industry critic Jerry Mander writes that it was only after he retired from a successful career as an advertising executive that he realized that his work had been to try to get people to buy things they did not want.[6]

Others in the advertising fraternity symbolized by the words "Madison Avenue" dispute this characterization. They insist that it is customers who determine what companies make, and that marketers' ads help these customers find what they want. This sounds like a win-win situation. But anyone who thinks twice about the ads that surround us and invade our space every day—the junk mail, the television spots, the billboards, and the web displays—has come to recognize that much of what inundates us is a relentless effort to create desires where none existed before. Like the confessional of old, the process not only uncovers existing cravings, but instills new ones.

Foucault believed that the ritual of confession inevitably placed those who confessed within the power orbit of the individuals and the institution to whom they were confessing. In one intense passage, he writes that it produced "a twofold effect: an impetus was given to power through its very exercise; an emotion rewarded the overseeing control and carried it further; the intensity of the confession renewed the questioner's curiosity; the pleasure discovered fed back to the power that encircled it.... Power operated as a mechanism of attraction; it drew out those peculiarities over which it kept watch." Neither confession nor the opinion sharing that takes place in market research offers a neutral, or win-win, proposition. Both are power transactions.[7]

Foucault also finds in confession a good example of how practices that originated in religion migrate into the larger society, or—put the other way—how The Market annexes these practices for their own purposes. He writes that "never have there existed more centers of power; never more attention manifested and verbalized; never more circular contacts and linkages; never more sites where the intensity of pleasures and the persistency of power catch hold, only to spread elsewhere."[8]

We can assume that when it instituted Confession, the Catholic Church wanted its people to be able to search their consciences and to experience the relief that accompanies being absolved. But it seems clear that the Church also had as one of its objectives bringing people more securely under its spiritual power. More desires meant more sins, more sins meant more confessions, and more confessions meant reinforcing, deepening, and widening the Church's influence.

But why does The Market need to create desires? A brief glance at the recent history of advertising helps us to answer this question. The cultural studies scholar Raymond Williams traces the beginning of modern advertising to the late nineteenth century when, with the invention of new technologies and the formation of monopolies, the challenge corporations faced was no longer how to increase production, but how to cope with overproduction: how could they possibly sell all the stuff they were turning out?[9]

The challenge became even more acute after World War II. Factories that had been building fighter planes, tanks, and cannons were now free to produce consumer goods at unprecedented levels. But were there enough consumers to absorb it all? Clearly, people needed to buy more or the economy would be in serious trouble. The problem was not entirely new. As long ago as 1934, Edwin Nourse, who later became the first chairman of the President's Council of Economic Advisors, played a leading role in a Brookings Institution study. Its report, "America's Capacity to Produce," singled out "market saturation" and "excess productive capacity" as serious challenges.[10] Several mechanisms were devised to cope with them. The first was to create a range of credit instruments, like layaway plans, installment buying, long-term mortgages, and eventually credit cards. All these encouraged people to buy things they might never have thought of—and they did. This meant that, in the religious sphere, certain moral virtues like thrift, simplicity, and delayed gratification that had been cultivated in a previous period were not only no longer needed: they had become bothersome obstacles to The Market. Now, churches were expected to encourage people to "live in the moment," to be less uptight and more "laid back." Many religious institutions did. Consumer debt skyrocketed and savings accounts dwindled. Some called the process a "war against savings and for consumption." Between 1982 and 1990, the average debt load of consumers in the United States increased by 30 percent. But corporate profits soared.

Another tactic to expand sales was to speed up the rate of obsolescence. Household devices were designed to wear out sooner, so replacements would have to be bought. Style changes, especially in women's wear, were sped up. Runways in Milan and Paris, with their sleekly cool models, were brought into people's homes by television and glossy magazines. Automakers continued to introduce a new model Ford or Dodge every year. Companies poured more and more artistic talent and imagination not so much into improving their products (although there was some of that) but into making their packaging more alluring.

The expansion of the financial sector, discussed in Chapter 7, resulted in the invention of a host of new "products" such as derivatives and mortgage-backed securities. The beginning of the Cold War boosted the business of languishing armaments factories which could once again mass-produce weapons both for America and for its far-flung allies.

But among all these devices to counter jaded demand and the saturation of markets, the creation and instilling of desires by the advertising guild became the most powerful. Innovative techniques for expanding sales by generating desire arrived on the scene just as television was vastly enlarging its scope and its penetration. It was The Market's equivalent of the perfect storm. And it was a towering success, maybe because, as Steve Jobs once remarked, "a lot of people don't know what they want until you tell them." People, as it turns out, once they were told, certainly did have a taste for apples, especially those whose logo had a piece bitten out.

Researchers have learned that, like Pavlov's famous dog, most people do not need to think for a familiar sight or sound that they associate with a favorable or unfavorable memory to penetrate their cerebral cortex. Advertisers know this. Their ads are not intended to provoke thought. Quite the contrary, they are designed to circumvent reflection and to appeal directly to emotion. This has led to what has come to be called "brand loyalty." But the use of the word "loyalty" in this context is worth pondering, especially when applied to a carefully promoted attitude of thoughtless, almost instinctive, response to a trademark. Calling this non-reflective reaction "loyalty" represents another appropriation, and dilution, by The Market of a concept that was born and developed elsewhere. Traditionally, we have spoken of loyalty to one's family or tribe or nation—maybe even to one's favorite baseball team. But loyalty to a brand of breakfast cereal or an automobile maker is something different. Loyalty, even misplaced loyalty, has motivated people to sacrifice their lives and very often other people's lives as well. It has also become a key term in religion. The American philosopher Josiah Royce once wrote an influential book on the subject, and sketched out the theory that human beings learn loyalty at a low and particularistic level (limited to family or tribe, for example). He argued that they should then move on to higher and more inclusive levels, culminating in loyalty to the whole human race and to an absolute being. He suggested that loyalty, not credulity or obedience, was Christianity's way of describing the appropriate relationship of the individual to God.[11] But one wonders if someone could really graduate from their loyalty to Campbell's tomato soup or to Heineken beer to a loyalty to humanity?

The marketers who work so tirelessly to craft brands and logos do not spend much time thinking about such issues. These experts are in high demand not only to contrive brand symbols that will capture people's loyalty, but to protect them jealously from copycats and thieves. In the old days of the wild west, it is said that someone could be hanged for rounding up a steer marked with some else's brand. Today, as well, the names of familiar products are sometimes drawn into nasty fights. A recent such fracas erupted over what can and cannot legally be labeled "mayonnaise." Only one of many hundreds that break out, this battle appeared to some to be a possible rematch of David and Goliath. The giant Philistine warrior in this case was Unilever, a true Titan in the food industry and the owner of Hellmann's. The downy-cheeked lad with the sack of smooth stones was a fledging upstart called Hampton Creek, which it seems was selling an eggless spread, presumably to serve a growing public that prefers to avoid them.

The tussle began when Unilever learned that Hampton Creek was calling its spread "Just Mayo." In this rerun, however, Goliath—instead of boasting that he would kill both David and the whole Israelite army—took the matter to court. Unilever pointed out, correctly, that the Food and Drug Administration required anything labeled "mayonnaise" to contain eggs and a certain amount of oil. No eggs, not mayonnaise. It further claimed that using the word "mayo" instead of the full "mayonnaise" was nothing but a dodge; anyone who hears "mayo" interprets that to mean mayonnaise. But just as Goliath seemed to be winning, the shepherd boy found another stone in his pouch. Hampton Creek discovered that Hellmann's, also eager to serve customers concerned with diet and health, had been marketing a "Cholesterol-Free Mayonnaise." It also lacked the required amount of oils required by the FDA. Now, the duel moved into a new stage. Hellmann's quickly added the word "dressing" to "mayonnaise" in its ads and on its labels, so that the "m" word was reduced to a mere modifier. Unlike Hampton Creek, which had been mislabeling its product for months, it stressed that it had changed its labeling immediately upon discovering the violation of FDA requirements.[12]

I have never gone back to determine how this David-Goliath match was decided. Undoubtedly, hundreds of gallons of mayo or mayonnaise were slathered on cheese and lettuce sandwiches by diners blissfully unaware of the struggle raging over what to call what they were eating. Still, if we retrace their paths to the supermarkets where they bought the containers, the power of a brand might become evident. Hurriedly loading a cart, did they reach without thinking for a familiar label—either one whose content they had enjoyed before or one that had appeared on television? Was their action almost automatic, not to say Pavlovian? If so, what the branders are trying to accomplish has succeeded.

Again, there may be a parallel in religion, but it is valid only up to a point. History's most prominent Roman Catholic theologian, Thomas Aquinas, wrote extensively about cultivating what he called *habitus*, a form of ethical behavior that over time becomes unreflective and almost automatic. This manner of acting was, the angelic doctor contended, superior to one that requires constant calculation and deliberation. His writing on the subject has influenced a current school of moral philosophy called "virtue ethics," which also holds that acting from a cultivated ethical core is better than weighing the right or wrong of each decision we face. This artless manner of living a moral life might be viewed with disfavor by anyone who has seen the horrid results of some of the unreasoning, often duty-bound conduct of those who have internalized blind loyalty to a cause or a leader. Aquinas, of course, did not have in mind this kind of fanatic behavior. His description of habitus appears within his long discussion of the classical virtues derived initially from Plato's scheme, discussed in Book IV of *The Republic:* wisdom, justice, prudence, and courage. He integrates these with the Christian "theological virtues" in an impressive demonstration of how, at least in Aquinas's view, Christianity and classical antiquity had much in common. What is important about the seemingly odd parallel of branding and virtues ethics is that, in their own ways, both Christianity and The Market have striven to implant the posture and bearing they advocate and also encouraged acting on these internalized attitudes as something we do without long or arduous deliberation. Both encourage habitus.

On the face of it, there seems to be nothing essentially wrong with this. But the real question is: What attitudes, habits, and reflexes do these techniques foster? The intention of the Christian and other religious traditions, at their best, is to cultivate what are called the fruits of the Spirit: love, joy, peace, patience, kindness, goodness, and faithfulness. Clearly, no religion has fully succeeded in nurturing these virtues at all times and in all their followers. But the attempt persists, and succeeds often enough to continue with it—even though religions also sometimes foment xenophobia and bigotry. The Market, at its best, has encouraged habits of creativity, risk-taking, and entrepreneurship. But at its worst, The Market, especially since its apotheosis to divinity, has also inspired wastefulness, cupidity, and avarice. Its endless quest for growth and expansion has brought the planet to the edge of a climate catastrophe of unprecedented proportions. It is always instructive to ponder Jesus's warning that we cannot serve both God and Mammon. But is this really the choice we must make?

It has been my contention throughout this book that there is nothing essentially wrong with markets. But markets are not part of the natural order, like the changing of the seasons or gravity. They have been constructed by human beings to serve certain stipulated purposes, which in many cases they have done quite well. But in the past couple of centuries, markets have become bloated, and they have swelled into The Market. The result has been that they not only fail to serve their intended purpose, but they intrude on and distort other vital institutions such as the family, the arts, education, and religion. They have become victims of their own stunning success, and have seriously damaged other aspects of the fragile human enterprise in the process.

Could the relationship between religion and the markets ever be one of reciprocity? Jesus also said that "the Sabbath was made for man, not man for the Sabbath" (Mark 2:27). Might the word "economy" be substituted for Sabbath in this saying? In his brilliant book on science and religion, *Rocks of Ages*, the late Stephen Jay Gould addressed another rivalry that has at times become destructive and acrimonious. He argues persuasively, however, that there need be no "warfare between science and religion" if these two human endeavors understand their appropriate vocations. Science observes, measures, and sometimes hazards predictions based on its investigations. For centuries, religions have deliberated over questions of meaning and value. The two need each other, and they fall into unnecessary contentiousness when they stray into the other's turf—when the Church tells a Galileo that he should not believe what he sees through his telescope, or a Russian cosmonaut declares there is no God because he has soared as high into the heavens as anyone ever has and not seen one. When each understands the powers and the limitations of its purpose and methods, not only is no clash necessary, but the two can inform and strengthen each other.[13]

Gould's recipe for a creative mutuality between science and religion suggests an appropriate example for the relationship between religion and business. But it will require adjustments on the part of both parties. Scholars of religion could help by foregoing both the sycophancy of serving as an acolyte in the temple of The Market, and uninformed attacks on what they sometimes dismiss as the inherent wickedness of the commercial enterprise. They could instead try to understand the world of business as so many theologians have patiently studied science. There can be little doubt that, despite a few holdouts on both sides, the relationship between science and religion is vastly better than is was at the time of the Tennessee "monkey trial." But the dialogue between religion and business is still stalled, in part because of ignorance, but also because The Market has still to be dethroned—perhaps the word should be "liberated"—from its incongruous and destructive aspirations to divinity.

17

The Market and the End of the World

> And he said unto me, It is done. I am Alpha and Omega,
> the beginning and the end. I will give unto him that is
> athirst of the fountain of the water of life freely.
>
> —Revelation 21:6

> This is the way the world ends
> This is the way the world ends
> This is the way the world ends
> Not with a bang but a whimper.
>
> —T. S. Eliot

All religions have some notion of how and why the world began and of how and why it might end, if indeed it ever began or will end at all. Some scenarios even specify *when* the world will end. But engaging in timetables and predictions carries with it a considerable risk since, epoch after epoch, the prophesied deadlines seem to arrive and pass while the world stubbornly ignores the schedule. Theologians have an elegant term for the study of ideas about world endings. We call it "eschatology." The word is derived from the Greek word *eschata*, or "end things," but since the end is often a return to the beginning—and in some theologies, "end" can mean *telos*, or purpose, as well as *finis*, or culmination—eschatology has gradually become what might be called the "theology of history."

Some people are fascinated by the often grisly details of end-time scenarios, as was proved by the recent immense popularity of the *Left Behind* series of religious-fiction books and films. But what eschatological doctrines do for the most part is portray the direction in which history is thought to be moving, and describe where we are on its arc at this moment. The chart of the seven "dispensations" that was tacked onto the wall of the Sunday School I attended as a youngster absorbed my interest not so much because of how it described the "last days," but because its indication of where I was located in the relentless flow of the ages gave me a strange comfort. It positioned me in a long and large story. I think this is why so many people are attracted to eschatologies, even those projecting cataclysm. They provide a sense, albeit often a false sense, of meaning, direction, and significance. Sometimes they inspire people to work hard for some goal like the peaceable kingdom. But they also sometimes inspire people to do cruel and crazy things, as when the Japanese end-time sect Aum Shinrikyo released poisonous Sarin gas into the Tokyo subway system in March 1995, killing or wounding over a thousand people. Devotees of a seething brew of elements plucked from Buddhist, Muslim, and Christian end-time teachings, they said they were trying to hasten the epochal conflict that would usher in the end time.

History abounds with wildly differing ideas about the beginning and the end, all responding to persistent human questions. What are we to make of the tumultuous events that constantly impinge on us? Are we approaching the Kingdom of God, the Second Coming, or the Final Judgment, as some Christians have claimed? Are we going nowhere in a world that has no beginning or end, as many Buddhists believe? Are we headed for a recurrent cosmic decline and catastrophe, to be followed by another turn in the wheel of time, which is the Hindu vision? Is history edging toward the "final crisis of capitalism" and the classless society, as Marxists have taught? Or are we on the way to the worldwide triumph of democratic capitalism, as Fukuyama predicted in *The End of History and the Last Man*?[1] Maybe we are going nowhere; "the rivers run into the sea and there is no new thing under the sun," as the biblical book of Ecclesiastes says.

Like any other religion, faith in The Market also has a theology of history. As we have seen in previous chapters, it has its own doctrines on what is happening in the world today, where it is headed, why things go wrong, and how to put them right. In the introductory chapter of this book I compared The Market as God to Zeus, most potent and preeminent of the Greek gods. But in the Greek imagination there was one divine force even more powerful than Zeus. It was Moira—that is, fate or destiny. Not even mighty Zeus could go against the will of Moira. In one famous passage, Homer has Zeus's wife Hera taunt him with a question to which she already knows the answer. If Fate has decreed the death of someone, could Zeus countermand it? The thunderbolt-hurling sovereign of Olympus offers no reply.[2]

Beginning roughly in the eighteenth century, there arose in the western psyche, and then around the globe, a Moira-type deity even more powerful than The Market: the idea of Progress. This theology appears in various expressions. Some people discern a line, although not a very straight one, moving upward. Others see a jagged line of ups and downs, but the overall direction is up. In both cases, these views have emerged only in the past few centuries. Ancient peoples tended to look at nature and see an endless cycle of growth, maturation, and decay, and they tended to inscribe the same pattern onto human history. But Jewish historical reflection, picked up and amplified by Christianity and Islam, rejected such cyclical thinking. The world had a beginning—Creation—and an end in the Final Judgment. Still, for thinkers drawing on this biblical tradition, direction definitely did not mean progress; there could be both positive change and retrogression in human history. Things were not "getting better all the time," with only setbacks here and there.

The "progressive" view, whereby Moira (or Progress) achieved its predominance, emerged only in modern times. But it arrived bearing a pre-history. It is the indirect descendent of the Christian doctrine of Providence. It took full command of the modern mind in the period of the Enlightenment and the Industrial Revolution, and it gradually absorbed and displaced its predecessors in the modern economic, religious, and intellectual credo. Adam Smith was a believer in progress in this sense. Both Hegel and Kant articulated versions of a kind of progress view. But it quickly became almost a creedal test case for the truly contemporary mind. Until quite recently, "believing in progress" was tantamount to being a reasonable modern person. Capitalism, socialism, communism, science, democracy, technology, and mass literacy eagerly attached their wagons to its ascending star. Like Moira of old, its directives could not be contradicted. Not to "believe in progress" was to be illiterate, ignorant, uninformed, and just not sufficiently civilized. Even when the promises of the devotee of progress did not always materialize, people still spoke of having "faith in progress." It was, and is, undeniably a religious concept.

How did this unprecedented elevation of Progress to its religious status occur? In his *Faith and History*, the Protestant theologian Reinhold Niebuhr suggests it emerged from a confluence of kindred currents. Many people had confidence that advances in the natural sciences, and later the social sciences, all relying on empirical and inductive methods, would inevitably propel the world forward. Social Darwinians thought progress was an extension of the theory of natural evolution. Even Karl Marx, although he foresaw class conflict as the mechanism, still held that history was moving toward a new and liberated humanity.

The occasional eruption of pessimism in certain romantic writers and in philosophers such as Schopenhauer and Nietzsche did not derail the overall consensus.[3] Many theologians, both Protestant and Catholic, bought into this optimistic vision. Protestant theologians saw the human drama advancing through ups and downs toward a world of peace and justice, and at the beginning of the twentieth century they inaugurated a journal ingenuously named *The Christian Century*. In 1907, Walter Rauschenbusch, the foremost exponent of the "social gospel," wrote on the first page of his most influential book, *Christianity and the Social Crisis:*

> If the twentieth century could do for us in the control of social forces what the nineteenth did for us in the control of natural forces, our grandchildren would live in a society that would be justified in regarding our present social life as semi-barbarous.

Rauschenbusch went on to claim that humanity was "gaining in elasticity and capacity for change." He asserts that "the swiftness of evolution in our own country proves the immense latent perfectibility in human nature." If, he continued, "we can rally sufficient religious faith and moral strength to snap the bonds of evil and turn the present unparalleled economic and intellectual resources of humanity to the harmonious development of a true social life, the generations yet unborn will mark this as that great day of the Lord for which the ages waited, and count us blessed for sharing in the apostolate that proclaimed it."[4]

Among Catholics, the leading proponent of the confident, albeit in his case very long-term, view was the paleontologist Pierre Teilhard de Chardin, who saw history proceeding in spurts but always toward increased complexity culminating in an "Omega point" which he identified with the ultimate victory of Christ.[5] Niebuhr sums up this dominant mood as follows: "Though there are minor dissonances the whole chorus of modern culture learned to sing the new song of hope in remarkable harmony. The redemption of mankind, by whatever means, was assured for the future. It was, in fact, assured by the future."[6]

The phrase "by the future" supplies the key here. In the religion of Progress, unlike Moira of old, the future assumes a redemptive power. When Moira is defined by the idea of Progress, the future becomes something we can look to with faith and in confident expectation. As the Epistle to the Hebrews states, in the classical King James translation: Now faith is the substance of things hoped for, the evidence of things not seen (Hebrews 11:1). Or as a more contemporary translation has it: Now faith is confidence in what we hope for and assurance about what we do not see.

The Bible, of course, is not talking here about "progress." So where does Moira as Progress now stand as the reigning divinity of contemporary civilization? It is almost heartbreaking to read the hopeful words of Rauschenbusch from 1907, realizing what happened only a few years later. And one must have a very long view indeed to be inspired by Teilhard's vision. Yet it must be said that, to the question of where the sovereignty of Progress now stands, the answer is that its influence seems to be shaken and teetering, but not fallen—at least not yet.

One of the liveliest conversations among scientists, bordering on what must be seen as an argument, is the one being carried on now regarding evolution. This is entirely appropriate since much of the fuel for the modern belief in progress comes from interpretations of the nineteenth-century work of Charles Darwin. The dispute is often both heated and complicated, but the core question is a simple one: is the process of evolution going anywhere? Does it have a direction? And if so, should that direction be understood as improvement—in other words, as progress?

Three of the main voices in this cosmos-sized squabble are those of the late paleontologist Stephen Jay Gould; the evolutionary theorist and outspoken atheist Richard Dawkins; and the paleontologist Simon Conway Morris, who is an avowed theist and anti-materialist. Gould contends that not only does modern evolutionary science fail to reveal any progress in the development of organisms from metazoans to human beings, it indicates no directionality of any kind whatsoever. There is no confirmation in the fossil record either for optimists or pessimists about where we have been and where we may be headed. Gould refuses to concede that the increasing complexity of organisms (which Teilhard builds on) necessarily makes them better able to cope with difficult environments, and therefore superior or more advanced than their predecessors. He refers to concrete examples—parasites, for instance—in which simplicity rather than complexity enhances survival. After all, he points out, the most successful life forms on the planet are bacteria, which have thrived for one hundred million years, while human beings have only been at it for a few hundred thousand.

For his part, Dawkins does see direction in evolution. He makes a distinction between the larger patterns of evolutionary history and the particulars. The first he sees as built-in and inevitable, but the second as the result of chance and contingency. Therefore he finds what he calls a "progressive trend" in evolutionary history, one in which "there are no reversals, or if there are reversals, they are outnumbered and outweighed by the dominant direction." He suggests therefore that evolution does indeed "exhibit progress," in the direction of what he cautiously calls "somebody's value system."[7]

Of the many books and articles Simon Conway Morris has written, the one that has attracted particular attention is *The Deep Structure of Biology: Is Convergence Sufficiently Ubiquitous to Give a Directional Signal?*[8] The term "convergence," which is also discussed by Gould and Dawkins, is the key to his argument as well. The word refers to common features, such as eyes, that are found among different species that evolved separately from each other. Morris relies on convergence to demonstrate that there is indeed a direction, and therefore what could be called a purpose, in evolution. He goes on to suggest this all leads to the inevitable appearance of human beings. In one of his books, he uses the term "inevitable humans." Some other scientists complement Morris's idea with the observation that, were the atmosphere and temperature of the earth even a little bit different than they are, human life could not have emerged or survived. This idea is called the "anthropic principle," and also sometimes includes the observation that the universe seems ideally suited to be studied and understood, while human beings, and not metazoans, are appropriately equipped to study it.

This thinking makes human beings into the crowning accomplishment of a millennia-old evolutionary process—a claim ridiculed by Mark Twain, who compared it to suggesting that the entire Eiffel Tower was constructed just to support the coat of paint that clings to the ball on its top. This sardonic Twainian comment was called to my attention some years ago when Gould and I, along with the legal scholar Alan Dershowitz, taught a course together on Science, Religion, and Law. Gould said he had a particular dislike for any psalm or other biblical passage that enthrones man as the apex of Creation. He enjoyed when I pointed out that the Book of Job takes a very different view, with God speaking from a whirlwind to wary Job, telling him in sarcastic and derisive tones that he is not as important or as central in the scheme of things as he might think (Job 38–39).

Gould differs from both Dawkins and Morris, and notes wryly that since they approach the question of progress in evolution from radically differing starting points—atheistic materialism and theism—they must not be building their conclusion on the observable facts, which both agree on, but on a bias, maybe an emotional proclivity, which they impose on those facts. Of course, Gould agrees, consciousness, and especially human consciousness, is vastly important, but that does not make it necessary. It might well have been different. He writes:

> There's a common tendency to equate importance with necessity. Just because something is important—which consciousness clearly is to the history of the planet—doesn't mean it was meant to be. There's never anything in the history of life that's had such an impact on the earth as the evolution of human consciousness, but that doesn't mean it was meant to be. It could still be accidental.[9]

This debate among scientists who study evolution is absorbing even though it is inconclusive. Progress still awaits the verdict. But the debate also falls short of supplying a satisfying answer for another reason. It does not address the crucial difference between natural history and human history. Is the latter just an extension of the former? Or could there be dynamics at work in human history, with all its seeming advances and obvious setbacks, that cannot be reduced to the narrative of nature's developmental course from the Big Bang to the present?

The argument, in science and in the humanities, continues. It has also gone on in the writing of history. Oswald Spengler went back to a somewhat cyclical view when he wrote *The Decline of the West*. Empires rise and fall, he argued. They always have and they always will, and the age of western dominance has reached its inevitable phase of deterioration. Arnold Toynbee, on the other hand, although he also charted the rise and fall of past empires in *A Study of History*, thought that the West still had an opportunity for renewal, but only if an "internal proletariat" gained influence. But few historians today risk venturing into the territory Spengler and Toynbee explored. By and large, they stick to documenting and interpreting limited ranges of the long human story; most avoid making predictions. The future, insofar as it appears at all, is more a matter of mystery than of hope.

So can we still call the idea of Progress the Moira of our age, the power to which even the almighty Market God must prostrate itself? Progress, in its religious role as a redemptive future, has lived through a hard century. After a hundred years of wars, gulags, genocides, and terrorism—and now the impending climate collapse—faith in inevitable even if sporadic human advance has been severely shaken. Speculation about whether we are approaching the final chapter of human history expresses itself in novels, films, music, and poetry. Robert Frost weighed in with these familiar lines:

> Some say the world will end in fire,
> Some say in ice.
> From what I've tasted of desire
> I hold with those who favor fire.
> But if it had to perish twice,
> I think I know enough of hate
> To say that for destruction ice
> Is also great
> And would suffice.

Worries about nuclear war, death by terrorism, or the threat of an uninhabitable planet due to climate change are now common currency. But this change in mood has not yet knocked the idea of Progress from its pinnacle. It still clings to its diminished throne, even though its voice is more muted. And The Market, when pressed for its continuing claim to our fealty despite its obvious flaws and failures, often claims that it is the humble gatekeeper of Progress in our time. Zeus is in the service of Moira.

One intriguing question is this: Could The Market as God survive without its spiritual dependence on Progress? Could the two be unpaired? What if the controlling myth of the coming century were not endless growth, but stability and equilibrium, and not a profit-making but a sharing economy—as improbable as that now seems? I have contended throughout this book that markets serve an important function in human life, and at their best they are creative, flexible, and venturesome. Is it beyond feasibility that the gods of markets could even become the servants of all people, especially those with urgent needs?

There is a passage in the Psalms that surprises many people when they come across it. It depicts God presiding over an assembly of the gods, making clear what being a real god requires of them. Some people wonder: wasn't the ancient Israelite faith monotheistic? What is this about gods? The answer is that the Hebrew faith was not monotheistic, but rather what is termed henotheistic. It recognized other gods but warned the Israelites that they should not serve them. But the key point in this passage is its spelling out of the duties of real gods, to which these deities seemed to be falling short. It might serve as a warning to The Market, or to any other pretender to divine status.

God has taken his place in the divine council;
in the midst of the gods he holds judgment:
"How long will you judge unjustly and show partiality to the wicked?
Give justice to the weak and the fatherless;
maintain the right of the afflicted and the destitute.
Rescue the weak and the needy;
deliver them from the hand of the wicked."

They have neither knowledge nor understanding,
they walk about in darkness;

254

all the foundations of the earth are shaken.
I said, "You are gods, sons of the Most High, all of you;
nevertheless, like men you shall die,
and fall like any prince." (Psalm 82)

Given these criteria for authentic godhood, clearly The Market does not make the cut. It does not do what any self-respecting god should do. Either it must start performing these duties toward the weak, the afflicted, and the destitute, or it must give up its position as a deity and be just a market again. We turn to this option in our last chapter.

18

Saving the Soul of The Market

> A religion is (1) a system of symbols (2) which acts to estab-
> lish powerful, pervasive and long-lasting moods and moti-
> vations in men (3) by formulating conceptions of a general
> order of existence and (4) clothing these conceptions with
> such an aura of factuality that (5) the moods and motiva-
> tions seem uniquely realistic.
>
> —Clifford Geertz

I believe that what Pope Francis has called "the deified market" is the lodestar in a total system, and it is a system that fulfills all the qualities set forth in Clifford Geertz's widely accepted definition of a functioning religion. But it is far from my intention to suggest that therefore The Market should be viewed, as it often is today, with the reverential respect some people still accord religion. On the contrary, in this book I have hoped to show two things.

First, the godlike role The Market now exercises is misplaced, and the web of values, narratives, and institutions it anchors needs to be critically reexamined. Second, precisely because The Market, despite its disavowals, does operate as a surrogate religion, the kind of criticism that is needed has been deflected and discouraged. The Market system is not part of nature. We as human beings constructed it, and we can renovate, dismantle, or transform it if we want to. Laying hands on it might not make one widely popular but, unlike touching the Ark of the Covenant, it will not be punished by instant death. The Market must be deprived of its sacred aura so we can think about it clearly. We do not need to take off our shoes or our hats when we enter its sanctuary.

But can The Market be saved? The ancient Christian philosopher Origen taught that even Satan would eventually attain salvation—but one does not have to reach that far back to venture an affirmative answer. I started this book with the recognition that markets of one sort or another have existed for a very long time and that they will be with us, in one way or another, for a very long time in the future. There is nothing essentially wrong or bad about them. Even financial markets, which at this moment in history are undergoing withering and largely well-deserved criticism, fulfill a crucial purpose in a complex modern economy. What exactly is at issue in this book?

Sheila Bair, who chaired the Federal Deposit Insurance Corporation (FDIC) during the 2008 financial crisis, put it exactly right. Near the end of her term, in 2011, she urged a group from the American Bankers Association to remember that "the success of the financial sector is not an end in itself, but a means to an end—which is to support the vitality of the real economy and the livelihood of the American people."[1] Bair was obviously in a good position to know how the components of the market economy should function, and how they had been malfunctioning. Martin Wolf, chief economics correspondent for the *Financial Times*, puts it this way: "Financial systems are important servants of the economy, but poor masters."[2] Then what is the problem with The Market?

In short, The Market, aptly symbolized by its most visible embodiment, Wall Street, has become an end and not a means. One of the major causes of the catastrophe of 2008 was that the megabanks entered into dicey deals designed to garner profits for themselves, and often even "bet against their clients" to do so. The servants of the economy became the masters, or tried to. But their strategy not only drove the economy into a disastrous recession, it pushed one of the biggest investment banks, Lehman Brothers, into bankruptcy, and others precariously near the cliff. The massive bailout that saved them began with about $700 billion from the US Treasury. Beyond that, just how much of taxpayers' money has actually been poured out is only gradually becoming known. In 2010, the Federal Reserve released data revealing that the initial $700 billion, as *The Nation* put it, "was a small down payment on an secretive 'backdoor bailout' that saw the Fed provide roughly $3.3 trillion in liquidity and more than $9 trillion in short-term loans and other financial arrangements."[3] During this turbulent time, while unemployment lines snaked around street corners and nearly a million houses displayed foreclosure signs, the financial giants continued to pay huge bonuses to the same executives who had led them—and a large part of the world—into the morass.

Meanwhile, back in the "real economy," popular anger at the big bankers simmered and threatened to boil over. It was hard for the many ordinary people who watched their pensions shrink and lost their family homes to think of The Market in any but the darkest terms. Would it ever be possible for these people, or anyone else, to think of The Market as essentially good?

Discussions about the sources of good and evil, and the relationship between the two, have been going on in theology for centuries. Recalling some of them might cast a little light on The Market's fall from grace. Saint Augustine taught that evil has no real substance, that it is always a misplaced—in his word, a "disordered"—good. This is precisely the plight The Market finds itself in today. An essential feature of a healthy society, for centuries it was just "the market." It served a vital function, along with the family, the tribe, religion, and custom. It both nurtured these other institutions and was nurtured—and constrained—by them. In Wolf's words, it was a servant.

But now something else has happened. As Michael Sandel writes in *What Money Can't Buy*, "we drifted from *having* a market economy to *being* a market society."[4] And, I would add, a market culture with a market religion. The change came when the market became "The Market"—when, like Adam and Eve in the Garden, it grew dissatisfied with its appropriate place in the human enterprise and strove to elevate itself to the status of a deity.

In the long travail of history, this kind of grasp for power is not an unusual turn of events. Throughout the centuries, various institutions—royalty, the military, and the priesthood—have reached for supreme sovereignty. Kings asserted their divine right to the throne. But soon thereafter royal heads began to roll. The late medieval popes, culminating in Pope Boniface VIII in his bull "Unum Sanctum," claimed supreme papal authority over both spiritual and secular realms. But not long after that, the papacy fell into division, with rival popes excommunicating each other and, during the Reformation, a whole section of Europe declaring its independence from both the spiritual and the secular authority of Rome. In the past two centuries, military coups have come and gone. But every time any of these aspirants have reached for the apple of god-like supremacy, they have inevitably become swollen and distorted. By trying to be more than they were, they became less. They stopped serving a necessary, if limited, purpose, and began to undermine the society they were supposed to serve. As *New York Times* business-page columnist Floyd Norris observes, "Having a big financial industry was viewed as a sign of success before 2008; now it is seen as a risk to the economy."[5] This is also the sad story of the modern market as a whole. Now what is to be done?

Again, there is an old but useful phrase from theology that may help answer this question. In Latin it is called the *restoratio humani*, the restoration of the human being to his or her appropriate place in the scheme of things: neither god nor devil, but human. This doctrine tries to answer Anselm's famous question *Cur Deus homo?* (Why did God become man?) According to some theories, God became incarnate in human life so that man could become divine. This idea, called *theosis*, found its way into some early Christian theologies (especially those affected by oriental mystical currents) and into certain strains of Greek and Roman religion, in which human beings did sometimes becomes gods. One theologian, Athanasius of Alexandria, said of the Incarnation, "God became what we are in order that we might become what he is." This idea, that God's purpose is to divinize humanity, still has some standing in Christian theology, especially in Eastern Orthodoxy. But the dominant motif that eventually emerged was something different—namely, that God entered into human history not to divinize human beings but to help them become what they are intended to be, which is truly human. This is what is meant by *restoratio humani*.

For our purposes here, *restoratio* raises the key question about the overstuffed Market: Can it once again become simply "the market?" Can it be restored to its important-but-not-divine place in the scheme of things? How can it be healed of its illusions of grandeur, its spiritual elephantiasis? The Market stands in need not of abolition but of a thorough recreation, a *restoratio*. But how can such a thing happen?

Again, there may be some hints to be drawn from religious history. First, redemption must always begin with repentance. The party seeking restoration must recognize the error of its ways and resolve to live differently. The classical invitation in the Book of Common Prayer is addressed to "All ye who do truly repent of your sins . . . and intend to lead a new life." What follows then is a welcome to the communion table ("draw near . . ."), and a symbolic restoration of the offender to his or her rightful place in the family of God and of humanity. Repentance precedes restoration.

But what should The Market confess? Has it "done things it ought not to have done," or "not done things it ought to have done"? It is never proper for anyone to confess someone else's sins, whether of pride or lust or envy or what the classical theologians called "vainglory"— or anything else. One might start, however, by confessing for The Market (or for any other would-be penitent) the transgression that is most severely condemned by the Hebrew prophets and by Jesus, and that is hypocrisy. Hypocrisy simply means pretending to believe or practice a moral or religious teaching, but doing so insincerely, and even misusing that practice for an ulterior purpose. The prophets inveigh against those who give lip service to God's covenant but then crush the poor underfoot. Jesus calls at least some of the scribes "hypocrites," and likens them to "whited sepulchers."

One of the most damaging accusations against advocates of The Market and their insistence on unimpaired competition is the charge that they do not really believe their own gospel—that while they celebrate competition rhetorically, in practice, they try their best to get rid of it. While brandishing the banner of an unimpeded Market (especially by government regulators), they try in many ways to limit and circumvent competition. John D. Rockefeller, for example, constantly extolled the free market but did everything possible to eliminate his rivals in the oil business. Monopolies and cartels were invented by business not to enhance competition but to limit it.

There is every indication that modern businesses have not left behind the Rockefeller era of verbally extolling the free market while at the same time inventing countless ways to subvert and delimit it. On May 21, 2015, the *New York Times* carried a front-page headline that read "Banks Admit Scheme to Rig Currency Prices: Wave of Manipulation in Foreign Exchanges." The story describes how four of the world's leading banks conspired with each other, often using online chat rooms, to manipulate the foreign exchange currency market so as to minimize risk and competition and maximize profits. This is a glaring example of using limited cooperation in order to cripple competition. The scheme was eventually uncovered by regulatory agencies, and the fines were large enough to wipe out whatever gains had been realized. But for many readers, it was the content of those chatroom machinations that revealed the disingenuousness of the bankers. The Justice Department noted that one bank trader had remarked, "the less competition the better."[6]

A careful reading of the biblical drama suggests that *restoratio* is a continuation of creation. After the six days of creation recounted in Genesis, God "rested" on the seventh. But after that first Sabbath, God did not stop his creative—or possibly "re-creative"—activity. Instead, God is depicted in Scripture as continuously creating and recreating. "Behold," he says. "I am doing a new thing; now it springs forth, do you not perceive it? I will make a way in the wilderness and rivers in the desert" (Isaiah 43:18–20).

New and unprecedented realities constantly emerge. One theologian, Gordon Kaufman, even proposed that instead of speaking of God as "creator," with the image of a craftsman nailing boards together in our minds, we might think of God as "creativity," the divine energy that in the words of the book of Revelation constantly "makes all things new." Some people find this image too impersonal and wonder how one can sing a hymn to a cosmic energy field. But at least it has the virtue of capturing the ongoing nature of creation.

The Genesis story of creation confirms this open-ended interpretation. Scholars of Hebrew now agree that the first sentence of the Bible, which is usually rendered as "In the beginning God created the heavens and the earth," is more accurately rendered: "When God began his creative activity . . ." The process took six days to complete what turned out, however, to be only the first phase. Of course, "days" in this account might not be units of twenty-four hours. The word probably did not mean that for the writer of Genesis, and only the most intractable fundamentalists insist on such a reading today. But such literalists constitute a tiny minority even in their own camp. Indeed, the redoubtable William Jennings Bryan (who is called "The Great Commoner" but also sometimes called, because he led the prosecution of Scopes in the famous monkey trial, "The Great Fundamentalist") was no literalist. He suggested that the "days" of Genesis might have been whole eras. Also, the "seven" in the days of creation has a symbolic meaning. It conjures to what many ancient peoples considered to be the perfect number. Today, centuries later, "seven" still retains some of the archaic aura. It is regarded by some as a lucky number, just as thirteen, even in the twenty-first century, is still so suspect that hotel and office building managers skip it in their numbering of floors.

Given the suggestiveness of "seven," and the idea that the creation and recreation of the universe and of history continue apace today, it may be valuable to think of the recreation of The Market's place in the world—its restoration—as proceeding in seven steps or "days." It is also important to understand exactly what is going on in the biblical story. The Hebrew word in the text for "create" is *bara*. The word is used exclusively for the activity of God, and it does not mean "to make" in the sense of "to build or construct." There is another word for that. Rather, *bara* has the sense of "to order" or "to assign a place or role." God's work in creation is to compose an unfinished symphony of diverse sounds and tonalities into what is intended to be a harmonious whole, complete with counterpoint and chords. But unlike the deist conception of the "clockmaker God," who constructs a complex mechanism and then leaves it to run on its own, this image of God is more like that of a composer-director who constantly re-arranges the balance as the trumpets or the bass violins start to drown out the flutes and the violas. Further, he must do so delicately while the orchestra continues to play. To carry the metaphor farther (always a risky step), in addition to conducting, he might be seen to play along with the orchestra like some concertmasters have been known to do.

It is worth pointing out that, in the earlier Egyptian and Mesopotamian mythologies that preceded Genesis, a powerful deity had to contend with semi-divine forces (monsters) and win only by means of violent combat. This does not happen in Genesis. Here, God overcomes chaos and formlessness (in our metaphor, perhaps cacophony and discord) by ordering, balancing, and synchronizing. Even what were previously seen as the darkest forces are enlisted in the overall schema and assigned their apposite places. This is not such a far-fetched idea. Tchaikovsky brought cannons into his *1812 Overture*, and John Cage incorporates urban clatter and rattle into his works.

Now, with this brief background of the Genesis "creation" story in mind, let us see what it might suggest about saving the soul of The Market, and achieving its *restoratio humani*.

The Seven Days of Creation and Recreation

On the first day of creation in the biblical version, God "separated the light from the darkness," and in so doing he separated both of them from himself. In other words, the first action the Bible attributes to God is one of decentralization. As we will see below, this centrifugal process continues in the following days, throughout the rest of the Old and New Testaments, and according to many people's faith, has carried on ever since. The Israeli scholar Avivah Gottlieb Zornberg explains in her insightful book on Genesis that, from the beginning, God busied himself breaking up his unitary and monolithic power into other centers. God's work, she writes, is of "increasing complexity" and of "primal disintegration." Paraphrasing the great medieval rabbinic commentator Rashi, she continues, "the main business of that [first] day was the radical transformation of reality from the encompassing oneness of God to the possibility of more-than-one."[7]

Likewise for The Market, the goal of the "first day" or the "primary phase" in its recreation should be to begin restoring it to its fitting and healthy place—a process of decentralization. It involves dis-integrating the colossal banks and financial empires that are "too big to fail" and "too big to jail." This means dismantling the temples of The Market to clear the way for small-scale community or state banks, especially ones that are organized as cooperatives or owned by nonprofit groups dedicated to investing in local enterprises and home owning. Eventually, banks that specialize in international business could take their place among the others without crowding them out.

On the second day, the biblical account describes God as continuing the decentralizing. He separates the waters, so that land can appear. In other words, God did not stop with splitting off a reality other than his own. He also introduced the same process of what might be called "devolution" within that newly-constituted separate realm, and he instituted the nature of the mutual relationship that was to exist between and among these elements.

This same devolution needs to happen in our market-dominated economy and culture. Now, The Market imposes its will on more and more areas of life. Education is diced into saleable credit units; works of art are assessed as valuable investments; entertainment has been corrupted by money; making profit as the goal of the "health industry" is pricing the benefits it has to offer beyond the reach of many people; and even religion is increasingly shaped by consumer values as churches conduct market surveys and reshape their worship to cater to public whims. Not only do these institutions need to be freed from the distortions imposed on them by The Market (which they often so eagerly embrace), they also need to find ways to relate to each other mutually, without the God of The Market hovering and intruding.

In Genesis, on the third day, the trees and plants make their appearance. But God does not "create" them. His power to generate new life has by now already been widely distributed, so God instructs the earth to produce them on its own, and it does, "each according to its kind." This final phrase suggests that the process of subdivision continues. Onions produce onions and pears sprout more pears, and they do this on their own. God has given them the freedom and the responsibility.

This suggests that in the recreation of the market today, not only do financial power centers need to be decentralized, their governance must be "de-hierarchized" as well. Financial power should not flow down from the top (Wall Street and the Federal Reserve) but spread out horizontally. The organizational chart becomes a web instead of a pyramid. One can only imagine the immense creativity that might be released if the markets and financial institutions were free to experiment and try out new techniques and approaches.

The good news is that this *restoratio* of the American economy is already—quietly and often unnoticed—underway. Today, millions of

Americans are involved in co-ops and worker-owned firms. One hundred thirty million people participate in the ownership of co-op businesses and credit unions. More than thirteen million are worker-owners of eleven thousand companies which are employee-owned. We do not need to recreate the economy ex nihilo since it is already renewing itself. This garden just needs care and watering.

Once the grip of the big banks is loosened, these more localized financial units and employee-owned firms can develop various horizontal patterns of governance. In Cleveland, Ohio, a group of such employee-owned companies was helped by local universities and hospitals with more purchasing power to move into solar-panel installation and to construct a commercially successful hydroponic greenhouse that produces three million heads of lettuce a year. The group also started a "green" institutional laundry service that cleans the bedding of hospitals and other institutions. Small beginnings, perhaps, but larger systemwide changes often originate in obscure and overlooked places. Remember that inconspicuous stable in Bethlehem.

Now we come to the fourth day. On this day, yet a new expression of God's sharing his power comes into view. According to the biblical narrative, something quite noteworthy occurs: God decentralizes his own power. He not only creates the environment of light, heavens, sea, and earth. He also decrees that it will be these heavenly bodies (and not God himself) that will govern day and night. They will mark the seasons, the days, and the years—a critical responsibility for the ancient Hebrews, because these divisions indicated when the holidays, feasts, and rituals would take place. God does not directly engage in this governance. Rather, he delegates it. The heavenly bodies will now "rule over" these crucial matters. On the previous day, God had not made the trees and plants. Instead, he entrusted the earth to produce them. Now he does the same with the waters. They are delegated to

267

bring forth swarms of living creatures to crawl on the earth and birds to fly in the air.

Here is what could happen with The Market. In classical Catholic social teaching there is the idea of a "subsidiary." It suggests that, in both economics and politics, some things may be done best at a higher level but most things can be accomplished even better at a lower one. Our current rush to centralize everything from public schools to telecommunications companies to newspapers, even though it is often done in the name of efficiency, is mostly carried out in an effort to lower costs or increase profits. But it is often the consumer who suffers the consequences. This is why we now see so many people withdrawing their savings from international banking behemoths and patronizing local community banks.

On to the fifth day. By now, God seems to be enjoying himself, so "great sea monsters" appear—not, it should be noted, as dark semi-divine ogres as in the previous mythologies, but as creatures who are welcomed into the world. God explicitly declares them to be good. Along with their fellow creatures they can now propagate "each according to its kind." No, Ahab, Moby Dick is not the very embodiment of evil who must be harpooned. He is another fellow being to whom God has assigned a place in the universe—as the Psalmist writes later, "to frolic in the deep."

This fifth day can be read as a self-limitation that God imposes on himself. He decides to share with his creation even his power to create. Given what we have said above about the meaning of "create" (*bara*), this passage suggests that the assigning of roles and functions can now be carried on between and among many participants. Some modern biblical scholars, in dealing with the relationship of Genesis to the older myths that we have mentioned above, once argued that the big difference between them was the Israelites' introduction of mono-theism. It is one God who does all this. But a more recent and more persuasive reading suggests that the central point is not the oneness of God. Rather, it is the Hebrew God's determination to share power and authority. As noted above, Rashi says God wants to move away from all-encompassing oneness to more-than-oneness. In fact, when God says, "Let us make the human in our image," there is a suggestion that diversity, complexity, and relationship exist within the life of God, and his sharing them with the world is not just a generous ges-ture, but an outpouring of his own essential nature. God's life is a polyphony. Saint Augustine taught that these different internal features of God are not hierarchical but equal, and are held together by love. Yes, there is even a hint, however vague, of equalitarian democracy in this old story.

What does this mean for a restored and recreated market system? Simply stated, it means The Market would become the market, or maybe markets. It means the democratization of the economy. Ordi-nary people and local communities would be directly involved in not just political decisions but all the decisions that affect their lives, in-cluding economic ones. It means the current tendency of concentrating more and more power at the top, in the hands of CEO's and boards of directors, would be reversed. For example, when in early 2013 the SEC sought to require corporations to disclose their political con-tributions to their own shareholders, irate business leaders an-nounced they were ready to fight the idea. And yet these shareholders are hardly a mob of angry peasants with pitchforks. They are in fact the owners of the corporation, and at least on paper they elect its board of directors. It would seem that, at the moment, democratic participa-tion in the economy—even that of the shareholders in the corporations they own—is being choked off rather than encouraged. There is clearly a need for a thorough *restoratio*.

On the sixth day of God's shaping and assigning, he fashions human beings. The Hebrew word here is *ha-adam* which involves wordplay with the term for dirt or soil. "Adam" is not the given name of an individual and does not suggest a gender. In fact, in a later verse, it says, "male and female, created he them." Ha-adam carries a more corporate overtone. A good translation might be "humankind." Unlike his previous shaping, God here does not simply command. Instead he shapes the ha-adam from the soil and dust, sculpted "after our own image." But what does "image" mean and how does that "our" creep into the language of this allegedly monotheistic God?

What this *imago dei* means has been discussed and argued over for centuries. Does it mean that ha-adam has reason or intellect, or possesses creative powers or free will? There is no clear consensus. But from what God has just demonstrated about himself on the previous "days," it might well mean ha-adam has the capacity and the responsibility to share power and authority rather than trying to concentrate it and cling to it. The fact that ha-adam is given "dominion" over the other creatures can be misleading if we imagine the word to suggest how earthly tyrants dominate their subjects. We have just witnessed in the first five days that the biblical God does not govern in that way. Rather, he apportions and distributes his powers. This is the way God wants ha-adam to govern, and it is hinted at as God assigns ha-adam a fitting place in the scheme of things. This collective "Adam" is to nurture and tend the intricate self-reproducing plants and animals surrounding him in the Garden. God's purpose is to promote the health and well-being of the independent beings to whom he has assigned roles in the drama. When these living parts of the whole organism forget or neglect their particular tasks, when they usurp the responsibilities that have been assigned to other parts, the whole system becomes disfigured.

God, however, does assign ha-adam a very important responsibility that is shared by none of the other creatures: the naming of the animals. And "whatsoever ha-adam called every living creature, that was the name thereof." This naming is no trivial task. It is another step in God's divestment of his authority. In the first verses of the creation narrative, it is God who names the light and the darkness. Now things change. God shares this divine prerogative with ha-adam. It is a highly significant delegation of power. In the culture in which this account was written, naming something was fraught with weighty significance. Naming the animals gives them a place in the human meaning-world that even their assigned natural functions had not given them. Further, it links ha-adam in a strong tissue of affinity with his fellow creatures. The humans were drawn into the world of the animals, not now simply by their roles but in a network of shared meaning. Culture was being grafted onto the physical earth.

Building on his command of evolutionary theory, Pierre Teilhard de Chardin advanced an evocative idea. He suggests that, on top of geological and biological levels of the earth's formation, there gradually appeared what he termed a "noosphere," analogous to the atmosphere or biosphere. The word derives from the Greek νοῦς (*nous*, "mind") and σφαῖρα (*sphaira*, "sphere"). This third sphere has emerged through the interaction of human thinking, and has grown step by step with the organization of the human mass in relation to itself as it populates the Earth. Thus, as humankind organizes itself in more complex social networks, the noosphere grows in awareness. This concept extends Teilhard's "Law of Complexity-Consciousness" which asserts

271

that, as simple organisms develop into increasingly complex ones, consciousness increases in intensity and the need for the parts to relate to each other harmoniously also increases.

Drawing on theology more than paleontology (as discussed in Chapter 17), Teilhard goes on to speculate that the culmination of this vast cosmic evolutionary process is what he calls the Omega Point, the goal of history. This is an apex of thought and consciousness that he believes is symbolically foreseen in the idea of the "Second Coming" of Christ. I do not know of any commentary by Teilhard on Genesis, but his ideas comport well with Avivah Zornberg's interpretation of Genesis as a story of "increasing complexity." I also suspect that Teilhard might have seen ha-adam's naming of the animals as an expression of the emergence of the noosphere.

At first, Teilhard's writings did not sit well with many Catholic authorities, who thought they detected a whiff of heresy. Eventually he was prohibited from publishing them (though they circulated widely in mimeographed copies). After his death, however, and after the new and more open policies decreed by the Second Vatican Council in the early nineteen-sixties, the ban was lifted. Today, Teilhard is being granted a new and often enthusiastic reading. Some see him as a visionary who foresaw a new synthesis of science and religion, or as a prophet of ecological sustainability, even though many scientists prefer to eliminate the idea of the Omega Point and some discount the whole notion of a purposeful direction in an evolutionary process guided only by chance.

Of course, we cannot leave the venerable old biblical story of creation without being reminded that everything did not work out the way God intended. It never has. He took the immense risk of granting his newly ordered creation not only responsibility, but also the genuine freedom without which responsibility is hollow. It is possible to read the remainder of the Bible as the story of God's patient and unending search for an "other"—a partner in what he was trying to do. This is what he intended in the creation of a world that is separate from himself, and the creation of ha-adam. But time after time, his creatures misuse their freedom to act responsibly. A serpent slithers in, followed by a scene of nasty mutual incrimination between the man and the women. After that, things go downhill. Expulsion from the Garden is followed by the fratricide of Abel by Cain. Then things go downhill even further. God has to continue his creation, now a constant recreation. He sends a punishing flood and then a promising rainbow. He chooses a new man, Abraham, to make a new start that he vows will eventually prove to be a blessing of all the families of earth. He makes a covenant, a kind of treaty of mutuality, with a people who were to become a "light to the nations"—but who fail to live up to their calling. He sends prophets and teachers, and—in the Christian version—Jesus and a newly enlarged "people of God," to advance his purposes.

Are we talking here about a decentralizing God? I have a colleague who teaches the Greek classics and also nurtures a preference for Greek religion. He sometimes chides me with the accusation that the monotheism that Jews and Christians have foisted on the world is at the root of all our wars and conflicts. He argues that we would be better off if we had stayed with polytheism. My response, which has never convinced him, is that classical Christianity is not really monotheistic. It is Trinitarian, which by my reading of history is the result of an early Christian effort to blend elements of Jewish monotheism (which, as we have seen, may not have been all that monotheistic after all) with pluralistic elements in the Hellenistic culture in which the ancient church soon found itself.

It is important to recognize, however, that there is a difference between an array of deities on the one hand and, on the other hand, a God whose essential nature is itself pluralistic and who strives to compose a universe of free and responsible "others," such as the creation story of Genesis describes. Also, recent biblical scholarship strongly suggests that the same decentralizing God is still at work in the New Testament. I in Chapter 14 related the story told in the second chapter of Acts of the Apostles about the tongues of flame and the descent of the Spirit on the day of Pentecost. It describes a scene in which disciples from all around the Mediterranean Sea are suddenly able to understand each other even though all are speaking their own languages. Earlier interpreters have often read this as a miraculous reversal of the so-called "curse of Babel." In that incident, recounted in Genesis 11, human beings boastfully tried to construct a tower (probably a ziggurat) that would "reach up to heaven," in order to "make a name" for themselves. Pentecost has been seen as a kind of relaunching of the human enterprise, a bringing back together of the people who had been "scattered" by linguistic differences.

In the recent scholarly consensus, however, the Babel story is read not just as punishment for pride but also as an act of grace, saving humanity from the trap of centralization and the hubris that always seems to accompany it. In this reading, the Pentecost story is not simply a reversal of Babel, but a continuation in the same direction— toward a unity, or a "communion," based on diversification. The disciples are described as understanding each other not because they all speak the same language, but as they speak in their own tongues. Also, after the event, they are—like the people of Babel—scattered. But the scattering this time is for the purpose of announcing a new form of diverse community that will transcend the oneness-by-conquest of the Roman Empire.

Despite often fierce persecution, for three centuries this multifaceted new *koinonia* (from the Greek κοινωνία, for joint participation) flourished and spread, and did so without a uniform creed or a central hierarchy. Then, however, in the early fourth century, Emperor Constantine (with the collusion of some all too willing bishops) hijacked this loose web of local congregations for his own imperial purposes. He quickly insisted that this heterogeneous scattering of communities adopt a uniform creed. Under the imperial command to conform, most did. Soon after, the march toward a top-down church, which more and more resembled the structure of the empire, set in.

The early Christians found themselves up against a deep-set human tendency. Their vision of the decentralizing thrust of God's work in world history cut against what had happened before and what was still going on among them.

This still goes on today. The impression most people have of how world religions operate—namely, that they do not tend toward decentralization but rather do the opposite—is, alas, correct. Didn't Solomon decree that the altars in ancient Judah should be closed so that all worship would be concentrated in the Temple in Jerusalem? Didn't the popes try for centuries to focus final authority in the Christian movement in Rome? Didn't the different caliphates of Islam, in Baghdad, Cordoba, and elsewhere, struggle with each other to try to unite all the children of the Prophet into one *Umah* under one caliph? All true, of course. The acquisition of power, and then more power, seems to be a universal human failing. Emperors try to enlarge their empires. Huge banks buy merely big banks which have already absorbed small banks. The business pages of newspapers devoted to mergers and acquisitions never lack for news. Religions are not immune to the proclivity for this same titanism.

Still, there have always been countercurrents. The Sufi mystics of Islam and the Protestant reformers have challenged the imperial impulse in religion time and time again. We may be entering a period in which the centrifugal energy is once more at work. When he was spoken of as a strong candidate for the papacy, the late Cardinal Carlo Maria Martini of Milan gave a widely noted lecture in which he declared that what today's Catholic Church needs most is a pronounced dispersal of the authority that has accumulated over the past two hundred years in the Roman curia. Regions and dioceses, even local parishes, should be given more of a voice. The conclave, however, did not select Martini. He was passed over for Cardinal Joseph Ratzinger, who became Benedict XVI and, in stark contrast to Martini, strongly supported what he called "recentrage": the return to Rome of the decision-making that had begun slipping away after Vatican II. Still, even though Martini is now deceased, indications of what Pope Francis is trying to do suggest he stands more in the Martini camp.

Recalling the seven days of creation and its long sequel in world history may or may not help us to think about what needs to be done to save The Market from its own excesses. Yet, when a problem seems intransigent, which is certainly the case with the position of The Market today, sometimes looking at the question from a different perspective creates new openings. It should be remembered that, in the biblical record, the work of the Creator Spiritus is not confined to churches or to religion. The Spirit also moves "where it will" in history and in nature. The *restoratio* continues, and sometimes in unexpected places. It might well be at work in The Market.

Banks, although they may be "made of marble" as the old Woody Guthrie song puts it, are subject to change from unexpected quarters. For example, we could be watching the final few years of the traditional branch bank. Today, more and more people are doing their banking via smartphones. Some "millennials" say they have not set foot in a bank for a year and may not enter one at all for years to come.

But it is often hard for the muscle-bound banks to keep apace. A few years ago, Citibank proudly opened what it called its "branch of the future" in Union Square, New York, loaded with the latest technologies such as walls with interactive touch screen features. But mobile banking apps quickly made this "branch of the future" into a withered branch of the past.

Other banks watched and learned. Recently, Bank of America closed down hundreds of its branch offices, and JP Morgan Chase announced it would lay off five thousand workers. One forecaster, Peter Diamandis, told a conference on finance in June 2015 that, by 2025, bank branches would disappear completely. At first this could look like even more centralization, but the opposite may be the case. Who needs a branch bank when they can do their banking on an iPhone? So much for marble walls and steel vaults: they have been cracked open by tiny hand-held devices.[8]

Of course, so far, this quicksilver change is happening mainly in retail banking. But the pace and scope of the new technologies is such that the behemoths and traders should be wary. What appears to be a solid foundation could turn out to be quicksand, and the impressive edifices it supports may be vulnerable. A next wave of tiny gadgets is coming forth enabling people to take photos, listen to hip-hop, play games—and do their banking. Remember, these baubles are held in the palms of the fastest-growing demographic. Still, a lesson to draw from history is that the colossus of finance will not be subject to a quick fix. Even with new technologies popping up almost by the hour, each of the steps needed to restore The Market to its appropriate place is bound to be contested, often fiercely. But this need not be a struggle unto death. If, as people of faith hold, the same decentralizing God manifest in the Pentecost story is still present in the world today, then the improbable and the unexpected can happen.

How might it take place? The Market is staffed by a variety of people. For some, their driving motivation is just plain greed. They have been infected by the contagion of acquisitiveness. And acquisitiveness is a disease for which there is no known cure. No matter how much wealth one has, it is never enough. But there are also people who work in the current financial system who would like to see the market reclaim its role as servant to the larger economy and to society as a whole. These people, many of them young and idealistic, often feel trapped in a labyrinth with no visible exit. Its atmosphere is heady and addictive. Try as they will to do the right thing, they feel thwarted. They need help from outside their golden cage.

The soul of The Market needs to be saved, but The Market cannot save itself. Only the *restoratio* suggested here, or something like it, can do that. The result could be a kind of salvation for a wide range of people.

It is said that when the Roman emperor Vespasian lay on his deathbed, he breathed a sigh and said, "Well, alas, I suppose now I must become a god." No human individual or institution, not even The Market, is suited to be a deity. When The Market does not have to be God anymore, it might be a lot happier.

Notes

Acknowledgments

Index

Notes

1. The Market as God

1. Pope Francis, "Evangelii Gaudium: The Joy of the Gospel" (New York: Image, 2013), 44–45. See also Jim Yardley and Laurie Goodstein: "Pope Francis, in Sweeping Encyclical, Calls for Swift Action on Climate Change," *New York Times*, June 17, 2015, A6.

2. See Harvey Cox, "The Market as God," *Atlantic*, March 1999. This article provided the basis for the expanded and updated text of this chapter.

3. Karl Polanyi, *The Great Transformation: The Political and Economic Origins of Our Time* (New York: Farrar and Rinehart, 1944).

4. Alan Cowell, "Tiny Village in Germany Subdues a Goliath," *New York Times*, November 14, 1996.

5. Christine Y. Cahill and Matthew Q. Clarida, "With Naming Rights on the Table, Harvard Gave Its Price," *Harvard Crimson*, September 10, 2014, 3. See also Matthew Q, Clarida, "School of Public Health Renamed with $350 Million Gift, Largest in Harvard History," *Harvard Crimson*, September 8, 2014, 1.

6. Paul Krugman, "What Markets Will," *New York Times*, October 17, 2014, A27.

7. Editorial Board of the *New York Times*, "A Reckless Call From the Senate's Leader," *New York Times*, March 9, 2015, A16.

2. Sciences, Regal and Divine

1. John Y. Campbell, Andrew W. Lo, and Craig MacKinlay, *The Econometrics of Financial Markets* (Princeton, NJ: Princeton University Press, 1997), 4.

2. George J. Stigler, *The Economist as Preacher and Other Essays* (Chicago: University of Chicago Press, 1982).

3. The reference is to 1 Corinthians 14:8: "For if the trumpet give an uncertain sound, who shall prepare himself to the battle?"

4. Eugene F. Fama, *Foundations of Finance: Portfolio Decisions and Securities Prices* (New York: Basic Books, 1976), 136.

5. Hans Küng, *Infallible? An Inquiry*, trans. Edward Quinn (Garden City, NY: Doubleday, 1971). See also August Bernhard Hasler, *How the Pope Became Infallible: Pius IX and the Politics of Persuasion* (New York: Doubleday, 1981).

6. David Colander "How the Economists Got it Wrong," *Critical Review: A Journal of Politics and Society* 23, no. 1–2 (2011).

3. How The Market Became Divine

1. See Scott W. Gustafson's *At the Altar of Wall Street: The Rituals, Myths, Theologies, Sacraments, and Mission of the Religion Known as the Modern Global Economy* (Grand Rapids, MI: Eerdmans, 2015) for an incisive discussion of the myth of barter. I am grateful for Gustafson's brilliant insights which, had they been published earlier, would surely have informed more of the pages of this book.

2. Lewis Mumford, *The Myth of the Machine, Technics and Human Development* (New York: Harcourt Brace Jovanovich, 1967).

3. Kenneth Turan, "Movie Review: *Cave of Forgotten Dreams*," *Los Angeles Times*, April 29, 2011.

4. Henri Frankfort, *Kingship and the Gods: A Study of Ancient Near Eastern Religion as the Integration of Society and Nature*, Oriental Institute Essays (Chicago: University of Chicago Press, 1948).

5. David Graeber, *Debt: The First 5,000 Years* (New York: Melville House, 2011), 124.

6. Lewis Mumford, *The City in History: Its Origins, Its Transformations, and Its Prospects* (New York: Houghton Mifflin Harcourt, 1961), 411.

7. *Rerum Novarum: Encyclical of Pope Leo XIII on Capital and Labor,* Libreria Editrice Vaticana. Available at http://w2.vatican.va/content/leo-xiii/en/encyclicals /documents/hf_l-xiii_enc_15051891_rerum-novarum.html.

8. Walter Rauschenbusch, *Christianity and the Social Crisis* (New York: Macmillan Company, 1907), 422. Quoted in Sidney E. Ahlstrom, *A Religious History of the American People* (New Haven: Yale University Press, 1972), 785.

9. An argument for this possibility is made by Brazilian theologian Leonardo Boff, another leading thinker in liberation theology, in *Francis of Rome and Francis of Assisi: A New Springtime for the Church* (New York: Orbis, 2014).

4. How The Market Creates People

1. See Mary R. Lefkowitz, *Greek Gods, Human Lives: What We Can Learn from Myths* (New Haven: Yale University Press, 2003).

2. See Reinhold Niebuhr, *Reinhold Niebuhr: Major Works on Religion and Politics,* ed. Elizabeth Sifton (New York: Library of America, 2015), 198, 386; and Paul Tillich, *Systematic Theology,* vol. 2: *Existence and the Christ* (Chicago: University of Chicago Press, 1957), especially the section on "Estrangement" starting on page 47.

3. Robert A. G. Monks and Nell Minow, *Corporate Governance,* 4th ed. (Hoboken, NJ: John Wiley and Sons, 2008), 25.

4. Frederick Hallis, *Corporate Personality: A Study in Jurisprudence* (Oxford: Oxford University Press, H. Milford, 1930), xlix. Cited in *Collective Responsibility: Five Decades of Debate in Theoretical and Applied Ethics,* Larry May and Stacey Hoffman, eds. (Lanham, MD: Rowman & Littlefield, 1992), 137.

5. Devlin Barrett, Christopher M. Matthews, and Andrew R. Johnson, "BNP Paribas Draws Record Fine for 'Tour de Fraud,'" *Wall Street Journal,* June 30, 2014.

6. Matt Apuzzo and Ben Protess, "Justice Department Sets Its Sights on Wall Street," *New York Times,* September 10, 2015, 1.

7. Lawrence Kohlberg, *Essays on Moral Development,* vol. 1: *The Philosophy of Moral Development* (San Francisco: Harper and Row, 1981).

8. Quoted in Ralph Gomory and Richard Sylla, "The American Corporation," *Daedalus* 142, no. 2 (Spring 2013), 102.

9. Adolf A. Berle Jr., and Gardiner C. Means, *The Modern Corporation and Private Property* (1932; New York: Macmillan, 1948).

10. The Business Roundtable, "Statement on Corporate Responsibility," October 1981, 12, quoted in Gomory and Sylla, "American Corporation," 107.

11. "Statement on Corporate Governance," Business Roundtable White Paper, September 1997, pp. 1–2, quoted in Gomory and Sylla, "American Corporation," 110.

12. Interview with Jeffrey Immelt, *Manufacturing and Technology News*, November 30, 2007, quoted in Gomory and Sylla, "American Corporation," 115.

5. Biblical Sources of Conflict over Usury and Phishing

1. Dante Alighieri, *Inferno*, XI: 106–111. As translated by James Finn Cotter, *Dante, The Divine Comedy* (Stony Brook, NY: Forum Italicum, 2000), 71.

2. For a brief but excellent summary, see the entry on "Loans" in *Dictionary of Scripture and Ethics*, gen. ed. Joel B. Green (Grand Rapids, MI: Baker Academic, 2011), 488.

3. R. H. Tawney, *Religion and the Rise of Capitalism* (New York: Harcourt Brace, 1926), 49.

4. Ibid., 48.

5. To be clear, Thomas Wilson himself was no fan of banking. The quote is taken from a section of *A Discourse upon Usury by Way of Dialogue and Orations* (1572) in which he gives the opposing side voice to make its case.

6. Tawney, *Religion and the Rise of Capitalism*, 246.

7. George A. Akerlof and Robert J. Shiller, *Phishing for Phools: The Economics of Manipulation and Deceit* (Princeton, NJ: Princeton University Press, 2015).

8. On the centrality of narrative to human activity see also Randy Olson's *Houston, We Have a Narrative: Why Science Needs a Story* (Chicago: University of Chicago Press, 2015). In it, Olson outlines the universal structure within narratives and shows how they have helped humans make sense of ourselves and our world from the beginning of history.

6. Biblical Sources of Conflict over Redistribution

1. See "Covenant" in *Dictionary of the Bible*, ed. James Hastings, rev. ed. by Frederick C. Grant and H. H. Rowley (New York: Charles Scribner's Sons, 1963), 183.

2. Thomas Piketty, *Capital in the Twenty-First Century* (Cambridge, MA: Belknap Press of Harvard University Press, 2014), 422–424, 569.

3. As the King James Bible translates the tenth verse, it reads "Proclaim Liberty throughout all the Land unto all the Inhabitants thereof." The words are familiar to many Americans not necessarily because they have read them in the Bible but because they are inscribed on the Liberty Bell in Philadelphia's Independence Hall.

4. Roland H. Bainton, *Here I Stand: A Life of Martin Luther* (New York: Penguin, 1995), 58–59.

5. Pope Francis, *Misericordiae Vultus*, Bull of Indiction of the Extraordinary Jubilee of Mercy. Vatican, April 11, 2015. Available at https://w2.vatican.va /content/francesco/en/apost_letters/documents/papa-francesco_bolla _20150411_misericordiae-vultus.html.

6. Pope Francis, "Letter of His Holiness Pope Francis According to Which an Indulgence Is Granted to the Faithful on the Occasion of the Extraordinary Jubilee of Mercy," Vatican, September 1, 2015. Available at https://w2.vatican.va /content/francesco/en/letters/2015/documents/papa-francesco_20150901 _lettera-indulgenza-giubileo-misericordia.html.

7. James S. Henry and Laurence J. Kotlikoff, "Let's Make the Vatican Bank a Bank," *American Interest*, October 2, 2015.

7. Top-Heavy Short Circuits

1. William Tabb, "The Criminality of Wall Street," *Monthly Review* 66, no. 4 (September 2014), 13.

2. Thomas Piketty, *Capital in the Twenty-First Century* (Cambridge, MA: Belknap Press of Harvard University Press, 2015), 297.

3. James Tobin, "On the Efficiency of the Financial System," *Lloyd's Bank Review*, no. 153 (1984), 14–15. Cited in John Bellamy Foster, "The Financialization of Capitalism," *Monthly Review* 58, no. 11 (April 2007), 3. Also see Rana Foroohar, *Makers and Takers: The Rise of Finance and the Fall of American Business* (New York: Crown Business, 2016).

4. Kevin Roose, *Young Money: Inside the Hidden World of Wall Street's Post-Crash Recruits* (New York: Grand Central Publishing, 2014).

5. Ibid., 249.

6. Steve Lohr, "Refocusing, G.E. Reports Growth in Industrial Businesses," *New York Times,* April 18, 2015, BI.

7. Quoted in Peter Brown, *Through the Eye of a Needle: Wealth, the Fall of Rome, and the Making of Christianity in the West, 350–550 A.D.* (Princeton, NJ: Princeton University Press, 2012), 509–510.

8. Barbara Tuchman, *A Distant Mirror: The Calamitous Fourteenth Century* (New York: Alfred Knopf, 1978), 26.

8. Big, Big Banks and Big, Big Churches

1. Michael Corkery and Nathaniel Popper, "Goldman Plans Online Lending for Consumers," *New York Times,* June 16, 2015, A1.

2. Stephen G. Checchetti and Enisse Kharroubi, "Why Does Financial Sector Growth Crowd Out Real Economic Growth?" Working Paper no. 490, Bank for International Settlements, February 2015. Available at http://www.bis.org/publ/work490.htm.

3. Gretchen Morgensen, "Smothered by a Boom in Banking," *New York Times,* March 1, 2015, BI.

4. Luigi Zingales, *A Capitalism for the People: Recapturing the Lost Genius of American Prosperity* (New York: Basic Books, 2012), 48.

5. Marion Maddox, "In the Goofy Parking Lot: Growth Churches as a Novel Religious Form for Late Capitalism," *Social Compass* 59, no. 2 (2012): 146–158. The surprising title of this article comes from one pastor's comparison of his megachurch's parking lot to Disneyland's.

6. Daniel Bell, in *Cultural Contradictions of Capitalism* (New York: Basic Books, 1976), strongly contends that culture is not just a byproduct of the economy, as traditional Marxists have believed, but that culture does influence the economy. He argues that the cultural turn from delayed gratification to encouraging impulse-buying was generated by the change in the economy itself from its period of capital accumulation to consumer capitalism.

9. The Bishop and the Monk: Augustine and Pelagius

1. For an overview of the church in this period see Judith Herrin, *The Formation of Christendom* (Princeton, NJ: Princeton University Press, 1987).

2. See Peter Brown, *Augustine of Hippo*, new ed. (Berkeley: University of California Press, 2000).

3. Brinley R. Rees, *Pelagius: A Reluctant Heretic* (Woodbridge, Suffolk, England: Boydell Press, 1988), 20.

4. Ian C. Bradley, *The Celtic Way* (London: Darton, Longman & Todd, 1993), 62.

5. Peter Brown, *Through the Eye of a Needle: Wealth, the Fall of Rome, and the Making of Christianity in the West, 350–550 AD* (Princeton, NJ: Princeton University Press, 2012), 371.

6. See John A. F. Thomson, *Popes and Princes, 1417–1517* (Boston: Allen and Unwin, 1980) for an excellent treatment of the Renaissance papacy.

10. Adam Smith: Founder and Patron Saint?

1. Glass paste medallion of Adam Smith, sculpted by James Tassie, 1787, National Galleries of Scotland. Image available at https://www.nationalgalleries .org/collection/artists-a-z/t/artist/james-tassie/object/adam-smith-1723-1790 -political-economist-pg-1949.

2. Murray N. Rothbard, "The Adam Smith Myth," Mises Daily blog, Mises Institute, January 13, 2006. Available at https://mises.org/library/adam-smith-myth.

3. Ibid.

4. Shaun Walker, "Why a Giant Statue of Vladimir is Causing a Public Outcry in Moscow," *The Guardian*, June 11, 2015.

5. Adam Smith, *An Inquiry into the Nature and Causes of the Wealth of Nations*, 1776, Book I, Chapter 2.

6. Paul Valelly, "A Victory for Pope Francis," *New York Times*, May 22, 2015.

7. David Rohde, "Her Legacy: Acceptance and Doubts of a Miracle," *New York Times*, October 20, 2003.

8. For example, Brian Kelly, "Patron Saint for the Internet, Isidore of Seville," blog post, January 8, 2010, Catholicism.org, Saint Benedict Center, New Hampshire. Available at http://catholicism.org/patron-saint-for-the-internet -isidore-of-seville.html.

9. Adam Smith, *The Theory of Moral Sentiments*, quoted in Paul S. Williams, "A Visible Hand: Contemporary Lessons from Adam Smith," in *Adam Smith as Theologian*, ed. Paul Oslington (New York: Routledge, 2011), 135.

10. Adam Smith, *The Theory of Moral Sentiments*, new ed. (London: Henry G. Bohn, 1853), Chapter III, Part I, Section I.

11. Simone Weil, *The Need for Roots: Prelude to a Declaration of Duties toward Mankind*, trans. Arthur Wills, preface by T. S. Eliot (New York: Putnam, 1952; orig. French 1949).

12. Adam Smith, *The Theory of Moral Sentiments*, "Of Virtue" Chapter I, Part VI, Section II, 329.

11. Adam Smith: Theologian and Prophet?

1. Jacob Viner (Philadelphia: American Philosophical Society, 1972), 81–82, quoted in Paul Oslington, "Introduction: Theological Readings of Smith," in *Adam Smith as Theologian*, ed. Paul Oslington (New York: Routledge, 2011), 1.

2. Adam Smith, *The Theory of Moral Sentiments*, pt. II, sec. III, ch. III, 106.

3. Ibid., 236.

4. Robert L. Heilbroner, *The Worldly Philosophers*, rev. 7th ed. (New York: Touchstone, 1995).

5. Abraham Joshua Heschel, *The Prophets* (New York: Harper and Row, 1962).

6. Robert Bellah, *Religion in Human Evolution: From the Paleolithic to the Axial Age* (Cambridge, MA: Belknap Press of Harvard University Press, 2011). The relevant material on China can be found in Chapter 8, "The Axial Age III: China in the Late First Millennium BCE," 399–480.

7. John Kenneth Galbraith, *A Short History of Financial Euphoria* (Knoxville, TN: Whittle Direct Books, 1990).

8. Karl Jaspers, *The Origin and Goal of History* (New Haven: Yale University Press, 1954); Eric Voegelin, *Order and History*, vol. 1: *Israel and Revelation* (Baton Rouge: Louisiana State University Press, 1956). Jaspers and Voegelin are cited and quoted by Robert Bellah, *The Axial Age and Its Consequences* (Cambridge, MA: Belknap Press of Harvard University Press, 2012), 375.

9. Heschel, *The Prophets*, 5–6.

10. Adam Smith, *Theory of Moral Sentiments* (1759), Part I, Section III, Chap. III.

12. Banker, Philosopher, Trickster, Writer

1. John B. Thompson, *Studies in the Theory of Ideology* (Berkeley: University of California Press, 1984), 6, quoted in Jean-Christophe Agnew, "Banking on Language: The Currency of Alexander Bryan Johnson," in *The Culture of the Market: Historical Essays*, ed. Thomas L. Haskell and Richard Teichgraeber III (New York: Cambridge University Press, 1993), 231.

2. Agnew, "Banking on Language," 239.

3. Ibid., 241.

4. A. J. Ayer, *Philosophy in the Twentieth Century* (London: Weidenfel and Nicholson, 1982), 74–75. Quoted in George Cotkin, "William James and the Cash-Value Metaphor," *Et Cetera, A Review of General Semantics* 42, no. 1 (Spring 1985), 37.

5. See, for example, Victor H. Matthews and Frances Mims, "Jacob the Trickster and Heir of the Covenant: A Literary Interpretation," *Perspectives in Religious Studies* 12 (1985), 185–195; and John E. Anderson, "Jacob, Laban, and a Divine Trickster: The Covenantal Framework of God's Deception in the Theology of the Jacob Cycle," *Perspectives in Religious Studies* 36 (2009), 3–23.

6. "The 'Confidence Man' on a Large Scale," *New York Herald*, July 11, 1849, quoted in Johannes D. Bergmann, "The Original Confidence Man," *American Quarterly* 21 (Autumn 1969), 563–564.

7. Herman Melville, *The Confidence-Man: His Masquerade*, Modern Library edition, ed. John Bryant (New York: Random House, 2003), 208.

8. Melville, *The Confidence-Man*, xxxiv.

13. The Breath of God and The Market Geist

1. Max Weber, *The Protestant Ethic and the Spirit of Capitalism*, trans. Talcott Parsons (Boston: Unwin, 1985; trans. 1930; orig. 1905).

2. Michael Novak, *This Hemisphere of Liberty: A Philosophy of the Americas* (Washington, DC: AEI Press, 1990), 26.

3. Novak, *This Hemisphere*, 78.

4. For a succinct summary of Michael Novak's thought on The Market, see Linda Kintz, *Between Jesus and the Market* (Durham, NC: Duke University Press, 1997), 217–229.

14. "Go Ye into All the World"

1. Michiko Kakutani, "A Soft-Focus Look at Fox's Tough-Talking Tough Guy," review of Zev Chafets, *Roger Ailes: Off Camera*, *New York Times*, March 19, 2013, C1.

2. Nielsen Comparable Metrics Report, Q4 2015, accessed at http://www .nielsen.com/content/dam/corporate/us/en/reports-downloads/2016-reports /comparable-metrics-report-q4-2015.pdf.

3. Jerry Mander, *The Capitalism Papers: Fatal Flaws of an Obsolete System* (Berkeley: Counterpoint, 2012), 176.

4. Frederick J. Zimmerman, Dimitri A. Christakis, and Andrew N. Meltzoff, "Television and DVD/Video Viewing in Children Younger than Two Years," *Archives of Pediatrics and Adolescent Medicine* 161, no. 5 (2007), 473–479.

5. See Sydney E. Ahlstrom, *A Religious History of the American People* (New Haven: Yale University Press, 1972); an account of Noyes and the Oneida Community starts at page 498.

6. Eric Schlosser, *Fast Food Nation: The Dark Side of the All-American Meal* (New York: Mariner Books, 2012), 279. Note that the McDonald's website is quoted in an afterword in the book's paperback edition, not in the text as it was originally published.

7. Thomas Hine, *The Total Package: The Secret History and Hidden Meanings of Boxes, Bottles, Cans, and Other Persuasive Containers* (Boston: Little, Brown, 1995), 238.

8. Jonathan D. Spence, *The Memory Palace of Matteo Ricci* (New York: Viking Penguin, 1984).

9. Sturla J. Stålsett, ed., *Spirits of Globalization: Growth of Pentecostalism and Experiential Spiritualities in a Global Age* (London: SCM Press, 2006).

10. Ibid.

15. The Liturgical Year of The Market

1. Andrew Adam Newman, "Beauty Brand Creates Campaign to Combat Mental Illness," *New York Times*, November 28, 2014, B2.

2. Numa Denis Fustel de Coulanges, *The Ancient City: A Study on the Religion, Laws and Institutions of Greece and Rome* (1873; Boston: Lee and Shepherd, 1877).

3. Ruth La Ferla, "Courting a Different Shopper for Ramadan," *New York Times,* June 25, 2015, D8.

4. Morgan Rousseau, "Black Friday, Bloody Black Friday upon Us Again," *Boston Metro,* November 28–30, 2014, 2.

5. "Target Shoppers Nationwide Score Doorbusters as Black Friday Gets Underway," Target Press Release, November 28, 2014.

6. Rousseau, "Black Friday."

7. Hiroko Tabuchi, "Black Friday Fatigue? Thanksgiving Weekend Sales Slide 11 Percent," *New York Times,* November 30, 2014.

8. Julia Zorthian, "Black Friday Sales Down More Than $1 Billion," *Time,* November 29, 2015.

9. I am grateful to Eric Young, who enrolled in a course I offered at Harvard on "God and Money," for the rich insights in his superb unpublished term paper on Santa Claus, on which I have relied in this section.

10. Stephen Nissenbaum, *The Battle for Christmas* (New York: Alfred Knopf, 1996), 90.

11. Max A. Myers, "Santa Claus as an Icon of Grace," in *Christmas Unwrapped: Consumerism, Christ, and Culture,* ed. Richard Horsley and James Tracy (Harrisburg, PA: Trinity Press International, 2001), 190.

12. Steven D. Hales, "Putting Claus Back into Christmas," in *Christmas: Philosophy for Everyone,* ed. Scott C. Lowe (Malden, MA: Wiley-Blackwell, 2010), 161–171.

13. Carl G. Jung, "Answer to Job," in *Psychology and Religion: West and East,* trans. R. F. C. Hull (New York: Pantheon, 1958), 464.

14. Leigh Eric Schmidt, "The Commercialization of the Calendar: American Holidays and the Culture of Consumption, 1870–1930," *Journal of American History* 78, no. 3 (December 1991), 887–916. See also Katherine Lane Antolini, *Memorializing Motherhood: Anna Jarvis and the Struggle for Control of Mother's Day* (Morgantown: West Virginia University Press, 2014).

16. All Desires Known

1. Michel Foucault, *The History of Sexuality Volume 1: An Introduction* (New York: Vintage Books, 1978).

2. Michael Schudson, *Advertising, the Uneasy Persuasion: Its Dubious Impact on American Society* (New York: Basic Books, 1984), 54.

3. Karen Shapiro, "The Construction of Television Commercials: Four Cases of Interorganizational Problem Solving," PhD diss., Stanford University, 1981, 197, quoted in Schudson, *Advertising*, 54.

4. Schudson, *Advertising*, 55.

5. John Bellamy Foster and Robert W. McChesney, "Surveillance Capitalism: Monopoly-Finance Capital, the Military-Industrial Complex, and the Digital Age," *Monthly Review* 66, no. 3 (July–August 2014), 19.

6. Jerry Mander, "The Privatization of Consciousness," *Monthly Review* 64, no. 5 (October 2012), 18.

7. Foucault, *History of Sexuality*, 45.

8. Ibid., 49.

9. Raymond Williams, *The Long Revolution* (Cardigan, UK: Parthian Books; Reprint edition, 2012).

10. Foster and McChesney, "Surveillance Capitalism," 3.

11. Josiah Royce, *The Philosophy of Loyalty* (New York: Macmillan, 1908).

12. Stephanie Strom, "Unilever, Suing Over Rival's Use of 'Mayo,' Changes Own Website," *New York Times*, November 17, 2014, B6.

13. Stephen Jay Gould, *Rocks of Ages: Science and Religion in the Fullness of Life*, Library of Contemporary Thought (New York: Ballantine, 1999).

17. The Market and the End of the World

1. Francis Fukuyama, *The End of History and the Last Man* (New York: Free Press, 1992).

2. In the *Theogony* of Hesiod, the three Moirai are personified, and are acting over the gods. In Plato's *Republic*, the Three Fates are daughters of Ananke (necessity). It seems that Moira is related to Tekmor (proof, ordinance) and to Ananke (destiny, necessity), who were primeval goddesses in mythical cosmogonies. Note that the concept of a universal principle of natural order has its

equivalents in other cultures, such as the Vedic Rta, the Avestan Asha (Arta), and the Egyptian Maat.

3. Included in Reinhold Niebuhr, *Reinhold Niebuhr: Major Works on Religion and Politics,* ed. Elizabeth Sifton (New York: Library of America, 2015), 770.

4. Walter Rauschenbusch, *Christianity and the Social Crisis in the 21st Century: The Classic That Woke Up the Church* (New York: The Macmillan Co., 1907), 422, quoted in Sydney Ahlstrom, *A Religious History of the American People,* 785–786.

5. Pierre Teilhard de Chardin, *The Phenomenon of Man* (New York: Harper Perennial, 1976).

6. Niebuhr, *Rheinhold Niebuhr,* 775.

7. Richard York and Brett Clark, "Stephen Jay Gould's Critique of Progress," *Monthly Review* 62, no. 9 (February 2011): 31.

8. Simon Conway Morris, *The Deep Structure of Biology: Is Convergence Sufficiently Ubiquitous to Give a Directional Signal?* (West Conshohocken, PA: Templeton Foundation Press, 2008).

9. Stephen Jay Gould, interviewed in Wim Kayzer, *A Glorious Accident* (New York: W. H. Freeman, 1977), 92–93, quoted in York and Clark, "Stephen Jay Gould's Critique," 35.

18. Saving the Soul of The Market

1. Bair tells the story of the speech and how it was received in her memoir, *Bull by the Horns: Fighting to Save Main Street from Wall Street and Wall Street from Itself* (New York: Simon and Schuster, 2012), 313–314. For a fuller exploration of the need for markets to serve society, see Robert Reich, *Saving Capitalism: For the Many, Not the Few* (New York: Knopf, 2015).

2. Martin Wolf, "The Challenge of Halting the Financial Doomsday Machine," *Financial Times,* April 20, 2010.

3. John Nichols, "Fed's 'Backdoor Bailout' Provided $3.3 Trillion in Loans to Banks, Corporations," *The Nation,* December 2, 2010.

4. Michael J. Sandel, *What Money Can't Buy: The Moral Limits of Markets* (New York: Farrar, Straus and Giroux, 2012), 10.

5. Floyd Norris, "The Perils When Megabanks Lose Focus," *New York Times,* September 6, 2013, B1. (Note that the title of the article was changed in the *Times'* online edition.)

6. Michael Corkery and Ben Profess, "Rigging of Foreign Exchange Market Makes Felons of Top Banks," *New York Times,* May 21, 2015, I.

7. Avivah Gottlieb Zornberg, *The Beginning of Desire: Reflections on Genesis* (New York: Schocken, 2011), 4.

8. Angela Yi, "Money Messages," *Harvard Political Review* 42, no. 4 (Winter 2015), 8.

Acknowledgments

Several people helped and supported me as I wrote this book. My old friend Dr. Robert McKersie of the Sloan School of Management at MIT read and commented helpfully on key chapters. My world-class Teaching Fellow, Scott Rice, helped with reading and feedback. Richard Parker of the John F. Kennedy School read and made constructive suggestions on various sections. The International Christian University in Tokyo, Japan, gave me the opportunity to lecture on this subject while there was still time for making changes. My wife Dr. Nina Tumarkin and my son Nicholas listened to my gripes as I wrote, with no visible indication of impatience. But mainly, the students who took my Harvard course "God and Money" kept me on track with their questions and criticisms. I am grateful to all of them.

Index

Index